Introduction to
VALUE THEORY

Nicholas Rescher

Research Professor of Philosophy
University of Pittsburgh

PRENTICE-HALL, INC., ENGLEWOOD CLIFFS, NEW JERSEY

PRENTICE-HALL INTERNATIONAL, INC. *London*
PRENTICE-HALL OF AUSTRALIA, PTY. LTD. *Sydney*
PRENTICE-HALL OF CANADA, LTD. *Toronto*
PRENTICE-HALL OF INDIA PRIVATE LTD. *New Delhi*
PRENTICE-HALL OF JAPAN, INC. *Tokyo.*

Library of Congress Catalog Card Number 68-9384

Printed in the United States of America

Current Printing (last digit):
10 9 8 7 6 5 4 3 2 1

For KURT BAIER,
Colleague, Friend, and Helpful Critic

Preface

The principal innovation of this philosophical introduction to value theory is its focus upon *values* as they are dealt with in everyday-life situations, and have sometimes been studied by sociologists and social psychologists*, rather than upon *Value* (with a capital V) as has been standard in the philosophical tradition. Its point of departure is, not a philosophical theory about "the nature of value," but a philosophically informed scrutiny of the workings of the value concept with which we operate in everyday affairs. From here the treatment of values is developed in the light of relevant work in the social sciences, particularly economics. The result is a book suitable as a textbook for upper-class and graduate courses in the theory of value and as supplementary material for both courses in normative ethics in philosophy departments and foundations-oriented courses in economic theory (and also for a course in methodological issues in the social sciences).

The conception of values reflected in this book came into focus in the wake of my participation in a project of interdisciplinary inquiry into the impact of technological change upon American values. Centered at the University of Pittsburgh but involving collaborators from many institutions, this project was supported by grants from the Carnegie Corporation of New York and the International Business Machines Corporation and was directed by Prof. Kurt Baier and me. The findings of the project, published in K. Baier and N. Rescher (eds.), *Values and the Future: The Impact of Technological Change on American Values* (New York, The Free Press, 1968),

*I say sometimes, because some social scientists do not concern themselves with values as they function in everyday-life contexts, but with artificial technical value-constructs often so far removed from our informal concept of "Values" as even to cast doubts upon their claims to this characterization. However, the school of Clyde Kluckhohn (for example) approaches values in just the way that is adopted here.

v

provide a backdrop against which the ideas of this book came to be developed. Specifically, Chapter IX of the present work is adapted from my own contribution to that volume. Moreover, Chapters III, IV, VII, and VIII of this book all draw upon materials from previous publications written in connection with the project. Detailed acknowledgments are given in the footnotes.

I am much indebted to my associates in the Pittsburgh Values Project, in particular my philosophical colleagues David Braybrooke, John Robison, and Jerome Schneewind, for the exchange of ideas about the nature and workings of the value concept. Above all, I gratefully acknowledge the help of my colleague Kurt Baier, both on points of detail and general stimulus. I am grateful to Prof. Roderick M. Chisholm for reading the book in manuscript and affording me the benefit of constructive criticism.

I wish to thank Miss Judy Bazy for preparing the typescript for the printer and for helping to see the book through the press. I am grateful to Mr. Bliss Cartwright and Miss Sandy Roper for help in preparing the bibliography. I am very grateful to Miss Hazel Johnson, Consultant for the Development of Collections at the University of Pittsburgh Library, for cooperative and competent bibliographical assistance.

N.R.

Pittsburgh

Contents

vii

VI

VII

VIII

IX

X

Appendix
I

Appendix
II

I

The Study
of Values

1. WHAT IS A VALUE?
THE PROBLEM AND THE APPROACH

The dictionary defines *value* as "the quality or fact of being excellent, useful, or desirable";[1] although when we say that loyalty to superiors is one of a man's values, we are not automatically saying that this in fact is one of his qualities. In the English language the word is used in a somewhat loose and fluctuating way. Philosophers and social scientists concerned with value questions have long recognized the need for a more precise value terminology to facilitate the exact formulations needed in scholarly and scientific contexts. But this desideratum seems to be the only point of agreement. All workers in the field echo this complaint. Nevertheless, all their positive efforts have failed. No proposal for a delineation of value terminology has been able to generate any significant degree of concurrence, let alone become a focus of settled consensus. The sociologist Clyde Kluckhohn, who strove for decades to put value studies on a firm conceptual footing, has surveyed the field of proposed characterizations of "value" on several occasions with the same

[1] *Webster's New Collegiate Dictionary* (Springfield, 1961 edition).

1

dreary upshot of confronting a chaos.[2] (He himself later characterized his own principal attempt at a rigorous definition of *value* for social science purposes as "not very successful."[3])

2. THE DETERMINATION OF VALUE

We shall start with a deliberately oblique approach to the question *What is a value?* Rather than considering what a value *is*, let us begin with the problem of how a value *is manifested*. How is the presence of a value detected? When we impute to someone (N = Smith, Jones) subscription to a certain value (X = "love of country," or "devotion to duty," or "the worship of Mammon"), what grounds can we possibly have for this claim?

It is clear that value subscription can manifest itself in two easily distinguishable overt modes: First on the side of *talk* (or thought), in claiming that N subscribes to a value, we give grounds for expecting a certain characteristic type of verbal action, namely, that he would "appeal to this value," both in the support or justification of his own (or other people's) actions and

[2] See E. M. Albert and C. Kluckhohn, *A Selected Bibliography on Values, Ethics, and Esthetics (1920–1958)*. Glencoe, Ill. (1959).

I quote the following definitions of "value" from a longer list compiled by my colleague Kurt Baier. Though comparatively short, the list is long enough to exhibit the great diversity in the conception of "value" as well as the looseness with which various writers use the term.

"A thing has or is a value if and when people behave toward it so as to retain or increase their possession of it." (George Lundberg)

"Anything capable of being appreciated (wished for) is a value." (Robert Part and E. W. Burgess)

"Values are the observe of motives . . . the object, quality, or condition that satisfies the motivation." (Richard T. LaPiere)

"Values are any object of any need." (Howard Becker)

"[A value is] a desideratum or anything desired or chosen by someone, at sometime—operationally: what the respondent says he wants." (Stuart C. Dodd)

"By a social value we understand any datum having an empirical content accessible to the members of some social group and a meaning with regard to which it is or may be an object of activity." (Florjan Znaniecki)

"[A value is] a conception, explicit or implicit, distinctive of an individual or characteristic of a group, of the desirable which influences the selection from available means and ends of action." (Clyde Kluckhohn)

"[Values are] the desirable end states which act as a guide to human endeavor or the most general statements of legitimate ends which guide social action." (Neil J. Smelser)

"[Values are] normative standards by which human beings are influenced in their choice among the alternative courses of action which they perceive." (Philip E. Jacob and James J. Flink)

[3] "Have There Been Discernible Shifts in American Values During the Past Generation," in E. Morison (ed.) *The American Style* (New York, 1958), pp. 145–217.

in urging upon others the adoption of actions, courses of action, and policies for acting. Moreover, in addition to such overt verbal behavior we would of course expect him to take the value into proper account in the "inner discourse" (*in foro interno*) of deliberation and decision making. In imputing a value to someone, we underwrite the expectation that its espousal will manifest itself, in appropriate ways, in his reflections regarding the justification and recommendation of actions. The prime indicators of value subscription are those items which reflect the *rationalization* (defense, recommendation, justification, critique) of aspects of a "way of life."

But second, on the other hand, we also expect the value to manifest itself on the side of *overt action*. We would draw back from saying that "patriotism" ("financial security," "the advancement of learning") is one of *N*'s values unless he behaves in action—and not just at the verbal level—so as to implement the holding of this value by "acting in accordance with it" himself, by endeavoring to promote its adoption by others, etc. In saying that prudence, for example, is one of *N*'s values, we *underwrite the presumption*—this does not, of course, *guarantee*—that *N* behaves prudently (is a prudent person). This would apply to statements about other values, such as patriotism or intelligence. (The converse, of course, is by no means true. To say that *N* is prudent no more implies that prudence is one of his values than to say that he is impatient implies that impatience is one of his values.)

A value is thus bound up with a Janus-headed disposition cluster, and we expect it to orient itself in two directions, that of discourse and that of overt action. There is, of course, the problem of the hypocrite and the dissimulator, the man who merely talks the value but does not implement it in action. *Per contra,* there is the man who acts in accordance with a typical pattern of value subscription (for reasons of conformity, by happenstance, etc.) but who does not subscribe to the value at the verbal level, and may even explicitly reject subscription to it. In either event we would have to refrain from a value imputation of any *unqualified* kind. In imputing a value to someone we underwrite the expectation that its espousal will manifest itself in practice as well as in thought.

Subscription to a value is consequently a two-sided affair, and value imputations have a double aspect: both verbal and behavioral. When we impute to the person *N* subscription to the value *x*, we underwrite the grounds for expecting from *N* a reasonable degree of conformity with the characteristic manifestation patterns of subscription to *x* both in discourse and in action.

We thus impute a value to someone to characterize his vision of "the good life" or at any rate his vision of how life ought appropriately to be lived— be this in his judgment "for the good" or not, in some more fundamental sense of the term. "His vision" indicates that we are concerned with how he looks at the matter; "how life is to be led" indicates that we are concerned with *conduct* (action). His way of looking at the matter would be expected to manifest itself—at any rate under ordinary circumstances—by his *dispositions to talk* (to approve, disapprove, recommend, encourage, etc.). Moreover, his view of how life is to be led would generally be expected to manifest itself—again, under ordinary circumstances—by his *dispositions to act*, by the things he does and the ways in which he chooses to expend his resources of time, energy, etc.

On the basis of these considerations, we may readily see that there are two major avenues of approach to the analysis of the value pattern of a person or a society. The tools of inquiry can be shaped with a view to either of the two principal ways in which values manifest themselves. Because of the dual aspect of values in manifesting themselves in both the spheres of talk and action, we can seek to determine values from either of these directions.

On the side of behavior, the principal tool of value study will be *budget analysis*, i.e., a scrutiny of patterns of resource investment. Here the idea of a *resource* must, of course, be construed broadly, including not merely material resources, but also time (time-budget analysis), and the expenditures of energy, effort, toleration for inconvenience, etc.

On the side of talk, the primary tool of investigation will be *content analysis*. Thus, when the values of a society are at issue, one appropriate measure is a scrutiny of the pronunciamentos of various publicly recognized spokesmen for values: newspaper editorialists, graduation-exercise speakers, religio-moral sermonizers, and political orators. Nowadays, the data provided by such more or less spontaneous verbal reactions are often extended and supplemented by the content analysis of that methodologically important artifact, the questionnaire.

Like all other techniques of empirical investigation, these two are not foolproof. Budget analysis shows what people *do* spend, and not what they are *prepared* to spend (which may, of course, be much more). Again, content analysis may let us down in value studies because of the "hypocrisy problem" of talk that gets out of joint with action (in lip service or the like). These techniques, like most of the methods of inquiry, have to be used with subtlety and care.

3. THE RELEVANCE OF VALUES

Values are intangibles. They are, in the final analysis, things of the mind that have to do with the vision people have of "the good life" for themselves and their fellows. A person's values—such as "loyalty" or "economic justice" or "self-aggrandizement"—represent factors that play a role in his personal welfare function, the yardstick by which he assesses the extent of his satisfactions in and with life. Values, of course, manifest themselves concretely in the ways in which people talk and act, and especially in the pattern of their expenditure of time and effort and in their choices in the marketplace. And it is primarily through these concrete manifestations that values secure their importance and relevance. This, however, does not alter the fact of their own abstract and mentalistic nature, nor does it mitigate their methodologically problematic character.

People's values function both as constraints and as stimuli. A man's adherence to a certain value, say "patriotism," motivates him in doing some things (e.g., resenting an aspersion upon his country) and in refraining from doing others (e.g., any disloyal action). The prevalent values of a society—particularly of a democratic society—significantly condition the ways it conceives of, and goes about discharging its business. The flat rejection of the prospect of preventive war by the United States and the no-first-strike policy maintained through several successive administrations reflect in significant part the appreciation by America's political leadership of certain fundamental value commitments of the American people. (Somewhat similar value-inherent restraints were operative in circumscribing American actions during the Bay of Pigs adventure and the subsequent Russo-Cuban missile crisis.) Values are thus an important element, not merely for the sociologist's understanding of national traits and character, but even for the appreciation of political realities. Values are important for politics, that "art of the possible," because they play a significant role in the determination of what *is* possible.

4. THE LANGUAGE OF VALUES

The language we speak provides us with actual names for some values but not others. Thus, in English, we have such named values as "loyalty," "justice," or "self-aggrandizement," and such named disvalues as "tyranny," "discrimination," or "nepotism." Other values (or disvalues) cannot be named by single words but must be indicated by more complex formulas: "the freedom of the press," for example, or "the promotion of literacy," or "the diffusion of the amenities of life." All such values—those that can be indicated by a single word and those that require a more complex formula—are natural to the modes of life and speech of a people (hence their potential role as slogans for the guidance or critique of action).

It would seem that no definite apparatus of value terminology that departs extensively and markedly from ordinary usage stands much chance of becoming established on a widespread basis. Only a conception of value that relies heavily on the factor of preformalistic familiarity seems to offer a sufficient basis for agreement in this particular sphere. In other branches of science, the introduction of a highly technical concept—far removed from ordinary discourse—may be desirable, nay, essential for progress. But when it comes to confronting the idea of value itself, this seems to be a futile step. Since our interest lies with values as we have in fact come to conceive of them, it will be a good policy to stick close to the vocabulary of everyday value talk. This, at any rate, will be our starting point. In the end, the need for greater precision will no doubt force us to introduce a special terminology of more-than-ordinary exactness. (Moreover, it may well prove desirable to undertake various refinements for special purposes.)

The disadvantage of the technical "value constructs" that some social psychologists present by artifical coinages is that—apart from the inevitable fact that they are harder to grasp and to study—they would have to embody a conception of value (but *which* conception?) radically different from the one we adopt here. For it is a consequence of our emphasis upon the overt role of values in the rationalization of action that *the language of value* must be part of *the language of common life*. The fabric of value is woven of the thoughts people entertain about their actions within the framework of their view of the good life.

It is worth noting in this regard that the possession of values is a pervasive human phenomenon—at any rate in the setting of societies and cultures that have reached a certain level of development. Man, as a rational animal, exhibits a fundamental tendency to plan his actions (thus comparing alternatives), and to pass judgment on the doings of himself and his fellows. In providing the basis for such rational appraisals, values are consequently ubiquitous in human affairs. Man, being a reflective creature, is sufficiently sensitive to the disadvantages of the actual conditions of life, and of the shortcomings of his fellows, to have at least a vague glimmering of a vision of the good life. It would be difficult to conceive of a person who "rejects values *as such*," although the idea of a person who "rejects" the values of his society—i.e., rejects certain *specific* values—is readily accepted.

5. SOME TECHNICAL TERMINOLOGY

At the "object level" of value talk itself we shall—as just indicated—adhere to the language of common life. But at the "meta-level" of talk *about* values, a certain amount of technical terminology will prove most conducive to the interests of precision, clarity, and concision. A modest installment of this technical vocabulary may as well be put before the reader at the outset.

Value subscribers. A person who "subscribes" to a certain value (i.e., has, holds, accepts, is dedicated to, gives his adherence to it, or the like) will be characterized as a *subscriber* to this value. This idea can obviously be applied to groups of persons as well. "Dietary propriety," for example, is a value for Catholics (Muslims, orthodox Jews—all, to be sure in different ways), but not at all for Protestants.

Evaluations and their ascription. When Jones says, "Social justice is one of my values," he *manifests his subscription* to this value. When Smith says, "Social justice is one of Jones's values," he *ascribes* or *imputes* this value to Jones. When Jones says, "That is a bad policy" (say, because it goes against social justice), he *makes an evaluation* of the policy at issue. When Smith says, "Jones regards that as a bad policy," then he ascribes or imputes this evaluation to him. Value *subscriptions* are undertaken by the person who says, "Neighborliness is a great virtue" or "No scholar can do better than to throw new light into unexplored sectors of his discipline." By contrast some examples of value *ascriptions* are: "The Founding Fathers placed primary emphasis on life, liberty, and the pursuit of happiness" or "Among the politically sophisticated men of his circle, greater stress was placed upon economic welfare than upon personal considerations." It is thus significant to distinguish between:

1. *Subscribing to* (*generic*) *values* on the one hand and *making* (*specific*) *evaluations* on the other.
2. A person's actual *subscription* to a value or making of an evaluation on the one hand, and on the other his *ascription* of a value or an evaluation to someone.

This second distinction is particularly important: to subscribe to values and make evaluations is to assume positions that are *value-committal,* whereas an ascription of a value is *value-neutral* on the part of the person who puts it forward (the ascriber, though not, of course, the ascribee). The man who says, "Jones regards that as a bad policy because it goes against his self-interest" does not himself take any stand on the merits or demerits of either the policy or the value of self-interestedness.

The loci of value. When an *evaluation* is made, one element that inevitably enters in is an item in respect of which the evaluation proceeds and through which values enter upon the stage. For example:

Smith's friendship was of the greatest value for the advancement of Jones's career.

The Wiggins tract is of little value for purposes of cultivation.

Brodia is a splendid mare for breeding.

But whenever something is held to be of value, there is always to be found somewhere on the sidelines a value with respect to which this thing is prized. Thus "the advancement of his career" is of value to Jones presumably because such items as "success," "financial security," "the respect of his peers," and the like, are among his values. Again, "the cultivation of crops" is of value presumably because it conduces either to profit ("financial security," etc.) or to comfort ("being adequately nourished," "health," etc.). Thus the full *exposition* of an evaluation—in which we specify the exact respect in which something is held to be "of value"—will have to include three factors:

1. The *value object* that is being evaluated (Smith's friendship, the Wiggins tract).
2. The *locus of value* (the advancement of one's career, the cultivation of land).
3. The *underlying values* that are at issue ("financial security," "wealth").

We shall refer to this particularizing factor that intervenes in an evaluation between an abstract *value* and the particular, concrete *thing* under consideration (the value object) as the *locus* of value. (It should, incidentally, be noted that the value object may be any of an endless variety of things: inanimate things, animals or persons, the actions of people, states of affairs, plans and policies, etc. There is no hope of finding a coherent classification scheme at this level of generality.)

This distinction between a value, a value object, and a locus of value is helpful in avoiding serious confusion. A person can value nearly anything (e.g., Aunt Hattie's lorgnette), but only a rather limited number of desiderata are sufficiently general and remote from concrete particularity to count as loci of value (e.g., "the possession of works of fine craftsmanship"). And values proper (e.g., "craftmanship" as such) are yet more remote, abstract, and ideological.

6.   A FORMULA FOR VALUE

In the preceding sections we deliberately deemphasized and backed away from the question of *defining* a value. The approach was that of the precept: To see what values *are,* let us consider what they *do.* But having done this, let us now return to the endeavor of capturing the essential nature of values within a formula.

A value represents a slogan for the "rationalization" of action (but a slogan that is positively oriented; otherwise we would speak of a *disvalue*). It represents a slogan, because it is specifiable by a catchword ("economic justice," "the rights of minority," "economic welfare," etc.). And it is invariably a formula that relates to the "rationalization" (justification, critique, defense, recommendation, etc.) of action. Correspondingly:

> *V* is one of *N*'s values if, and only if, *N* is prepared to invoke *V* favorably— and to acknowledge the legitimacy of its invitation by another—in the rationalization of action.

But a person *N* can subscribe to a value *V* rationally only if he has grounds for such a favorable view of its involvements. This requires closer scrutiny. With any value *V* there is associated a certain possible state of affairs, the *realization of V*, whose attainment is promoted by the actions being rationalized by the invocation of the value at issue. Thus the value of "political equality" has as its realization state the condition that men in general are politically equal, or likewise the value of "racial supremacy" has as its associate state lording it over other men by the members of one "master race." In this manner, every value corresponds to a possible state of affairs or condition of the world which represents its state of full (or at any rate substantial) realization. When we say that *V* is one of *N*'s values, then this "associated state of affairs" must be such that:

1. *N* has (and holds his interlocutors to have) a favorable attitude toward this associated state of affairs, doing so
2. because in his (*N*'s) view its realization provides a benefit for someone (not necessarily *N* himself or his interlocutors).

This somewhat more refined view of the matter enables us to restate our earlier formula in improved form: *A value represents a slogan capable of providing for the rationalization of action by encapsulating a positive attitude toward a purportedly beneficial state of affairs.*

This formula accurately conveys the fundamentally ideological character of values: Values are banners under which one can fight (however mildly), being bound up with man's vision of the good life through his conceptions of the beneficial.

His espousal of values is inextricably bound up with the two aspects of man as a "rational animal," his having needs and desires and his capacity for reason. Value is rooted in the fact that man is a goal-oriented organism seeking to achieve satisfactions and avoid dissatisfactions; valuation is pos-

sible only by a being who is capable of feeling relatively positively and nega-
tively toward things—of having "pro-feelings" and "con-feelings."[4] The
polarities of pleasure and pain and of benefits and costs provide the possibilities for certain things being in a man's interests and others not. These
polarities provides the indispensable groundwork for valuation. But the
capacity to have values requires more than mere seekings and avoidances:
it requires the capacity to *rationalize* these actions. To have a value is to be
able to give reasons for motivating goal-oriented behavior in terms of benefits
and costs, bringing to bear explicitly a *conception* of what is in a man's
interests and what goes against his interest: to operate within reason-giving
contexts with reference to a "vision of the good life." Valuation is an instru-
mentality of a "life world" (*Lebenswelt*) of rational agents endowed with
pro-feelings and con-feelings and thus possessing the capacity for goal-
directed behavior in a social (i.e., reciprocally communicative) setting.

7. FACTS VERSUS VALUES: THE IMPERSONAL NATURE OF VALUES

It is often argued by philosophers and social scientists alike that value claims
are nonempirical, and consequently incapable of being established as true,
and as a result wholly subjective. This statement, of course, is argued when
applied to the *subscription* to values by a person, not when applied to their
ascription to some person. The claim that "social justice" is one of Jones's
values is a contention that everyone on all sides is prepared to concede as
an empirical issue. But that "social justice" is a value, i.e., is a genuine or
appropriate or correct value, is held to be a purely subjective thesis.

Put into the briefest possible compass, our own view is as follows. No
sharp line of separation can be drawn between statements of value and statements of fact: value theses are always shot through with factual considerations. Value theses are not matters of taste, but are either well founded or
ill founded, either right or wrong. In our own view, values are founded upon
a vision of how life ought to be lived. The quality of the sorts of lives that they
facilitate thus becomes the arbiter of values. Perfectly objective standards are
operative here, revolving about the concept of human welfare: health, well-
being, comfort, security, freedom of action, etc.

[4] There is little harm in calling these feelings "pleasures" and "pains," although this
is somewhat misleading since (1) it exaggerates the requisite degree of intensity, and (2) it
wrongly suggests that the feeling be physical in nature, which is not necessary. Even a
"pure intelligence" can in principle be value-appreceptive, albeit perhaps only over the
more limited range of intellectual and aesthetic values.

Values whose espousal conduces—under the available circumstances—to an enhancement of the "quality of life" are to be classed as well founded. What is at issue here is certainly not a matter of idle choice or personal preference (hence the difference between the ascription that X subscribes to the value V, and the claim that V is an authentic value—one to which men *ought* to subscribe). This is an issue to be settled by objective—indeed largely empirical—means. For example, that "racial supremacy" is an ill-founded value that undermines the quality of people's lives (including those of the purported "master race") is something that can certainly be argued on the empirical basis of historical evidence: It is not a matter of "subjective preference" at all.

An important aspect of the "ideological" nature of values is that their standing is interpersonal and in this sense *impersonal*: value-grounding considerations are not respecters of persons. Of course, something (say, a jack) can be "of value" for X (who owns a car) that is not of value for Y (who does not). Or again, a value can be subscribed to by X and not by Y. But if X's contention that V is a value is correct and well founded, then V's status as a value is just as compelling for Y as for X. Something cannot be a value for one person and fail to be a value for another (though it can, of course, be *valued* by the one and not the other, or be *of value* to one person and not to another). If something is a proper value, the considerations which establish this fact will have to be equally compelling for all.

This impersonality is the basis for the essentially objective nature of value, according to our conception of the matter. That a certain rationale of action can genuinely conduce to a better life in terms of the actual welfare of the people involved is something that can be settled in principle—and in very large measure in practice—by quite objective considerations. To the extent that this is so, the purported subjectivity of values collapses, and the supposedly insuperable fact-value dichotomy along with it.

8. THE RATIONALIZATION OF ACTION

The principal role of values—so we have urged—resides in the rationalization of action. A somewhat closer scrutiny of this is desirable.

The rationalization of action can be viewed from three principal perspectives:

1. The first-person perspective of *deliberation* and *decision making* in the context of the question: What am I (are we) to do?
2. The second-person perspective of *advising* and *counseling* in the context of the question: What are you to do?

3. The third-person perspective of the *justification* and *critique* of action: What are the merits (or demerits) of what *X* is doing (has done)?

All these patently go back to one uniform underlying question: What is the best thing for me (you, him) to do: what is the relative merit of this course of action in comparison with that alternative? Thus, the fundamental role of a person's values is, not surprisingly, to underwrite the *evaluation* of his actions—to support "practical reasoning," that is, his purposeful thinking about actions in their broadest ramifications (including the means by which and the circumstances under which he performs them). A closer look at actions and practical reasoning about them is indicated, and this will be the task of Chapter IV. Meanwhile we must, in the next chapter, take up the problem of the classification of values.

II

The Dimensions
of Values

1. THE PROBLEM OF VALUE CLASSIFICATION

Why classify values? The question of the classification of values may strike the reader as a purely academic exercise of relatively little practical worth. But it is not so. One cannot begin a really coherent, well-informed discussion of any range of phenomena (dogs, games, diseases, etc.) until some at least rough classification is at hand. For classifications embody needed distinctions, and confusion is the price of a failure to heed needed distinctions. And, of course, in any practical application of the theoretical discussion— already at the level of gathering data—the mechanisms of classification are a virtually indispensable guide.

Owing to the inherent complexity of the concept of a value—the numerous and varied facets involved—value classification can be approached from many sides. Different principles of classification will, of course, be associated with these various angles of approach. This proliferation of perspectives from which values can be regarded serves in good measure to account for the absence of standard and widely accepted principles of value classification. Our own conception of value, set forth in the preceding chapter, lays the basis for a diversified family of interlocking cross-classifications of values. It is fitting to set these out in some detail, both because it is useful to have these classifications at our disposal and because the consideration of such classifications sheds further light upon our understanding of the value concept.

It should perhaps go without saying that the handful of value classifications to be considered here is by no means exhaustive; these classifications are but key examples. The most that can be claimed for them is that they represent some of the most urgent requisites for a systematic survey of values that is to be precise in articulation on the one hand and fruitfully applicable on the other.

2. CLASSIFICATION BY THE SUBSCRIBERSHIP TO THE VALUE

Perhaps the most obvious classificatory distinction regarding values relates to the *subscribership* to the value. Is the value held—or is it such that it ought to be held—by a person or by a group, and then what sort of a group? Is the value (say, "self-esteem") put forward in the context of discussion as a value *of* Smith in particular, or *of* scientists in general, or *of* Paraguayans in general? Among what group of people is the value "at home," as it were; what is its appropriate setting? We correspondingly obtain such classificatory groupings as *personal* values, *professional* (professionwide) values or *work* values, *national* (nationwide) values, etc.

Like some of the other classifications to be introduced here, this is not a classification of values as such pertaining to their *content*, i.e., the subject matter with which the value deals. Rather, the value is taken as already given and fixed so far as its meaning-content is concerned; the only question is: Who holds it?

3. CLASSIFICATION BY THE OBJECTS AT ISSUE

In evaluation something is evaluated with reference to a certain valued characteristic: men, say, are evaluated *in point of* their intelligence, or nations *in point of* the justice of their legal arrangements, or precious stones *in point of* their purity. A value, say, "intelligence" or "justice" or "purity (in precious stones)," is thus correlated with a certain valued state of affairs in which it comes to be realized: men's being intelligent, society's being just, precious stones being pure. This state of affairs is specified in terms of the relevant mode of evaluation applied to the *object items* or *objects* at issue (men, nations, things).

Thus one of the ways of classifying values is with reference to the appropriate group of objects to which the value is taken to have application. Some of the main categories in a classificatory system of this type would be as follows:

Name of value type	Explanation of what is at issue	Sample values
1. Thing values	desirable features of inert things or of animals	purity (in precious stones) speed (in cars or horses)
2. Environmental values	desirable features of arrangements in the (nonhuman) sector of the environment	beauty (of landscape or urban design) novelty
3. Individual or personal values	desirable features of an individual person (character traits, abilities and talents, features of personality, habits, life patterns)	bravery intelligence (in man)
4. Group values	desirable features of the relationships between an individual and his group (in family, profession, etc.)	respect mutual trust
5. Societal values	desirable features of arrangements in the society	economic justice equality (before the law)

On the basis of this classification, it is readily seen that what is at first blush a single value may come to be differentiated with respect to its objects. So with "respect": *self-respect* belongs to category 3, but the *mutual respect* of associates falls into category 4. Again, the *justness* of an individual belongs to category 3, but the *systematic justice* of a nation falls into category 5.

The question at issue throughout this classification relates to the *domain of applicability* of the value. This is a matter of introducing—indeed of defining—the specific value at issue. Thus if what *X* values is "spaciousness in gardens," we cannot simply speak of "spaciousness" as one of the values he holds, for he might, for example, prefer compactness rather than spaciousness in, say, dwelling-houses. In indicating the domain at issue, then, we are actually *not so much classifying a given value as specifying which value is given.* These examples, moreover, show that the list given above is only a starting point. The specification of a domain lends itself to indefinitely greater ramifications.

4. CLASSIFICATION BY THE NATURE OF THE BENEFIT AT ISSUE

As a conception of the beneficial, a value is invariably bound up with a *benefit:* namely, that which is seen to ensue upon the realization of this value. Values can thus be classified according to the types of benefits at issue. To implement this prospect, we need to be able to effect a prior classification of benefits themselves. But how are benefits to be classified?

This question is a relatively simple one, for the notion of a benefit is correlative with that of human wants, needs, desiderata, and interests. Insofar as something conduces to the latter, it is to be classed under the rubric of the former. Thus, since we have a reasonably reliable view of human wants, needs, desiderata, and interests, we also have a plausible survey of potential benefits. This can be projected into a corresponding classification of values, somewhat along the following lines:

	Category of value	*Sample values*
1.	Material and physical	health, comfort, physical security
2.	Economic	economic security, productiveness
3.	Moral	honesty, fairness
4.	Social	charitableness, courtesy
5.	Political	freedom, justice
6.	Aesthetic	beauty, symmetry
7.	Religious (spiritual)	piety, clearness of conscience
8.	Intellectual	intelligence, clarity
9.	Professional	professional recognition and success
10.	Sentimental	love, acceptance

In this classification we group values according to the generic *qualitative nature* of the benefit they involve—e.g., being in good standing with ourselves (7) or with our group (4) or with our professional colleagues (9); having welfare of mind (8) or of body (1); enjoying pleasantness in the condition of labor (2), or of life (8), or in the attractiveness of the environment (6). The guiding concept of this group of classifications is to differentiate values according to the nature of the benefit at issue—that is, according to the human wants, needs, and interests that are served by their realization.

We might, incidentally, compare the benefits at issue not in point of their *type,* but simply in point of their *magnitude.* This gives rise to another "dimension" of values, viz., their *height.* For one may assess values comparatively with respect to the extent of the benefits that accrue from their realization. It is just in this sense that "health" is a higher personal value than "comfort" or that the value of "courtesy" is lower in contrast to "justice."

5. CLASSIFICATION BY THE PURPOSES AT ISSUE

Values can also be classified with respect to the specific type of purpose served by realization of the valued state of affairs, as with *food value or medicinal value*, to cite paradigm examples. Thus we may speak of the *exchange value* of an artifact, i.e., its value for exchange purposes or again of the *deterrent value* of a weapon, i.e., its value for purposes of deterrence. Comparably, we might speak of the *bargaining value* of a certain resource, or even of the *persuasive value* of an argument. Again, monetary value can be grouped in this class: the monetary value of something being its value for purposes of acquiring money, its exchange value *vis-à-vis* money. (On the other hand, if *monetary value* is construed, as is perhaps more natural, as the value of something *measured in monetary terms*—so that the units of comparative evaluation are at issue—then a yet different mode of value classification is clearly at hand.)

Whenever the value under discussion is characterized in terms of the formula "value for___ ___purposes," then we have a classification that proceeds with a view to describing the *mechanism* through which the benefit at issue in the value is to be realized (be it exchange, bargaining, persuasion, etc.). Again, something of the same sort is at issue with a locution of the type: "His counsel was of great professional value to me." For this way of speaking is presumably to be construed as: "His counsel was of great value to me for professional purposes, i.e., in facilitating my attainment of some of the elements of professional success." Here then, the classification of values proceeds in terms of groupings of the *loci* of value that are at issue, that is, the specific human purposes to the attainment of which the value is relevant. (On this conception of "*loci* of value" see Sec. 4 of Chapter I.) This mode of value classification would come to the fore in the analysis of a statement of the type: "The literary value of Samuel Pepys's *Diary* is limited, but its documentary and historical value is enormous."

6. CLASSIFICATION BY THE RELATIONSHIP BETWEEN THE SUBSCRIBER AND THE BENEFICIARY

In general, a person subscribes to a value because he sees its realization as beneficial to certain people. Consequently yet another approach to the classification of values takes its departure from this point and classifies values according to the "orientation" of the value, that is, according to the relationship that obtains between the person who holds the value, the subscriber, on the one hand, and on the other, the presumptive beneficiaries who benefit from the realization of the value.

This approach leads to a classification of the following sort:

I.   Self-oriented (or *egocentric*) values
        (Examples: "success," "comfort," or "privacy"—that is, one's own success, comfort, or privacy)
II. Other-oriented (or *disinterested*) values
     A.   Ingroup-oriented (or parochial) values
             1.   Family-oriented values (family pride)
             2.   Profession-oriented values (the good repute of the profession)
             3.   Nation-oriented values (patriotism)
             4.   Society-oriented values (social justice)
     B.   Mankind-oriented values
             (Examples: aesthetic values or humanitarian values in general)

Again, this classification can serve in the identification (or individuation) of certain blanket values that spread over a wide area. For example, consider the fact that the rubric value "loyalty" covers such rather diversified values as *family* loyalty, or *professional* loyalty, or *national* loyalty.

7.   CLASSIFICATION BY THE RELATIONSHIP THE VALUE ITSELF BEARS TO OTHERS

Certain values are viewed as systematically subordinate to others. For example, "frugality" can scarcely be viewed as a self-subsistent value, but as subordinate to "wealth," or to "self-sufficiency," or to "simplicity (of life style)," or some such other value or combination of values. Or again, "generosity" may be prized for its conduciveness to the "happiness" of others. In such cases, the benefit seen to reside in a realization of the value is looked upon as residing in some other, "larger" value or values to which the initial value is subordinate. Values of this subordinate, other-facilitating sort may be characterized as *instrumental* values or *means* values. Such values come to have this status not so much (or at any rate not primarily) because of their inherent nature, as because their realization conduces to the realization of other values that are regarded as more fundamental.

A second category of values stands in contrast to these instrumental values. The values of this second category are not viewed as subordinate but as self-sufficient. "Loyalty" or "honesty" are, in general, to be prized primarily on their own account, not because acting on them conduces to the realization of other, "larger" values. These, then, are the *intrinsic* values or *end* values. The benefit of realizing a value designated in this manner is seen to reside primarily in this realization of itself and for itself.

8. FURTHER CLASSIFICATIONS

The preceding list by no means exhausts the range of perspectives from whose standpoint values can be classified. For example, one could also classify values by *how soon the benefit at issue comes to be realized.* "Familiarity with the terrain was of great *immediate* value to him," "A knowledge of French will be of *ultimate* value to her," that is, of value to her in the long run. Here the value of the item being evaluated is appraised in terms of the question: How immediate or deferred is the acquisition of the benefits to be accrued from bringing the valued state of affairs to realization?

9. CONCLUSION

Six main principles for classifying values have been examined. We have seen that values can be differentiated by:
1. their subscribership
2. their object items
3. the sort of benefits at issue
4. the sort of purposes at issue
5. the relationship between subscriber and beneficiary
6. the relationship of the value to other values

These six factors indicate distinct "dimensions" with respect to which values can be characterized so that some of their key features can be set out in a systematic fashion. They provide a relatively clear and precise mechanism for discussing significantly general and persuasive aspects of values. By the use of such classifications at least part of the enormous complexity of values can be reduced to orderly terms. It is, moreover, useful to heed these different dimensions of value because an awareness of the distinctions that underlie them enables us to avoid invitations to confusion in value discussions. At first thought, it might seem that when one speaks of "societal value," "aesthetic value," and "exchange value," one is talking about the same sort of thing—just so many different ways of classing values with respect to a long but homogeneous list of distinguishing labels. That this impression is quite incorrect—that very different sorts of things are at issue here—has become clear in considering the highly variegated "dimensions" of value.

III

The Role of Values
in the Explanation of Behavior

1. STATEMENT OF THE PROBLEM

The explanation of a man's behavior in terms of his values is a procedure frequently resorted to in historiography, in everyday discussion, and in the informal psychology of literature (especially in plays and novels). Nor has this useful process of ordinary life been abandoned in more rigorous and scientific settings. In the social sciences, it is, for example, commonly met with in readings in sociology, and in individual and social psychology. An analysis of the conspicuous role of values in the explanation of behavior is therefore quite obviously a question of substantial interest for philosophers, not only because of its bearing upon philosophical psychology, but also because the problem is a meeting ground of the traditional interests of philosophical value theory with concerns in the philosophy of social sciences.

In the reasoned analysis of the springs of human action, one expects to find an appeal to values primarily in two contexts: in deliberation and decision making on the one hand, and in the explanation of human behavior upon the other.[1] These two facets of values are, of course, closely connected. The connection between them is effected by the mediating principle that in maintaining that *x* (e.g., honesty) is one of *N*'s (e.g., Smith's) values we are prepared to claim that *N* would take his subscription to *x* into due account in making relevant choices. Consequently we expect that the outcome of these choices, viz., *N*'s actions, significantly reflect—and are thus in some measure explicable in terms of—his commitment to *x*. But just how are we to conceive of the holding of a value as being "reflected" in action, or as underlying an action? This key question must be answered if appropriate light is to be thrown upon the explanatory role of values.

We are concerned with the role of values in the explanation of *actions*. This is not to say that values cannot be invoked in the explanation of other sorts of things, such as behavior patterns ("Smith is a free-and-easy spender because 'liberality' is one of his values") or even the subscription to certain values themselves ("Smith values 'economic justice' because *justice,* i.e., 'justice in general,' is one of his values"). But such value-explainable items will, of course, in their turn be bound up with human behavior, that is, with actions.

2. MODES OF EXPLANATION

Our prime concern will be with the explanation of particular human actions—*N*'s reading a certain book, casting a certain vote, buying a certain item, speaking out for a certain policy. The focal question has the form—not "Why did *N* do *x in such-and-such a manner*?" (reluctantly, efficiently, swiftly, etc.), but—"Why did *N* do *x at all*?" Current philosophical analyses of the explanation of human actions place prominent stress upon two distinct alternative types of explanations:

1. Explanations in terms of *causes* ("He sat down because the shock was such as to make his knees buckle," "He fell asleep through the action of the sedative").
2. Explanations in terms of *reasons* or *motives* ("He mailed the letter because he wanted to set her mind at rest," "He took the 5:40 to get home in time for dinner").

Explanations of the latter sort proceed in terms of consciously espoused aims, goals, and purposes; those of the former type deal, rather, with accounts that proceed in terms, not of "reasons," but of biomedical "forces" (broadly construed to comprise the machinery of unconscious motives and the Freu-

---

[1] The perspective of the present chapter is restricted to the second issue; the ensuing chapter is devoted to the first.

dian springs of action).[2] It is at once clear that explanations in terms of values ("She refused his request for aid because of her devotion to duty") do not fit smoothly into this dichotomy.

Explanations in terms of reasons involve an explicit reference to specific (goal-oriented) *considerations* the agent "has in mind" in connection with his actions. Thus consider the claim that Smith ran "because he wanted to get to the train on time." Any explanation of this sort clearly cannot work out unless Smith gave explicit consideration to the train and the matter of getting to it. But if Smith stood his ground under fire "out of devotion to duty and love of country," we are not in a position to say anything specific about what sorts of things he envisaged and what sorts of thoughts he must have "had in mind" on the occasion in question. Value explanations do not indicate anything about specific reasons. Yet they are obviously not causal: they tell us nothing about the effective mechanisms or processes through whose functioning the actions came about.[3] Value explanations are highly nonspecific: they work in terms of something akin to reason patterns or motive patterns. How, then, can such explanations go about their work?

3. HOW VALUES FIGURE IN
THOUGHT ABOUT ACTION

As was remarked in the opening chapter, a value subscription can manifest itself in two distinguishable modes: First on the side of *talk* (or thought), in claiming that *N* subscribes to the value, we give grounds for expecting a certain characteristic type of *verbal* action, namely, that he would "appeal to this value" in discussion and thought-about action. In addition to actually overt verbal behavior, we would expect him to take the value into proper account in the "inner discourse" (*in foro interno*) of deliberation and decision making. In imputing a value to someone, we underwrite the expectation that its espousal will manifest itself in the appraisal, justification, and recommendation of actions. Here, the prime indicators of value subscription are those verbalizations that reflect the *rationalization* (defense, recommendation, critique) or action.

But second, on the other hand, we also expect the value to manifest itself

---

[2] For a clear analysis of the differences and kinships between these two modes of explanation see C. G. Hempel, *Aspects of Scientific Explanation* (New York, 1965), pp. 463–485. Cf. also R. S. Peters, *The Concept of Motivation* (London, 1958).

[3] In this regard, incidentally, value explanations do not stand alone, but are joined by explanations that invoke habits and dispositions generally.

nonverbally, at the level of *overt action*. We would draw back from saying that patriotism (financial security, the advancement of learning) is one of *N*'s values unless he behaves *in action*—and not just at the verbal level—so as to implement the holding of this value by "acting in accordance with it" himself, by endeavoring to promote its adoption by others, etc.

A value, as we saw, is a Janus-headed disposition cluster, and one expects it to orient itself in two directions: that of discourse and that of overt action. In imputing a value to someone, we underwrite the expectation that its espousal will manifest itself in practice as well as in thought. When we impute the subscription of *N* to the value *x*, we underwrite the grounds for expecting from *N* a reasonable degree of conformity with the characteristic manifestation patterns of *x* subscription both in discourse and in action.

Having a certain value is obviously different from having a certain goal or a certain preference. But, of course, the goals one adopts or the preferences one has are reflections of, and indications for, one's values. The connection between values and goals is not straightforward. Usually we can make very plausible presumptive inferences from values to goals (if someone "values money," its acquisition is presumably a goal of his). But knowing he has a certain goal, we may be quite uninformed about the operative values (e.g., if his goal is "making money," we cannot say what his values are—he may not, for example, be actuated by any "selfish" motives at all).[4] This point is well put by R. S. Peters in the context of character traits rather than values: "A man who is ruthless, selfish, punctual, considerate, persistent, and honest does not have any particular goals; rather he pursues whatever goals he has in particular sorts of ways."[5]

It is important to realize that values are related to action in categorically different ways that vary with the nature of the thing valued. One must distinguish between values that are related to the possession of such diverse items as:

1. a certain motive, habit, or disposition for action (e.g., bravery, generosity)
2. a certain physical state (e.g., health, good looks)
3. a certain capability, skill, or talent (e.g., agility, endurance)
4. a certain state of mind or attitude (e.g., indifference to money, patriotism)
5. a certain character trait (e.g., resoluteness)
6. a certain state of affairs (privacy, economic justice)

[4] It is, moreover, necessary to distinguish between valuing a thing (e.g., money) and valuing *the valuing of that thing* (viz., avarice). It is necessary to differentiate between "reputable" values (e.g., intelligence) whose *second-order* valuing *we would ordinarily expect* of the person who values the thing at issue, and "disreputable" values whose second-order valuing we would expect the person who has the value to gainsay.

[5] Cf. *The Concept of Motivation, op. cit.,* p. 5.

In each of these cases the characteristic pattern of value subscription will correspondingly be of a rather obviously different nature. Thus if *N* values a certain skill (of his), say, at tennis, he would be expected to cultivate and display it himself, whereas if he values, say, a certain state of affairs, he may well be expected to do various things that have little of self-relatedness, for example, by virtue of civic pride to work to promote the amenities of his town, or the like.

In this direction, moreover, one finds the distinction between the subscription to specific values and the positive commitment toward values in general, i.e., attaching importance *to the having of values as such*. Thus to say of someone that he is a person of high (or low) standards is not to impute a particular (first-order) value to him, but to claim that he attaches importance to the having of values—and consequently, of course, to endeavoring "to live up to" them in action.

The idea of a "characteristic pattern of value subscription" requires explanation and defense. We have said that to impute subscription to a value to someone is to attribute a composite, complex disposition to him—a disposition manifesting itself both on the side of verbal and of overt behavior. But just what sort of disposition? Let us consider a particular example. Suppose we say of someone that "patriotism" is one of his values. Think now of that great cluster of modes of behavior that relates to the holding, or nonholding, of this value (joining patriotic organizations, celebrating national holidays, inculcating the young with the principles of devotion to country, supporting patriotic causes, etc.). Now to some extent action along the lines of such modes of behavior is "only to be expected" on a person's part: that he should act in this way to a rather modest extent would "go without saying." Subscription to a value is imputed to people against such a background conception of *indifferent neutrality* with respect to a sizable body of "value-relevant" behavior patterns. The imputation embodies *inter alia* the claim that, on the side of both overt and verbal action, its subject would tend to display these patterns of behavior to a significantly "greater than ordinary" extent.

The pattern is the same regardless of the particular value at issue:

1. We have in mind the delineation of a category of "value-relevant" behavior—on both the verbal and the overt-action side.
2. We have in mind a "neutral" or "ordinary" (not by any means necessarily "the average") extent of engagement in the modes of behavior in this category, and then against this background,
3. We impute to the value subscriber a degree of involvement in actions of type 1 that significantly exceeds the level of type 2—or falls short of it, depending on the value at issue.

In imputing subscription to a value to someone, we thus do so against the background of a concept of a life style that is "neutral" or "indifferent" with respect to this value as regards the relevant categories of activity, both on the side of verbal behavior and on that of overt action. We claim that important characteristic modes of action are "value intensive" in certain relevant respects—intensive, that is to say, when appraised against the backdrop of a pattern of "neutral" behavior as with respect to the value at issue.

There is a striking parallelism between this view of values and Aristotle's doctrine of the "mean." Take money, for instance. There is the avaricious man who "overvalues" it (of whom we can say that "money is one of his values") and the improvident man who "undervalues" it (whom we can speak of as "heedlessly indifferent to money"). Both of these "value extremes" are, plainly, conceived of against the backdrop of a certain neutrally "normal" involvement with money. This illustrates the essentially Aristotelian perspective of our view of value subscription. It exhibits, too, the genesis of the phenomenon of a polarity of *contrary* values ("liberality"—"frugality"; "independence of action"—"conformity"; "indifference to public opinion"— "due heed of the opinions of one's fellows"). For in the case of most sorts of values,[6] there can be undervaluing and overvaluing: even as a man can act too much or too little prudently, so he can assign an inordinately high or low place to prudence in his system of values.

This general view, of course, leads to the problem of how this zero-point origin of the value-neutral life style is to be fixed. Is this a matter for sociological statistics? Surely not; the reference point is not fixed quite so easily and straightforwardly. (Otherwise, one could not sensibly say of the majority of people in our society—or even in the world—that they are devoted too much to some values and too little to others.) The matter is patently one that can be settled only from the standpoint of the theoretical considerations of a substantive ethical doctrine regarding "the proper life" for men. This issue clearly cannot be resolved without reference to the empirical study of actual human behavior, but, on the other hand, can equally clearly not be resolved simply and solely upon this basis.

4. THE EXPLANATORY INVOCATION OF VALUES

In the light of these considerations we can appreciate more sharply the explanatory force of an appeal to values in accounting for human behavior. Let us consider an example. Suppose that someone accounts for N's taking

---

[6] But not all! One must exclude here the *moral* values such as honesty, justice, etc. For the correspondingly *de trop* behavior patterns are not definable—a person cannot without "explanations" be said to act *too* honestly or *too* justly.

a certain action, e.g., joining a certain political organization, on the grounds that, say, the eradication of poverty ranks high in the roster of N's values, its prosecution being one of the primary objectives of this group. The explanatory grounds here adduced are both relevant and telling because they fit N's action into an *established pattern* of action or tendencies to action on his part.

In this way, the value invoked in an explanatory role plays a part in a long story. The formula that "Brutus joined the conspiracy against Caesar because of his devotion to the Republic" exfoliates into a complex narrative: "Brutus believed that Caesar's political machinations would weaken or destroy the Republic. He was persuaded that the conspirators' plot was the last remaining effective means for impeding this development. Eager to preserve the Republic at virtually any cost, etc." We have here much the same sort of complication as found in the explanatory unpacking of the purely *causal* formula "The house burned down because she left her lighted cigarette lying on the pillow."

Let us consider a more realistic instance of an explanation of this type. One biographer has given the following explanation of Lord Melbourne's support of the Reform Act of 1832.

> Melbourne had been quite right in thinking that the popular demand for reform was now so strong as to make it risky to refuse it. . . . [delay would] lead to the break up of the Government, he told Palmerston, and to a general exacerbation of feeling. The Ministers' chief aim should be to keep things together until people had a chance to cool down. Besides it would be letting down Lord Grey to assist in breaking up his Government. As often before in Melbourne's history, he felt strongly about personal obligations because he was so uncertain about any others. Doubtfully, reluctantly, resignedly he reverted to his old acceptance of reform.[7]

This explanation is clearly of the value-appeal type: In the main, so it is claimed, it was the value he placed upon *personal loyalty* that accounts for Melbourne's backing of a government measure about whose merits he was, with regard to the purely doctrinal side of the matter, profoundly skeptical. But again, the effective completion of the explanatory formula would be a long and intricate matter indeed.

Generally speaking, the imputation to someone of subscription to a value approximates very closely to ascribing a *character trait*—a character-descriptive disposition—to him (e.g., stinginess or susceptibility to flattery). The kinship here is brought out in ordinary usage, for in this area we can

---

[7] David Cecil, *Lord M.: The Later Life of Lord Melbourne* (London, 1954), p. 52.

generally paraphrase locutions of the form "He did x because ..." as "In doing x he acted out of ..." ("He shot his rival because he hated him" to "In shooting his rival he acted out of hatred"). In both cases, that of a character trait and that of a value imputation, we have to do with a general pattern of actions and tendencies to action that constitutes an "ideal type" of a certain sort of person (the stingy man or the patriotic man).[8] In both cases alike, the ascription at issue is thus to be articulated in terms of conformity in behavior to a certain "ideal type." This fact provides the setting for the explanatory force of the ascription as a basis for accounting for particular items of behavior, viz., those which represent continuing instances of those general tendencies to action that constitute the basis for the ascription in question.

The explanatory efficacy of such an account obtains through the mediation of a classificatory mechanism. We have as a background multiple groupings of diverse patterns of human behavior, falling within typical constellations [the *modus operandi* of "the patriotic man" or "the (politically) ambitious man"]. And in giving a value-oriented explanation of behavior ("In doing x, Smith acted out of partiotism"), we fit the action at issue (Smith's doing of x) into a classificatory niche (acts of patriotism, i.e., the modes of action of patriotic men) in such a way that, through the ideal type at issue the rough outlines of an explanatory account can be discerned (patriotic men tend to do x-type acts because these conduce to realization of their patriotic values).

It might be objected that a value explanation of this ideal-type variety is a circular procedure. "Look at what you are doing," the objector charges, "you are saying that N acts in this or that way (e.g., justly) because he espouses such and such a value (justice). But how do you know he has this value?—simply because he acts in this or that way. What is this but to say that N acts as he does (i.e., justly) because that's how he acts?" The objection overlooks the temporal aspect of the situation. We explain N's action in the present case with reference to his subscription to a value, but then justify this subscription claim with reference to *the pattern of past actions*. The underlying thesis is one of *stability* in behavior patterns: We suppose that a man's actions tend to be "true to type" so that present behavior conforms to past patterns. This temporal aspect, together with the stability thesis that provides its basis, prevents the ideal-type variety of value explanation from sinking into circularity.

[8] On explanation in the social sciences in terms of "ideal types," see C. G. Hempel, *op. cit.*, pp. 160–171.

Our finding of the close functional kinship between the ascriptions of values and of traits of character should come as no surprise. For it is clear that in the ordinary course of things our standard mode of procedure in depicting someone's character calls in large measure for the description of his values. It is only natural that value-explanations are akin in their logical structure to character-explanations. After all, the subscription to certain values is among the most significant features definitive of a man's character.

IV

The Role of Values

in Deliberation and Decision Making

1. INTRODUCTION

A man's values are both clues to guide another's explanation of his actions
and guides to his own deliberations in the endeavor to arrive at decisions.
This latter consideration introduces the theme of "practical reasoning"—the
lines of ratiocination people engage in when seeking well-based answers to
questions regarding what is to be done.

An active revival of interest on the part of philosophers in practical reasoning is currently in progress, as the list of references given in the bibliography
attests. This interest relates both to the history of the problem and to the
substantive issues. Recent discussions of the latter sort have, it would appear,
been seriously impeded by a failure to accord due recognition to the centrally
important role that must be given to *values* in any adequate theory of practical reasoning. The aim of the present chapter is to clarify this role and to
argue for the thesis that an adequate account of practical reasoning must
have at its very heart and center a mechanism for the application of a suitable
machinery of valuation.

2. A CHARACTERIZATION OF PRACTICAL REASONING

The conception of "practical reasoning" was first dealt with by Aristotle, and we shall understand it here in more or less the same way that he did, viz., as the reasoning involved in rational deliberation leading up to and providing the reasoned grounds for acting. It is necessary for our purposes to distinguish several conceptual facets involved in action and to introduce terminology to mark these distinctions.

A "generic action type" (e.g., the opening of a window, the sharpening of a pencil) leads to a "specific action type" (e.g., the opening of *this* window, the sharpening of *that* pencil) when the "particular operand" at issue in the action (*this* window, *that* pencil) is specified.[1]

A "concrete act" or a "specific action" (*simpliciter*) (e.g., Jones's opening of *that* window at 3 P.M. yesterday, Smith's present sharpening of *this* pencil) involves the specification of three items to fix the definite, concrete context of the action:

    (i)   the *agent* (Jones, the Board of Directors)
    (ii) the *specific action type* (the opening of *this* window, the sharpening of *that* pencil)
    (iii) the particular *occasion* of action (3 P.M. yesterday, now)

A specification of these three items suffices for the *identification* of a concrete act; much more is, of course, required for its full description.[2] In our intended sense of the term there can be possible as well as actual concrete acts.

Correspondingly, let us introduce, for the sake of both ease and generality of discussion, three sorts of appropriate variables:

    1. X, Y, Z (with or without subscripts) for agents
    2. x, y, z (with or without subscripts) for specific action types
    3. $t, t_0, t_1, t_2, \ldots$, for particular occasions

Furthermore, let us introduce the composite expression of the form

$$[X/x/t]$$

as an abbreviation for the "action performance statement":

The agent X carries out (performs) a specific action of type x on the particular occasion t.

---

[1] Certain action types are inherently specific because their particular operand is "built-in," as it were (e.g., frowning, scowling).

[2] For further details see N. Rescher, "Aspects of Action" in *idem* (ed.), *The Logic of Decision and Action* (Pittsburgh, 1967).

Thus,

[Smith/ starting Jones's car/2.55 P.M. yesterday]

becomes the shorthand abbreviation for:

Smith started Jones's car at 2.55 P.M. yesterday.

And correspondingly,

[Jones/starting Jones's car/10.30 A.M. tomorrow]

abbreviates:

Jones will start his (own) car at 10.30 A.M. tomorrow.

Given that p is an action performance statement in the technical sense just specified, we may introduce the technical concept of a "task thesis," symbolized by

$$T(X:p)$$

to be read and understood as:

One thing for X to do (under the existing—or postulated—circumstances) is to make it true that p.[3]

This verbal statement is itself somewhat ambiguous; it needs and will receive further explanation and elucidation in our subsequent discussion. For the present, two glosses must suffice:

1. "One thing ... to do" is to be construed as "a *good* or *sensible* or *well-advised* (and not simply a *possible* or *conceivable* or *feasible*) thing to do."
2. "To make it true that p" is to be construed as "deliberately so to act that *as a result of his action* it will or will in all probability be true that p."

A task thesis in our sense represents what might be called an *in-the-first-analysis consideration* (as opposed to an *in-the-final-analysis judgment*) regarding meritorious action.

This idea of a task thesis is central to our discussion because it is to serve as the basis for our definition of practical reasoning. We shall adopt for present purposes the following definition:

An argument (piece of reasoning) constitutes an item of *practical reasoning* if its premises present considerations adduced *in support of a conclusion that is a task thesis.*

Thus, a course of argumentation is paradigmatically *practical reasoning* in the somewhat narrow technical sense here at issue—if it leads to a conclusion of the type:

[3] We here and henceforward take the range of the propositional variables 'p', 'q', etc., to be limited to action performance statements of the type "$[X/x/t]$."

One thing for me (you, him, X) to do—under the existing or postulated circumstances[4]—is to do such and such a thing on such and such an occasion.

A plausible example of such reasoning (taken from G. H. von Wright's important 1963 paper cited in the Bibliography) would be:

X wants to make the hut habitable (in the near future)
Unless the hut is heated (now), it will not become habitable (in the near future)

Therefore, the thing for X to do is to heat the hut (now)

The conclusion here is the task thesis

$T(X: [X/\text{heating the hut}/\text{now}])$;

that is:

One thing for X to do (being circumstanced as he is) is to make it true that X heats the hut now.

Another example of a plausible piece of practical reasoning in our sense would be:

Unless I do x, I'm going to land in the soup

Therefore, one thing for me to do is to do x[5]

The problem of the implication relations between task theses is significant for philosophical ethics because of its bearing on the question: To what act is one committing oneself in evaluating a course of action or in deciding that a given course of action is best?

Before the logical ramifications of such reasonings can be discussed profitably, it is necessary to clarify further the conception of a task thesis.

3. MORE ABOUT TASK THESES

To indicate the intended interpretation of a task thesis more precisely, we will indicate how its construction varies according to the person (first, second, third) at issue. The task thesis

$T(I: [I/x/t])$

---

[4] We shall systematically suppress this rider. It is, however, essential and should, though left tacit, always be supplied.

[5] Notice that inference still seems to obtain when the premiss is replaced by "Unless I do x, we're going to land in the soup" and even by "Unless I do x, he's going to land in the soup." But the inference

Unless he does x, I'm going to land in the soup

Therefore, one thing for him to do is to do x

looks less persuasive. The differences here can be attributed to the different "practical principles" that underlie these several inferences.

is to be interpreted as

> One thing for me to do is to make it true that I do x at t.

or, less verbosely,

> One thing for me to do is to do x at t.

A first-person statement of this form will represent a *deliberation-derived judgment*. Statements of this type express the upshot of one's own concern with the question: "What would be a good thing for me to do at t?"

The task thesis

> $T(\text{You}: [\text{You}/x/t])$

is to be interpreted as

> One thing for you to do is to make it true that you do x at t.

or somewhat less verbosely,

> One thing for you to do is to do x at t.

A second-person statement of this sort represents an *advice-presenting judgment*. Statements of this type offer recommendations to act in response to someone else's (actual or hypothetical) question: "What—in your judgment —would be a good thing for me to do at t?"

Finally, the task theses

> $T(\text{He}: [\text{He}/x/t])$
>
> $T(X: [X/x/t])$ with $X \not\vdash \text{I}, X \not\vdash \text{you}$

are to be interpreted as

> One (good) thing for him (X) to do is to make it true that he (X) does x at t.

or less verbosely,

> One (good) thing for him (X) to do is to do x at t.

or even more simply,

> X would do well to consider doing x at t.

A third-person statement of this form represents an *act-advisability judgment*. Statements of this type offer answers to the question "What is a (good) thing for him (X) to do at t?"

Task theses of the form "$T(X: [X/x/t])$" will be termed *subject-uniform*, in contradistinction to those of the form "$T(X: [Y/x/t])$"—with $X \neq Y$— which will be termed *subject-diverse*. Subject-diverse task theses are, of course, possible and perfectly meaningful. Thus,

> $T(\text{the guard}: [\text{the prisoner}/x/t])$

represents the perfectly viable task thesis:

>   One (good) thing for the guard to do is to ensure (make it true) that the
>   prisoner does x at t.

We shall henceforth always drop the superfluous rider about the time t whenever $t = now$ is intended.

Some philosophers would balk at subject-diverse task theses. They might
argue: "Surely there can be no subject-diverse task theses, it being a truism
that one person cannot will or execute the actions of another. When the guard
'makes it true' that the prisoner 'makes it true' that he (the prisoner) does
x, the quoted phrase is equivocal. Two very different 'makings' are at issue.
The latter consists simply *in doing* this something (oneself), the former consists in *making* (forcing, inducing, causing) *someone do x*." We reply: This is
a possible view of the matter, but not necessarily the correct one. The following approach seems perfectly viable: There are (it holds) two ways of "making
it true that X does x." The one (open to X alone) is "to do x oneself." The
other (open in principle to anyone) is "to get X to do x." What is at issue
is simply a matter of two different *ways* of doing the same thing (viz., making
it true that X does x). The situation is (on this view) quite analogous to that
of two men (X, Y) who can both (say) put together a certain puzzle. For this
is not a matter of two different acts ("putting the puzzle together in the X
mode" and "putting the puzzle together in the Y mode"), but of one act (viz.,
"putting the puzzle together") that can be done in distinct ways (viz., by X's
doing it and by Y's doing it). In any case, the point is not a crucial one for
our purposes: attention will here be focused exclusively on subject-uniform
task theses.

* * *

A task thesis

$$T(X: p)$$

cannot be appropriate (perhaps cannot even be meaningful) if it does not lie
within X's power—if not entirely, at least to some contributive extent—to
make it true that p. It is an immediate consequence of this principle that

$$T(X: [Y/x/t])$$

cannot be appropriate under any of the following circumstances (among
many others):

1. X is "control-impotent" with respect to Y, i.e., is not in a position to
    make Y do anything, let alone x.
2. Y is "performance-impotent" with respect to x, i.e., the doing of x is
    something which in principle lies outside Y's power. (This will be so
    a fortiori if x is an *impossible task* that lies outside anyone's power.)

3. t is an "effectively inaccessible" time which lies in the remote future or in the past. (Even if X can easily make it true that Y does x today, he cannot now make it true that Y did x yesterday.[6])

* * *

Consider the subject-uniform task thesis "$T(X: [X/x/t])$" for "One thing for X to do is to make it true that X does x at t" or, more simply, "One thing for X to do is to do x at t." Suppose further that this is a third-person task thesis (i.e., $X \neq$ me, $X \neq$ you) and that it is a task-at-hand thesis in that the occasion at issue is the present, i.e., $t - now$. We thus have the task thesis:

One thing for X to do (now) is x.

But this is clearly open to a variety of distinct, alternative constructions of which at least five significant possibilities are as follows:

1. The *moral* or *deontic* construction: A thing for X to do *on grounds of moral considerations* is x (*inter alia*).
2. The *legal* construction: A thing for X to do *on grounds of legal considerations* is x (*inter alia*).
3. The *prudential* construction: A thing for X to do *on grounds* of *prudential considerations* is x (*inter alia*).
4. The *voluntaristic* construction: A thing for X to do *on the basis of his own wants and desires in the matter* is x (*inter alia*).
5. The *synoptic* construction. A thing for X to do, *everything*—and thus specifically 1 through 4—taken into account, is x (*inter alia*).[7]

We shall not opt here for any of these alternative bases for evaluation, but shall keep open the possibility of each of these distinct constructions of a task thesis. Our interest shall be focused upon the task itself, in abstraction from the particular source of task imposition (morality, the law, prudence, the will, etc.).

In taking this stance, we must, however, avoid lulling ourselves into thinking that the question of the exact interpretation of task theses has no consequences as concerns the logical points at issue. For example, the inference

X wants to make it true that p

$\therefore T(X: p) \cong$ One thing for X to do is to make it true that p[8]

---

[6] There is a trivial category of exceptions: if X makes p true today, then he *eo ipso* makes it true that yesterday is a day preceding one on which p is true, etc. Cf. N. Rescher and J. Robison, "Temporally Conditioned Descriptions," *Ratio*, Vol. 8 (1966), pp. 46–54.

[7] There are, of course, other possibilities for a "point of view" to provide a basis for evaluation. The considerations of Chapter II, "Dimensions of Value," can be brought to bear at this point.

[8] We use the symbol $\cong$ to indicate alternative formulations of the same proposition.

is clearly warranted on construction 4 of task theses, but is, equally clearly, invalid in any of the other three interpretations.

* * *

We shall limit our discussion to categorical (unconditional) task theses of the type "$T(X: p)$" with the intended interpretation:

One thing for X to do is to make it true that p.

We shall not here deal with hypothetical or conditional task theses of the type "$T(X: p/q)$" with the interpretation:

The thing for X to do if and when q is true is to make it true that p.

We do not dismiss these hypothetical task theses for lack of importance or interest (they are, of course, crucially important in contingency planning), but only because categorical task theses are a natural—and by themselves sufficiently complicated—starting point.

4.   PRACTICAL PRINCIPLES

Consider again two examples of practical reasoning adduced in Sec. 2 above:

1. X wants to make the hut habitable
     Unless the hut is heated, it will not become habitable
     _____
     Therefore, one thing for X to do is to heat the hut

2.   Unless I do x, I'm going to land in the soup
     _____
     Therefore, one thing for me to do is to do x

Note that it is easy to enunciate *general principles the addition of which as premisses will render these arguments deductively valid.* Consider:

(P1)   Whenever anyone wants to achieve an objective and cannot achieve this objective unless he performs a certain action, then one thing for him to do is to perform this action.

(P2)   Whenever someone will land in the soup unless he performs a certain action, then one thing for him to do is to perform this action.

Such a principle which can serve as an enthymematic premiss in "trivializing" (i.e., rendering deductively valid) a cogent piece of practical reasoning will be termed a *practical principle.* The analysis and reasoned assessment of practical principles is in our view one of the main tasks of a material, substantive theory of action in contrast with a merely formal logical theory of practical reasoning, which concerns us here.

The inferential transition from a practical principle (be it of a legal, moral, prudential, voluntaristic, or synoptic kind) to a task thesis invariably calls for a factual premiss. With (P1) and (P2) above these might be given by such purely factual statements as: "*X* wants to achieve the objective . . . ," "*X* cannot do *A* without first doing *B*," and "Unless *X* does *A*, *Y* will land in the soup."

5. PRACTICAL REASONING: SOME "PARADIGM" CASES SCRUTINIZED

G. H. von Wright has put forward as "the pattern of a primary practical inference" that is "logically conclusive" an argument of essentially this pattern:[9]

1. *X* wants to do *x*

    Unless *X* does *y*, he cannot do *x*
    ___
    Therefore, *X* must do *y*

If we change the "wants to" of the first premiss to "must," the cogency of this argument is greatly strengthened:

2. *X* must do *x*

    Unless *X* does *y*, he cannot do *x*
    ___
    Therefore, *X* must do *y*

Departing somewhat from this pattern, we would obtain the inference:

3. *X* would do well to do *x*

    Unless *X* does *y*, he cannot do *x*
    ___
    Therefore, *X* would do well to do *y*

A concrete example would be

X would do well to light the match

Unless *X* strikes the match, *X* will not light the match
___
Therefore, *X* would do well to strike the match

Thus, in symbolic form we have the (seemingly cogent, plausible, and "valid") practical inference

4. $T(X: X \text{ does } x)$[10]

    $\sim [X \text{ does } y] \longrightarrow \sim [X \text{ does } x]$
    ___
    $\therefore T(X: X \text{ does } y)$

This procedure would also enable us to validate such (patently plausible) practical inferences as:

5. *X* would do well to do *x*

    If *X* does *x*, then he must also do *y*
    ___
    Therefore, *X* would do well to do *y*

___
[9] "Practical Inference," *The Philosophical Review*, Vol. 72 (1963), pp. 159–218; see pp. 172–173.

[10] $T(X: X \text{ does } x) \cong T(X: [X/x/\text{now}])$.

An instance of this pattern would be:

> X would do well to open all the windows in the house
> If X opens all the windows in the house, then X opens all the windows on the north side of the house
> _____
> Therefore, X would do well to open all the windows on the north side of the house.

Thus *if we treat task theses as subject to such principles of inference as*

$$
\begin{array}{ccc}
T(X:p) & T(X:\sim p) & T(X:p) \\
p \rightarrow q & q \rightarrow p & \sim q \rightarrow \sim p \\
\hline
\therefore T(X;q) & \therefore T(X:\sim q) & \therefore T(x:q)
\end{array}
$$

the validity of the inference at issue, viz., inference 3, would be established. But of course the conditions under which this way of proceeding is legitimate have yet to be considered, and we shall see below that these principles are not unqualifiedly valid.

* * *

The theory of reasoned argumentation deriving certain task theses from others provides the rationale for a *logical* theory of practical reasoning. Let it be granted that some task theses are basic and nonderivative, capable no doubt of being "vindicated" by considerations of appropriate sorts, but not themselves inferentially derived from other task theses. Nevertheless, there will be some instances—cases of the sort illustrated in the preceding discussion—in which some task theses are to be derived ("logically" derived, if you please) from others. In our view of the matter, the exploration and elaboration of this possibility is the main task for a formal logical theory of practical reasoning. The theory governing inferences to conclusions that are task theses is *the key issue* in the logical theory of practical reasoning.

6. VALIDITY IN INFERENCE WITH TASK THESES

In Sec. 4 above we presented some examples of more or less plausible arguments deriving a task thesis conclusion from premises including task theses. We must now deal with the general question of the formal validity of such inferences.

The familiar criterion of validity of assertoric logic—that an argument is valid when it is the case that *if* its premises are true, then its conclusion must (given these premises) also necessarily be true—is not directly applicable to arguments containing task theses, since task theses cannot be characterized as "true" or "false" in any direct and unproblematic way. Given that "X is to make it true that p" or "X is to make it true that $\sim q$," there is nothing we can say about the truth or falsity of such "taskless," ground-floor propositions as 'p' and 'q'. The difficulty that lies in the way of direct application of the familiar conception of validity in the present context is that the way in which task theses may be "true" (or "false") is not commensurate with the way in which ordinary, factual statements are "true" (or "false"). How is this difficulty to be overcome?

Consider such (patently acceptable) inference patterns as:

$$
\begin{array}{ll}
T(X:p) & T(X:p) \\
\underline{T(X:p) \longrightarrow T(X:q)} & \underline{\sim T(X:q) \longrightarrow \sim T(X:p)} \\
\therefore\ T(X:q) & \therefore\ T(X:q)
\end{array}
$$

Such inferences are valid on grounds of standard logic without any reference to a "logic of practical reasoning" (by the meaning of '$\longrightarrow$'). Could we not take the step from accepting their validity to accepting as valid:

$$
\begin{array}{ll}
T(X:p) & T(X:p) \\
\underline{p \longrightarrow q} & \underline{\sim q \longrightarrow \sim p} \\
\therefore\ T(X:q) & \therefore\ T(X:q)
\end{array}
$$

The step is tempting, but one might hesitate in the face of such counter-examples as:

> X is to make it true that X writes his Aunt Martha a letter in the German language
> If X writes his Aunt Martha in the German language, then (necessarily) the German language exists
>
> Therefore, X is to make it true that the German language exists

This is asking a good deal of X: the existence or nonexistence of the German language is, of course, something that lies wholly outside his control (although his doing of certain actions, e.g., speaking to someone in German, hinges crucially upon it).[11] Another example of similar character is:

> X is to make it true that X shovels the snow off the driveway
> X cannot make it true that X shovels the snow off the driveway unless it is true that there is snow on the driveway
>
> Therefore, X is to make it true that there is snow on the driveway

[11] It might be well to differentiate between the inferences

$$
\begin{array}{ll}
T(X:p) & T(X:p) \\
\underline{p \longrightarrow q} & \underline{\vdash p \longrightarrow q} \\
\therefore\ T(X:q) & \therefore\ T(X:q)
\end{array}
$$

where the $\vdash$ indicates that in the second inference the entailment in question holds on grounds of formal logical relations alone (thus ruling out such presuppositional entailments as that from "X shovels the snow off the driveway" to "There is snow on the driveway").

Our acceptance of the "validity" of the inference patterns in question goes back to our interpretation of the p's and q's not as arbitrary but only as *action-performance* statements. Thus we propose to read "$p \rightarrow q$" as "to make it true that p also requires making it true that q," and thus as expressing the fact that q is a *practically necessary condition* for p. (This conception should be developed in such a way as to be relativized to the circumstances that obtain. But this and other necessary refinements in the idea of "practical necessity" will not be developed here.)

It is worth remarking that in putting forward as generically "valid" such practical arguments as the above, two sorts of detail may be regarded as immaterial:

1. It does not matter whether we have to do with the first, second, or third person (i.e., $X = $ I, $X = $ you, or $X = $ he, outsider), *as long as the identification of X is uniform throughout the argument*. The validity of the pattern of reasoning is thus the same, independently of the question of whether the reasoning involves deliberation, advice, or third-party judgments of act-advisability.
2. It does not matter how our task operator T is construed (be it with respect to moral, legal, prudential, or other considerations), *provided only that the construction be uniform throughout the argument* (and thus specifically the same in the first premiss and the conclusion).

We can, of course, distinguish between task theses with respect to the (conceptual) source of the task, i.e., the sorts of considerations from which it derives. Just this was the step we took earlier in distinguishing between moral, legal, prudential, and voluntaristic task theses. These labels indicate the sort of "sanction" involved in going against the several sorts of task theses: moral or legal transgression, violation of self-interest, or going against one's desires. It is through "sanctions" of this sort that task theses derive their "justification," in one manner of speaking.

We can now resume the question of validity. We propose to regard an inference from task premisses to a task conclusion as valid if the corresponding command inference is valid, "corresponding" in the sense that this command inference results from the initial practical inference when we uniformly translate all its task premisses of the form "$T(X: p)$" (The thing for X to do is to do p) as command premisses of the form "$X! \, p$" (X, do $p!$). This policy reduces the theory of inference among task theses to the theory of command inferences, where we have at our disposal a relatively better-established branch of logical theory.[12]

---

[12] See N. Rescher, *The Logic of Commands* (London, 1966), and note the extensive bibliography of the subject presented there.

7. PRACTICAL INCONSISTENCIES

Consider the case of a "conflict of duties" or a "conflict of desires." Suppose that X finds himself so circumstanced that he would be well advised to do A and to do B, where A and B are incompatible, or that he wishes to do A and to do B, where doing A is inconsistent with doing B. We have then, *ex hypothesi*, three premisses of the form:

$T(X: p)$

$T(X: q)$

$p \longrightarrow \sim q$

Instances of this sort leap readily to mind: X's meager funds may suffice to pay his debt to Y or to pay his debt to Z, but not to both. Or X may want to be king, although he can only become king by compassing his brother's death, and yet he wants his brother to live.

In failing to regard the above trio as an inconsistent triad, we shall have to deny the formal validity of the inference pattern:

$T(X: p)$

$\underline{p \longrightarrow \sim q}$

$\therefore \sim T(X: q)$

For the three statements S_1, S_2, and S_3 will form an inconsistent triad only if we can validly deduce $\sim S_2$ from S_1 and S_3. But now if we take the plausible view that $\sim T(X: q)$ entails $T(X: \sim q)$, then we must also reject the inference pattern:

$T(X: p)$

$\underline{p \longrightarrow q}$

$\therefore T(X: q)$

We must reject this at any rate for the particular conception of task thesis in terms of which we have thus far been working.

But a new line of thought now opens up: Is there no viable variant of this conception of the T-operator for which the very plausible inference represented by the last-named pattern would obtain?

8. OPTIMAL VERSUS MERELY MERITORIOUS TASKS

Suppose that X finds himself in a position in which both

    1. to make it true that p

and

    2. to make it true that q

are "good things to do," but the *joint* realization of these two desiderata is (logically) impossible. Here again we have the characteristic situation of a "practical inconsistency":

$$T(X: p)$$

$$T(X: q)$$

$$p \longrightarrow \sim q$$

The situation is such as to force us to a "choice," as it were, between the two task theses "$T(X: p)$" and "$T(X: q)$." But let us now draw the needed distinction between the ordinary *meritorious task thesis* of the familiar type

$$T(X: r)$$

for

    "One good thing for X to do is to make it true that r,"

    and the (circumstantially) *optimal task thesis* of the type

$$T^{\#}(X: r)$$

for

    "The very best thing for X to do (under the existing or postulated circumstances) is to make it true that r."

The distinctions at issue can be indicated in a very simple, nontechnical way. One must distinguish between the stages of:

    1. *Deliberation*
        "A good thing for me to do is A."
        "I would do well to contemplate doing B most seriously."[13]

    2. *Decision making*
        "All considered, the very best I can do under the existing circumstances is to do C."

    3. *Implementing resolution*
        "I shall do C."

    4. *Implementing action*
        I do C.

The process can of course, break down at any stage. The man who fails to get to stage 1 is impulsive, heedless, frivolous, or some such thing. The man who gets to stage 1 but stops short of stage 2 exhibits a kind of deficiency in practical intelligence, a failure in the capacity for intelligent choice and rational planning. The man who gets to stage 2 but fails at 3—who says

[13] There is, of course, also a prior stage of feasibility assessment involving such judgments as: "One *possible* and *feasible* thing for me to do is A."

"I realize that x is, all considered, the best thing I can do, but I shall not do it, I shall do y instead"—is snared into irrationality, be it by passion, perversity, or for some other reason. Finally, the man who gets to stage 3 but fails at 4 is a victim of impotence (weakness of resolution, spinelessness, Aristotelian *akrasia*, or the like).

In taking the step from T to $T^{\#}$ we automatically leave the problem of "practical inconsistency" behind; it is now clearly impossible that a situation of the type

$$T^{\#}(X:p)$$

$$T^{\#}(X:q)$$

$$p \longrightarrow \sim q$$

could ever arise: the trio represents a genuine "inconsistent triad." "The best thing to do" cannot possibly involve the performance of mutually incompatible tasks.

Consider two mutually conflicting practical arguments of the von Wrightian type (based on four perfectly co-feasible premises):

X wants to be king	X wants his brother to live
X can become king only by poisoning his brother	X's brother will not live if X poisons him
∴ X must poison his brother	∴ X must not poison his brother

Given this situation, it is necessary to "make a choice" between the two (voluntaristic) task theses out of which the conflict arises under the hypothetical circumstances at issue, viz.,

"X wants to be king"

"X wants his brother to live"

It must be decided—and presumably X must decide—which of X's wants is to be implemented and which is to be abandoned. In short, compatibility must be brought into being among the welter of (circumstantially) discordant task theses representing merely meritorious desiderata ("being king"; "having his brother live") by seeking out those desiderata to which primacy is to be accorded, i.e., by fixing upon the optimal task thesis.[14] Here in going

[14] The situation is, from the strictly formal standpoint, closely analogous to that of the resolution of the inductive inconsistencies that can arise in such cases as:

a is an F	a is G
Very few F's are H's	Most G's are H's
a is probably not an H	a is probably an H

For a discussion of the resolution procedure here, which is closely akin to that of the resolution of practical inconsistencies, see C. G. Hempel, "Inductive Inconsistencies," *Synthese*, Vol. 12 (1960), pp. 439–469.

from T to $T^\#$, we go (in the case of wants) from *prima facie* or first-order wants to ultimate or overriding wants.

9. OPTIMUM-DERIVATIVE TASK THESES

From the logical point of view and the standpoint of a theory of practical reasoning, optimal task theses, although very important for the reasons that have been indicated (i.e., as affording an essential means of avoiding practical inconsistencies), have a very serious shortcoming because of the renewed failure of the plausible inference pattern:

$$T^\#(X\!:p)$$
$$\underline{p \longrightarrow q}$$
$$\therefore T^\#(X\!:q)$$

Thus, for example, the very best thing that X can do under certain circumstances may be "to open every window in the house." And of course the fact that X opens every window in the house entails "X opens the living room window" (under the supposition that the house has a living room which has a window). But it by no means follows that the very best thing that X can do (under the circumstances at issue) is "to open the living room window." An optimal act may entail as its necessary component an act which, taken in isolation or in separation from it, is highly nonoptimal, but nevertheless has, *ex hypothesi*, the important characteristic of being a part of (or, if you like, "derivative" from) an optimal task. For this reason it is desirable to introduce

$$T^*(X\!:p)$$

as shorthand for

$$(\exists q)\,[T^\#(X\!:q)\ \&\ (q \longrightarrow p)]$$

Thus "$T^*(X\!:p)$" is true just in case making it true that p is—not the optimal task for X, but—a part of what X is required to do, *inter alia*, in the course of realizing the optimal task. Such task theses will be characterized as *optimum-derivative*.

As an instrument of the theory of practical reasoning, T^* has certain clearly marked advantages:

1. As against T, T^* has, like $T^\#$, the advantage of avoiding practical inconsistencies. We cannot be confronted by the situation:

    $$T^*(X\!:p)$$
    $$T^*(X\!:q)$$
    $$p \longrightarrow \sim q$$

2. As against $T^\#$, T^* has the advantage from the standpoint of logical operability of having the crucial "entailment transmissibility" property exemplified by the inference pattern:

$$\frac{\begin{array}{l} T^*(X\colon p) \\ p \longrightarrow q \end{array}}{\therefore\ T^*(X\colon q)}$$

In a sense, we want a theory of practical reason which, if it cannot deliver all of $T^\#$, at least gives us T^*, i.e., the parts or components of an optimal course of action.

10. VALUES IN DECISION MAKING

The step from the concern with "merely meritorious" tasks to that with specifically *optimal* tasks (or their derivatives) carries us, within the domain of what we have characterized as *practical reasoning* in general, to the region of *decision making* in particular. Here we have to do with conclusions not of the form "X would be 'well advised' (from such and such a point of view) to do A" but of the form "Everything considered, the best X can do under the existing circumstances is A." In establishing such conclusions, incompatible tasks must be meshed into a consistent whole, and the welter of possible "good moves" must be boiled down to one specifically best course of action. Here we have to do not only with procedures for dealing with the question of whether doing x would or would not be "a good thing" but also with the more demanding question of "*how* good a thing" it would be. We must deal in detail with the priorities, the merits and demerits, the advantages and disadvantages, the "costs"[15] of and the "returns" from alternative courses of action. It is at the point of "decision making" (in the sense here specified) that values most emphatically enter into practical reasoning. And they enter in an essential and indispensable way because of the conflicts and inconsistencies that almost invariably obtain when one is dealing with merely meritorious rather than optimal (or near optimal) tasks. Valuation is inevitable in situations of this sort, where at the point of decision a choice must be made among incompatible alternatives, since rational choice must not be random but guided by considerations of comparative merit, considerations in which values must play a pivotal role.

[15] Not only the resource costs, but also what the economists call the "opportunity costs" of investing these resources here, and so not being in a position to deploy them upon alternatives.

11. THE LOGICAL STRUCTURE OF THE
PROCESS OF PRACTICAL REASONING

The logical structure of the process of practical reasoning as we have conceived of it here is perhaps to be explained with the greatest clarity and precision by tabular means:

The starting point	Course of action	Possible goals
	1	G_1 (meritorious)
Where	2	G_1 (meritorious)
we	3	G_2 (nonmeritorious)
are	4	G_2 (nonmeritorious)
	5	G_3 (meritorious)

The first step—so basic that it underlies and conceptually precedes the process of "practical reasoning" as we conceive of it—is the recognition within the sphere of *possible and feasible* goals of those that are meritorious. (This step, of course, is also—and inescapably—a matter of evaluation.) We must next examine the courses of action leading toward those goals *and evaluate them* in the full realization that an ignoble course may well lead to a meritorious goal, or obversely. This process of course-of-action evaluation requires taking into account conjointly both the merits of the goals and the merits of individual actions as constituents of courses of action leading to these goals. Now a given course of action, say, course 2 to goal 1, consists of a sequential pattern of component actions:

First do *A*; then do *B*; then do *C*; . . .

It is thus that we would arrive at a "decision" of the form: The very best thing to do now is *A*, and then *B*, etc. In short, to determine the merit of an act we must assess it not simply in isolation but also *as part of a course of action leading to a certain goal* (and thus with reference to the other acts involved here).

The evaluation of an act is to be carried out *separatim* only in "the first analysis" and requires for its completion also the assessment of those actions which are its companions in the course of action of which it must—under the circumstances—be a part. To say this is not to say that the end justifies the means, but to insist that neither ends nor means can be assessed in isolation and to realize the truism that even a very good act (say, giving money for a good cause) can under certain circumstances (limited financial resources) lead to other acts (failure to redeem obligations) which should count as decisive grounds against its performance.

12. ANALYSIS OF AN EXAMPLE OF VON WRIGHT'S

To exhibit more clearly the conceptual architectonic of the problem of decision making, let us consider the piece of reasoning put forward by von Wright as a paradigm of valid practical reasoning:

> *X* wants to make the hut habitable
> Unless *X* heats the hut, it will not become habitable
> ―――――――――――――――――――――――
> Therefore, *X* must heat the hut

Let the premises be true. Does the conclusion follow: "must" *X* heat the hut? The answer is neither "yes" nor "no" but "yes and no" —*yes* if the "wants" of the first premiss is "wants-in-the-final-analysis" and *no* if it is merely "wants-in-the-first-analysis." If there is something one "must" do in the sense of "must do to attain one of one's aims or desires," this does not show that one "must" do this in any more far-reaching sense. For the situation that actually confronts *X* is one of a choice between two situations:

	Alternative 1	*Alternative 2*
Cost:	The labor, etc., involved in getting the hut heated	The discomfort of an unheated hut
Return:	A heated hut	The time, energy, etc., that would have gone to getting the hut heated but is now available for application to other ends

We confront a problem in cost-benefit analysis of the classical type. To draw the conclusion "*X* must heat the hut" from the premises of the first argument above is to ignore the fact that in a comparison of this sort, *X*'s want to make the hut habitable may be *overridden by other wants*. Only if the "want" (aim, desire) in question is taken to be an "in-the-final-analysis" (i.e., an *ex hypothesi* nonoverridden) want does the argument actually cogently yield its conclusion. The ranking of wants—their comparative *evaluation*, in short— taking full account not only of the goals themselves and the benefits at issue in their realization but also of the "costs" (both intrinsic costs and opportunity costs) inherent in the courses of action leading to their attainment, is a crucial part of the logic of practical reasoning and represents the point at which values must be brought upon the stage.

13. CONCLUSION

The upshot of this chapter lends itself readily to summarization. Practical reasoning has to do with rational deliberation regarding the "things to be done" by us or others in the circumstances in which we find ourselves. At this general level of plausible things to do we find ourselves confronted with alternative courses of action which, if not abstractly incompatible, are at any rate *circumstantially* incompatible in the face of finite resources of time, money, etc. The rational process of decision making involves the comparative assessment of these alternatives in the attempt to fix upon one alternative to determine a coherent pattern of action that represents "*the best* thing to do." At exactly this juncture of the comparative assessment of alternative courses of action, the logic of the situation requires recourse to values as the requisite means for effecting the necessary choice among mutually incompatible alternatives. A recourse to values is indispensable for making this evaluation. In the logic of practical reasoning values thus play the key role of providing the means of arbitration between incompatible alternatives, alternatives which are not necessarily incompatible in themselves *in abstracto* but mutually exclusive in the context of finite resources.[16]

---

[16] This chapter draws extensively upon the writer's paper of the same title in *The Philosophical Quarterly*, Vol. 17 (1967), pp. 130–136.

V

Axiology:

The General Theory of Values

1. INTRODUCTION

Thus far, the approach to the treatment of values in this book has concentrated upon "values" in the pluralistic way that one deals with them in everyday situations by means of the resources afforded by ordinary language. In contrast with this admittedly rather diffuse and multifaceted approach, stands a view which not long ago was standard among philosophers on both sides of the Atlantic. Rather than coping with a multiplicity of values, and treating valuation as an inherently diversified cluster of related phenomena, these writers sought to found a unified theory of value in general, purporting to discover a common core of valuing throughout the wide variety of settings in which evaluation takes place. Across the pluralism of *values*, this school of thought saw operative a unified conception of *Value*. The project was thus launched of setting up a general theory of value, viewed as one unitary, broadly inclusive whole.

The founding father of this value-with-a-capital-V movement in modern philosophy was the German philosopher Rudolf Hermann Lotze (1817–1881). Lotze's doctrine set up a dualism of two realms, that of *fact* (or being) and that of *value*. (In this regard, Lotze was not an innovator, but followed in a tradition of long standing that can be traced back to Plato.) In adopting this dualism, Lotze sought to maintain a realm of significance for human concerns outside the sphere of a scientific naturalism, although he did try to assimilate both facts and values under a generalized conception of validity (*Geltung*). Lotze's double-realm conception, conceived of along the lines of Hume's classic is/ought dichotomy, provided the framework of discussion for two generations of later value theorists but had the unfortunate effect of promoting the (Spinozistic) idea that the value point of view is somehow at odds with that of our scientific understanding of the world. This Germanic value theory was transplanted to the United States with the Harvard appointment (in 1897) of Hugo Münsterberg, a student of H. Rickert who had studied with Lotze's disciple, W. Windelband. Because of Münsterberg's German accent—according to R. B. Perry—American philosophers "heard of 'walues' before they heard of 'values'."[1] On the Continent the main figures in the later development of value theory were Franz Brentano (b. 1838) and his school[2] and the Baden school of neo-Kantians founded by Wilhelm Windelband (b. 1848);[3] in England G. E. Moore was especially influential, and in the United States, Ralph Barton Perry, and Wilbur Marshall Urban.

In his highly respected book on *Realms of Value*, Perry defined "value" as follows:

> A thing—anything—has value or is valuable, in the original and generic sense, when it is the object of an interest—any interest[4]

In line with such a conception of the "original and generic sense" of value, value philosophers of the Austro-German school—which substantially (if often indirectly) influenced most Anglo-American writers on the topic prior to World War II—had attempted to found a general theory of values, often referred to as *axiology*. The program of this global approach to values envisaged three primary tasks for value studies: (1) the grounding of a

---

[1] *Realms of Value* (Cambridge, 1954), p. 9.

[2] This school, often called the "Second Austrian School of Values," included Christian von Ehrenfels, Alexius Meinong, and Anton Marty, as well as Meinong's pupils Oskar Kraus and Ernst Mally. The "First Austrian School of Values" was a school of *economic* value theorists (Menger, Wieser, Böhm-Bawerk).

[3] Its principal later members were Heinrich Rickert and Hugo Münsterberg. For details regarding these schools and the works produced by them see the bibliography at the end of the book.

[4] *Op. cit.*, pp. 2–3. This "interest theory of values" goes back to Perry's earlier writings on the subject.

generic conception of value to provide a unified basis for the wide diversity of contexts in which evaluation takes place, (2) the study of the phenomenology of valuation in general, and (3) the development of a system of value axiomatics codifying the universal rules of valuation. We must at least briefly consider each of these projects in turn.

2. THE GROUNDING OF A GENERAL THEORY OF VALUE

In his lectures on ethics at the University of Vienna from 1876 to 1894, Franz Brentano developed the groundwork of a highly influential theory of value. Brentano saw the basis of valuation in man's emotions[5]—specifically in the contrast between the complex of favorable emotions (loving, liking, being pleased about, favoring, etc.), on the one hand, and of negative emotions (hating, disliking, being displeased about, etc.), on the other. The former class of emotional acts he characterized very broadly as *love* and the latter as *hate*. These, of course, are not solely polar opposites, but are capable of gradation, of degrees, and of relative preferability or relative disapproval. These generic attitudes, viewed in abstraction from their specific context of occurrence, define the realm of valuation. Thus, as Brentano and his many followers saw the matter, it makes good sense not simply to deal with a great mass of diverse values and the varied spectrum of contexts in which evaluation takes place, but to consider the general phenomenon of valuing in abstraction from its various specific manifestations.

A sophisticated analysis of evaluation along these lines was developed by Brentano's pupil Alexius Meinong, on whose theory a "value experience" involves four ingredients:

1. The *value subject* who experiences
2. A positive (or negative) emotion called the *value feeling* directed at
3. A real or an "intentional" (nonexistent) object, a *value object* that is the thing with respect to which the evaluation is made, the value feeling being produced in the value subject (not by the value object itself, but) by the value subject's entertaining (though not necessarily accepting)
4. An existence judgment about the realization or existence of this value object.[6]

---

[5] Perhaps "attitudes" would have been a better term.

[6] ". . . the value-object does not cause the value-feeling. The cause of the value-feeling is a judgment of the existence of the value-object. This judgment provides the linkage between the value-feeling and the value-object." *Psychologisch-ethische Untersuchungen zur Werttheorie* (Graz, 1894), p. 21. Cf. the entire discussion on pp. 14–35.

In the Brentano-Meinong approach, value is not an independent self-sustaining characteristic of things but a derivative characteristic arising out of their relationship to people who interact with them experientially. But despite its experiential involvements, value has an objective foundation in the characteristics of its objects. These either are such that a certain value reaction toward them is appropriate, and then the evaluation is correct, or they are such that it is not and then the evaluation is incorrect. Value thus has an objective basis independent of thought, emotion, and experience, with the consequence that value experiences are either appropriate (correct) or inappropriate (incorrect).[7] This conception of the objective validity of evaluation espousal by the school of Brentano was adhered to by the followers of Husserl in phenomenology (M. Scheler, A. Pfänder) as well as in the influential writings of Nicolai Hartmann.

Apart from its somewhat psychologistic setting in the context of *value experience*, Meinong's characterization of evaluation agrees closely with our own conception of the evaluation (positive or negative) of an item by someone with reference to a value (i.e., a tool of "rationalization," and so a standard of judgment).

One of the real strengths of the Brentano-Meinong school—*vis-à-vis* some phenomenologists, and also Nicolai Hartmann—lay in their de-emphasis of Lotze's "double-realm" theory, and their abandonment of the teaching that an acceptance of the reality of human values is at odds with the scientific view of the world. The existence of man, and the nature of the conditions requisite to his well-being and welfare—and thus the characteristics of the humanly beneficial—are, after all, genuine *facts* about the world that neither need to be nor should be taken as lying outside the cognizance of natural science.

An important counterview to the Brentano-Meinong approach was put forward by Christian von Ehrenfels. Denying that the basis of value is emotion—or rather, affection, viz., pleasure and pain—Ehrenfels saw the foundation of value in *desire*. Meinong (and his followers in value theory such as W. D. Prall[8] in the United States) viewed affection as fundamental to desire: in their view we desire something because the contemplation of its existence or possession gives us pleasure. According to this view, we desire something *because* we value it. Ehrenfels (followed in this regard by R. B. Perry in the

---

[7] Compare Brentano's characterization of *goodness* as: "That which can be loved with a right love, that which is worthy of love, is good." *The Origin of the Knowledge of Right and Wrong*, tr. C. Hague (Westminister, 1902), p. 19.

[8] Prall was substantially influenced by Meinong in his writings on value, though he was not a follower of Meinong's in other ways—he called himself a "nominalist," for example, so in ontology he was opposed to Meinong.

United States) saw the matter in reverse: we value something because we desire it. Desire is the basic thing: it governs value, since pleasure is subsequent to desire; once we desire something we desire pleasure from the contemplation of its realization or its acquisition. (Note that the Meinong-Ehrenfels controversy was a dispute *within* the theory of value-hedonism: both sides regarded pleasure as the key to valuing.)

3. AXIOLOGY AND THE PROBLEM OF INTRINSIC VALUE

Value theorists in the axiological tradition viewed the topic of their concern as something distinctive and special, something not on the order, say, of the decorative value of a vase or the economic value of a piece of land. One crucial emphasis was made to set the discussion off from the consideration of these more mundane types of valuing, the emphasis upon *intrinsic* value. The axiologists focused primarily upon *intrinsic value* as distinguished from *instrumental value*, upon what is valued "as an end" or "for itself" or "in its own right," as distinguished from something that is valued "merely as a means" or "for something else." This distinction was not, of course, invented by the axiologists but goes back to Plato and Aristotle. That there must be something valued in its own right rather than for another is implicit in Aristotle's classic limit argument:

> Further, the *final cause* [*telos*, viz., "what is good in itself," i.e., valued in its own right] is an end, that sort of thing which is not for the sake of something else, but for whose sake something else is; so that if there is to be a last such term, the series [i.e., the for-the-sake-of series] will not be infinite, while if there is no such [final] term, there will be no end. But those who make the series infinite unwittingly annihilate the Good (for no one would undertake to do anything if he were not going to reach a limit); nor would Reason exist, for the reasonable man always acts for an end, which is a limit, but the final cause is a limit.[9]

Aristotle thus argues that the for-the-sake-of series must terminate in something that is "for its own sake," and this standpoint with its corresponding doctrine of intrinsic ends, or, rather, of intrinsic values, became focal in axiological theory.

John Dewey and his followers have attacked the validity of the distinction between means values and end values. They did so on grounds which can be rejected as insufficient because they failed to meet head-on the full weight

[9] *Metaphysics*, 994b9–16.

of the impressive infinite-regress argument.[10] But even if the distinction is abandoned, that between the subordinate that-valued-for-the-sake-of and the superordinate that-for-the-sake-of-which-valued will remain. And correspondingly, the relation of subordination being transitive, there remains the question—not really so far removed from that regarding end values— of those very high-level values for the sake of which most other valuings take place.

The question "What sorts of things may reasonably be taken to be valued as ends?" is the grand-prize question of traditional philosophical ethics. Here we reach the dividing point of the great ethical systems. What is to be valued as an end is *pleasure* (the Cyrenaics), *happiness* (Aristotle), *knowledge* (Plato), *virtue* (the Stoics), *a good will* (Kant), *the general welfare* (the Utilitarians), and so on. These, clearly, are all *summum bonum* theories that seek to found a monolithic, inverted-pyramid structure of value upon one single, solitary end value to which all others are somehow means. But, of course, a doctrine of ends values need not take this monistic form; it can be polychromatic and envisage a plurality of distinct end values which, even if some are "higher" than others, are at any rate subordinated to them in a means-ends hierarchy. The merits of Dewey's attack in the traditional theory can be viewed to reside not in his assult against the distinction of means value and ends value as such, but in an opposition to a monistic concept of end value.

At any rate, the conception of intrinsic value (or "ultimate-end value," in contrast to an instrumental "mediate-end value") provided a cornerstone of axiology by furnishing the link between mundane garden-variety valuings and capital V Values. If someone, say Smith, subscribes instrumentally to a certain value, say "frugality," he does so largely or wholly because he believes it to be a means conducive to something else that is valued, say the mediate-end value of "the economic prosperity of the country." Now if he values this economic prosperity as a means to "the greatest happiness of the greatest number," but regards that value in turn as self-validating, then we arrive at the finding that "happiness" will be one of his values (with a capital V). In tracing out the means-end chain we arrive at the sort of *intrinsic value* upon which axiological theory placed its prime emphasis.

Such a stress upon end values is particularly important from the standpoint of philosophical ethics, in which the axiologists primarily interested themselves. For here our concern is not with means values (e.g., how good a certain procedure is for torturing people) but with end values (the value of hap-

---

[10] Monroe Beardsley's provocative recent article on "Intrinsic Value," *Philosophy and Phenomenological Research*, Vol. 26 (1965–66), pp. 1–17, does try to meet the argument head on.

piness, of freedom, of life, etc.). There is a good discussion of this point in Wittgenstein's "Lecture on Ethics."[11] Ethics, he says, is concerned with what is good, not in the sense in which a piece of furniture might be said to be good (e.g., for seating or decoration or firewood), but in the sense of "what is really important" in life.[12] And not only are the values that are of interest to ethics end values, but, conversely, it is clear that any definable end value must have an ethical aspect in representing an appropriate target for human aspiration. The pursuits of the axiologists thus consolidated themselves in the arena traditional to philosophical ethics.

4. THE METATHEORY OF VALUATION

One of the central tasks of such a theory of evaluation in general is to make a critical examination of the generic features of the mechanisms for applying the concept of value. Here two questions above all have been at the forefront of discussion: (1) Is value a *property* of objects (like color) or is it a *relationship* (like ownership) that arises out of circumstances linking the value object with the valuing subject in some special way,[13] in which case the further question of objectivity vs. subjectivity arises: is valuation personal and relative; does value reside strictly "in the mind of the beholder," or does it have an objective grounding? (2) Is the value of an object something to be apprehended only in subjective experience (like the taste of a food or a drink) intuitively—or is its attribution to be based on impersonally specifiable criteria whose satisfaction can be determined by some objective examination akin to the scientific investigation of things?

An enormous literature has sprung up around these metatheoretical questions regarding valuation. We cannot here pursue the matter at the length required for an adequate discussion. In consequence, we shall content ourselves with formulating our own position in a brief and dogmatic way. As we see it, a paradigm model of evaluation can be found in the work of the land appraiser. The assessed value at issue (that of land) is relational: it is not a property inherent in the land itself (like the rockiness of its soil) but arises out of its relationship to people in its environment and has to do with

---

[11] Ludwig Wittgenstein, "A Lecture on Ethics," *The Philosophical Review*, Vol. 75 (1965), pp. 3–11.

[12] *Ibid.*, p. 5.

[13] Thus W. Windelband wrote that value "is never found in the object itself as a property. It consists in a relation to an appreciating mind, which satisfies the desires of its will or reacts in feelings of pleasure upon the stimulation of the environment. Take away will and feeling and there is no such thing as value." *An Introduction to Philosophy*, tr. J. McCabe (New York, 1921), p. 215.

various attitudes that people have toward the features exhibited by this valued item. Evaluation is thus generally "principled," i.e., based on criteria that take account of objective features of the items (real or assumed) that are being evaluated. Value has, therefore, an objective basis and can be assessed, by impersonal standards or criteria that can be taught to an evaluator through training. Value—in this conception—is relational (in viewing the value of an object as something that arises from the nature of its interactions with people, or perhaps intelligent beings generally) but objective (since evaluation is, in general, based on objectively establishable and interpersonally operative standards).

The controversy about the objectivity of value comes down to this: Is something *valuable* because it is *valued* (and so, solely because it is regarded by people in a certain way), or is something *valued*—properly and correctly valued—when it is *valuable*, that is, when it is objectively possessed of certain value-endowing features?[14] The question can be put in another way by asking what type of valuing situation is to be taken as typical. Is the paradigm evaluation that of a postage stamp, whose sole value resides in the fact that men wish to own it? Or is the paradigm evaluation that of an apple whose value, quite apart from the fact of its being desired, resides in its possession of those characteristics that make for its being nourishing, palatable, hunger-appeasing, etc.? (Note that it is only in this second case—when having value requires the possession of certain features—that one can speak of something that is valued as being rightly or correctly valued.)

Put in these terms the question (it would seem) virtually answers itself. Both types of value situations arise. There are postage stamp cases, where value derives from being subjectively valued, and apple cases, where value inheres objectively in value-endowing features. There are *mere* valuings of the *de gustibus non est disputandum* kind that lie beyond direct criticism, and there are *well-founded* valuings that can be correct or incorrect on the basis of an objective foundation. An adequate theory of value has to be prepared to take both types of valuings into account.

5.   WHAT CAN BE VALUED?

One of the main problems for a general theory of value relates to the question: What kinds of entities are "bearers of value"? What can be valued? This

---

[14] The dispute is closely parallel to the medieval controversy over Scotism, the doctrine that something is good because God wants it so, and not that he wants it so because it is good (i.e., is objectively good, independently of God's wishes).

question has no compact or tidy answer. *Virtually anything can be valued.* The most ugly and common object can be converted into something of value if endowed through association with sentimental value, say, hallowed by association with a beloved. There are even problems in specifying the specific entity that is valued. Suppose we value Jones's health; just what is it we value? Is it the *concrete thing*—the healthy Jones? Is it the *property*, health, in the Jonesian context? Or is it the *state of affairs* of Jones's being healthy?

Such questions about the bearer of value agitated the axiologists. From our own angle of approach, however, their significance is diminished. When something is valued rationally, there exists, *ex hypothesi*, a *reason* for valuing it that constitutes a "rationale" for its positive (or negative) evaluation. Our own approach to evaluation through the *values* at issue fixes upon these value-attribution-supporting considerations.

Of course, valuing taken strictly in isolation and by itself is reason-neutral, i.e., if I know merely *that* Smith values *x*, I do not *ipso facto* know *why* he values *x*. But the reverse is not the case: if I know what his values are, then I can draw plausible inferences about the things he values. The very fact that values can be classified (see Chapter II) gives one a basis for handling the question of the bearers of value. This is why our own approach to valuation took its point of departure not from the (unmanageable) aspect of the *objects* of valuing but from that of the *values* involved.

A merely seeming exception to the rule that if one knows what a man values one does not thereby know why he values it is formed by such common examples of valuings of a ball-point pen, hunting dog, or a motor car. With such things evaluation is usually *sui generis* evaluation: this is a good ball-point—it is as good *as a ball-point*: i.e., it realizes in a reasonable degree the various values (reliability, functionality, etc.) that are at issue in the *modus operandi* of ball-point pens. When "the sorts of values generally at issue with something of that kind" can be understood as a tacit rider to the evaluation at issue, then the aforementioned value ambiguity of a positive (or negative) evaluation—its failure to be specific as to the values involved— will be removed thereby.

6. THE GENERIC AXIOMATICS OF VALUATION

One of the principal tasks that the Austro-German school of value theorists set for itself was that of devising a "logic of valuation" based on the discovery of formal general rules basic to the theory of value, rules that are objective in their grounding and universal in their unrestricted applicability throughout the whole value domain. Such value axioms may seem rather obvious and not very "interesting"—even as is the case with the principles of logic itself—but all the same they are to provide a solid rational underpinning for the enterprise of value theory. Examples of such axioms are:

1. When something has value, then its existence is valuable and is more valuable than its nonexistence. (Brentano)
2. When *A* is something of positive value and *B* is something of negative value, then *A* is more valuable than the conjunction of *A* with *B*, and this conjunction is more valuable than *B*. (Brentano)
3. When something has value, then the more there is of it the greater the value. (Kraus)

Rules of this sort can certainly be called into question. (Item 3, for example, is very definitely a candidate for dispute.) Suffice it here to indicate that this exploration of the formally valid rules of valuation in implementation of its concept of value axiomatics is one of the salient insights and main contributions of the Austro-German school of value theorists, and, in particular, represents one of the many important contributions of Franz Brentano to the field of value studies. We shall pursue this topic of logical theory of valuation in great detail in the next chapter. The formal theory of preference along the lines with which we shall here be concerned is definitely to be viewed as a significant part of the permanent heritage of this school.

7. MATERIAL RULES OF VALUATION

Some recent axiologists have attempted to go beyond the exploration of such *formal* rules of value to attempt the development of *material but yet generic* principles of evaluation. However, little that can be classed as securely established has been achieved along these lines. Consider the following circumstance. A valued item such as a pearl jewel will exhibit certain characteristic properties: its chemical composition, hardness, luster, rotundity of shape, etc. Noting such facts as these, R. S. Hartman has proposed to determine the value (merit, goodness) of an item in terms of the quantitative volume of property involvement, i.e., in terms of the relative number of such characteristic properties that the item actually exhibits.[15] For example, a pearl with all the specific properties save the appropriate hardness and luster would be a fairly good pearl, being deficient in two out of (say) a dozen relevant respects, but would nevertheless be distinctly inferior in value to

[15] Robert S. Hartman, *The Structure of Value: Foundations of Scientific Axiology* (Carbondale, 1967).

one that was deficient in only one of these respects. Hartman says, "A thing is good if it fulfills the definition of its concept,"[16] and that the more complex and property-laden this concept becomes, the better the things that instantiate it.[17]

Viewed (as Hartman intends it) as a synoptic concept of value-in-general, this approach has serious shortcomings. Some minor criticisms that can be made within the framework of this approach are: (1) that it treats all the properties of the thing being evaluated as fully on a par with one another (although some would clearly be much more crucial than others—the luster of the pearl being more important than, say, its specific gravity), (2) that it neglects the fact that possession of a property can be a matter of degree (e.g., the rotundity of the pearl), while others are on-off matters (e.g., the chemical composition of the pearl, which represents an absolutely crucial consideration because an item deficient in respect of this particular property is not a poor pearl, but no pearl at all). More major criticisms can be launched against this entire mode of approach: (1) that it does not get at value-in-general, but only at value *sui generis*—the value of something as an instance of a specific kind with well-determined characteristic properties,[18] (2) that it bases the process of evaluation upon an outmoded—and in fact untenable—essentialistic perspective that treats pearls and apples as characterized by a constellation of *essential* qualities that denominate them as the sorts of things they are, and (3) that it overlooks the fact that complex types of things (with many properties) need not be inherently better than simple ones, and that "bad" things too have their characteristic definitions that incorporate a multiplicity of properties (sinners as well as saints, poisons as well as medicines).

8. AXIOLOGY: AN APPRAISAL

Axiology as the project of a unified philosophy of value cannot be adjudged as impressively successful. The philosophical temper of the times has turned against it. Philosophers have nowadays turned increasingly to conceptual issues, to drawing distinctions and analyzing points of detail; they have tended to view askance the notion of an overarching, monolithic doctrine of value that unifies ethics, aesthetics, etc., and imports material from

[16] *Op. cit.*, p. 103.

[17] " 'Richer in qualities' is the definition of 'better,' 'poorer in qualities' is the definition of 'worse'." (*Op. cit.*, p. 114.)

[18] That is, we can use the property inventory to evaluate (say) a pearl *qua* pearl, but we cannot use it to evaluate pearls *versus* diamonds.

economics, psychology, and sociology.[19] Nevertheless, at least two successes must be credited to axiology, as far as philosophy is concerned: (1) It has established a central place in the arena of philosophical concern for the clarification of conception of value and the study of phenomenology of evaluation. (2) It has initiated inquiry into some of the technical sectors of the value field, such as the theory of value measurement and the elaboration of a formal theory of preference.

Moreover, quite apart from the question of its accomplishments as a philosophical project, axiology has scored a highly important success in a quite different sector. It has projected the *value point of view* into the social sciences, with enormously fruitful results. A substantial corpus of work on values has in recent years come into being in economics, in psychology (e.g., in the Allport-Vernon tradition) and social psychology, and in anthropology and sociology (e.g., in the school of C. L. Kluckhohn). It is, perhaps, in this empirical, scientific area (rather than in technical philosophy) that we should look for the major fruits of the axiological tradition, which has, after all, exercised a profoundly stimulative effect upon all phases of value research. The value theory of the German axiological school proved to be both a means for averting the total capture of value considerations by the economists and a stairway that brought value discussions down from their lofty philosophical height to the arena of the empirical concerns of psychology, sociology, and social psychology.

[19] See, for example, James W. Smith's essay, "Should the General Theory of Value Be Abandoned?" *Ethics*, Vol. 57 (1947), pp. 274–288.

VI

Evaluation, Preference, and the Assessment and Measurement of Value

1. VALUES AND EVALUATION

A value can be realized in a greater or a lesser degree in one instance of its application as compared with another: one chair can be the more "comfortable," one route the more "convenient," one hat the more "economical," one action the more "prudent." In evaluating items in this way, we can make a value assessment: a determination of the relative extent to which something represents or embodies a certain value. Of course, comparisons of degrees or measurements of extent can be effected in contexts into which values do not enter (comparing degrees of darkness, measuring lengths of tables). But "evaluation" in the strictest sense is e-*value*-ation: a comparative assessment or measurement of something with respect to its embodiment of a certain value.

Values are inherently benefit-oriented, as we have seen. People generally engage in evaluation, not as an abstract exercise, but to determine the extent to which the benefits accruing from realization of some values are provided

61

by the items at issue. This endows evaluation with a purposive aspect: we evaluate with a view to certain definite results in regard to potential benefits. Important distinctions to be drawn with respect to evaluation are rooted in this fact: differences regarding evaluation arise because of differences among the ways in which the benefits envisaged are to be realized (e.g., market value in contrast to entertainment value).

It is necessary to recognize that much evaluation is limited in its orientation; most of the time we evaluate the items at issue "in point of" some consideration or other. We evaluate cars in point of their "economy" or "reliability," clothes in point of their "fashionableness" or "durability," and the like. Evaluation is generally a special-purpose resort; only in rare circumstances is evaluation made "on balance," in a synoptic, toti-comprising manner.

The evaluation of things is generally undertaken *sui generis*, with reference to an explicit or tacit reference class. It is in this sense that we speak of a valuable personal contact or a valuable item of information. (Of course, *valuable* often just means "high-priced of its kind.") We intend here to say that the benefits generally to be derived from items *of this sort* are present in the specific items at issue in an unusually high degree.

There is, moreover, the important distinction between the generic value of something and its specific value to someone for certain purposes at a certain time. A key that has very little value may prove of the greatest value to me on some particular occasions.

Most of these complications in the processes of evaluation—i.e., in the particular *applications* of value—do not concern us much in the present context of discussion. Our prime concern here is with the values themselves that provide the foundation requisite to evaluation.

2. THE DIVERSITY OF EVALUATION

When one says that a sunset is beautiful, one has made the evaluation that a certain mode ("the beauty of sunsets") of a certain value ("natural beauty") *is present in* a particular instance (viz., that particular sunset). By contrast, when one says that a certain procedure is convenient, one does not mean that the value of convenience is somehow "present in" that procedure, but rather that its realization is somehow *facilitated* by this object of evaluation (i.e., by its use or possession or the like). These examples show that evaluation can lead to rather diversified results with regard to the role of values in their relation to the object at issue. In placing the evaluated object within the valuation framework it may indicate either:

1. the extent to which *the value is embodied in* the object, or
2. the extent to which *realization of the value is facilitated by* the object, i.e., the relative extent to which the value is realizable through the object.

Certain values (beauty, health) are standardly realization values, whereas other values (safety, economy, wealth, clarity) are standardly facilitation values. (This distinction is closely related to the standard distinction between intrinsic value or end value on the one hand and extrinsic value or means value upon the other.)

3. ORDINAL VS. CARDINAL VALUE SCALES

Any value is generally associated with a corresponding "value scale," reflecting the fact that this value is to be found to be present in particular cases to varying degrees. Thus we have, for the sake of illustration, such examples as the following:

1. patriotism: disloyal ⟶ unpatriotic ⟶ indifferently patriotic ⟶ patriotic ⟶ superpatriotic
2. health (giving): unhealthy ⟶ harmless ⟶ healthful ⟶ highly beneficial
3. health (having): seriously ill ⟶ unwell ⟶ well ⟶ healthy ⟶ in blooming health
4. wealth: destitute ⟶ poor ⟶ of adequate means ⟶ well off ⟶ wealthy

Value scales of this type can differ in various important respects. Sometimes they are purely comparative, like item 1 (patriotism); sometimes they represent differences in degree that can be represented numerically, like item 4 (wealth). In the latter case we are dealing with a *cardinal* value scale, whereas in the former case a merely *ordinal* value scale is at issue.

Note also the following important differences:

1. Scale 1 relates to the comparative extent to which a certain value *is subscribed to* (and displayed) by a person (or persons).
2. Scale 2 relates to the comparative extent to which a specific item is capable of *conducing to the realization* of a certain value.
3. Scales 3 and 4 relate to the extent to which a person (or persons) *have been able to realize* the benefits at issue in a certain value.

All these represent very different sorts of "value scales." In general when we speak of evaluation we have in mind item 2—realization-facilitation—as the standard case.

4. MONOPOLAR VS. BIPOLAR
VALUE SCALES

A *bipolar* value scale is one that covers the entire range of negative to neutral to positive. In this case, a value comes to be viewed as opposed to a corresponding *disvalue* on the model:

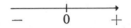

Here, the value at issue admits of an opposite, so that the scale has a negative range as well as a positive. At the root of the matter lies the distinction between a merely privative condition indicative of a lack of something (as poverty indicates the *absence* of wealth) and a condition that is the contrary extreme to another (as sadness is the contrary to joy). Some examples of bipolar value scales are:

    harmful ⟵ harmless ⟶ beneficial
    ugly ⟵——— indifferent ⟶ beautiful
    disloyal ⟵ lukewarm ⟶ loyal
    hostile ⟵—— neutral ——⟶ friendly

A *monopolar* value scale covers only half of such a spectrum of negative-to-positive: the range from neutral to positive. A disvalue does not enter in, only the absence of something positive and beneficial. Such a scale is pictured on the model:

         +——————⟶
         0   +

The value at issue with such a scale admits of privation, but not of a contrary opposite, and thus its scale lacks the negative range. Some examples are:

    unimaginative ⟶ imaginative
    unintelligent ——⟶ intelligent
    outmoded ———⟶ up to date

In such a range the value-deficiency terminus does not present a "neutral" state at all, but has a markedly negative connotation, since it represents the condition of maximal absence of something that is a genuine value.

The distinction between *value* and *worth* may be regarded illuminatingly in the light of this distinction between a bipolar and a monopolar value scale.

At first view it might seem that these concepts come very close to coinciding: that to evaluate something is to determine its worth, and conversely. But this is not so; the idea of value is considerably broader than that of worth. Value, unlike worth, admits the negative pole of *disvalue*: something can be *worthless* or "not worth talking of," but we do not speak of things as having *negative* worth (the locution "worth less than nothing" notwithstanding).[1] Moreover, we can also, of course, evaluate things in ways that have little bearing on a determination of their worth, as in assessing the accuracy of a marksman's fire.

5. TERMINATING VS. NONTERMINATING VALUE SCALES

Certain value scales are *terminating* in a positive (or negative) direction, there is a natural limit to the extent to which the value (or disvalue) at issue can be achieved. Thus, "wealth" can go on and on to accumulate in even greater and greater piles (in principle *ad infinitum*), but "health" can be carried only so far. Although one can be ever more "charitable," one can be only so "just" (i.e., *perfectly* just). Certain values come to a stop at the positive pole (health and justice), others come to a stop at the negative pole, for example, "health" again (one can be "sick unto death," but no more), unlike others which, like "justice," are nonterminating at the negative end of the scale (injustice knows no limits).

6. VALUATIONS AND VALUATION FUNCTIONS: "PREFERENCES," GRADING, AND METRIC VALUATIONS

We shall refer to the systematic apparatus by means of which the realization of a value is assessed as a *valuation*. Evaluation—with the initial E— is then to be understood as the result of the application of a valuation to certain items in a specific case.

A valuation may be *purely comparative* (e.g., more or less "just," or more or less "loyal" or devoted to "patriotism"), or it may be *metric* and afford machinery for actually numerical measurements. The difference here is just

---

[1] We can contrast someone with the "worthy man" as a "worthless scoundrel," but here the negative aspersion of noxiousness is cast, not by the evaluative label, but by the more descriptive epithet.

that between an ordinal comparision and a cardinal measure. And it is clear that a valuation can involve a fully metric mechanism for evaluation. Degrees of "wealth," for example, can be measured in monetary terms, or a society's commitment to "culture" might be measured (say) in terms of the amount of time its members devote to cultural activities (attending plays or concerts, reading literature, etc.).

The features of an ordinal and purely comparative valuation are as follows: We begin with a set of objects

$$x_1, x_2, x_3, \ldots$$

which serve as the subject items of the evaluation at issue (e.g., the individuals whose comparative wealth is being assessed or the societies whose comparative justice is being evaluated). Then we introduce an ordering of the $>$ type (or the $\geqslant$ type) where

$$x > y$$

represents the thesis that x outranks y in the value ordering at issue. The difference between the two types of ordering resides in the fact that whereas "$x > y$" *precludes* that "$x \approx y$" (i.e., "x and y are *indifferent*" in ordering, i.e., equal in value), "$x \geqslant y$ & $y \geqslant x$" guarantees that "$x \approx y$." Thus a comparative valuation of the $>$ type is antisymmetric, irreflexive, and transitive, whereas a valuation of the $\geqslant$ type is nonreflexive, nonsymmetric, and transitive.

Evaluation of this comparative sort has come to be tied closely to the idea of *preference*: in one (very broad) sense of the term one theory may be said to be "preferable" to another (in a certain respect) when its involvement with a (appropriately relevant) value is comparatively greater.

The linkage between preference and value is sometimes claimed to be closer than the facts warrant. First, however, it should be stressed that it is not *preference* but *preferability* that should be held in view when values are at issue, and the road from the former to the latter is neither direct nor easy. (We shall return to this point in Chapter VIII below.) More crucially, values cannot be extracted from preferences until one comes to consider the *rationale* of preference, i.e., the reasons or grounds that provide its basis. It is only then that we can arrive at the plausible equation:

preferable to (in such and such a respect) = more valuable than (on the relevant grounds)

Values, as instrumentalities for the rationalization of action, come upon the scene less when we ask what a person *prefers* than when we ask what he regards as *preferable*. This is why values come more clearly to the fore when we examine in breadth *dispositions* to choose (i.e., systematic, clustered preferences) than when we analyze in depth some individual choices (i.e., particular "acts of preference"). (It is certainly true that the rational person's preferences reveal or "manifest" or "reflect" his values at the operative level, but this is a remark not so much about *values* as about *rationality*.) It is exactly at this gross methodological level that the theoreticians' concept of Preference (with a capital P) makes contact with the concept of Value (with a capital V). In such contexts "preference" must be construed in a very objective sense. What is at issue is that something is "prefer*able*," not that it is "preferr*ed*."

The situation in the case of a metrized valuation function is as follows. We again begin with a set of items

$$x_1, x_2, x_3, \ldots$$

which serve as the subject items of the evaluation at issue (e.g., the persons whose comparative wealth is being assessed or the societies whose comparative degree of commitment to culture is being evaluated). Then we introduce a measure function or mensuration such that

$$\mu(x)$$

represents the numerical μ-quantity of the item x.

A comparative valuation can, of course, always be superimposed (trivially) upon a metric valuation by the rules:

$$x > y \quad \text{FOR} \quad \mu(x) > \mu(y)$$
$$x \geqslant y \quad \text{FOR} \quad \mu(x) \geqslant \mu(y)$$

A halfway house, as it were, between a purely comparative and a metrized valuation is a *grading*. Here we have an ordered family of grades

$$G_1, G_2, \ldots, G_n$$

ranked (say) with the convention that $i > j$ indicates that grade G_i outranks G_j. Then we introduce a grade-assignment function γ such that

$$\gamma(x)$$

represents the specific G_i grade that pertains to x.

Given such a grading, we obtain a corresponding comparative valuation by the rules:

$$x > y \quad \text{FOR} \quad \gamma(x) \; outranks \; \gamma(y)$$
$$x \geqslant y \quad \text{FOR} \quad \gamma(x) \; equals \; \text{or} \; outranks \; \gamma(y)$$

We could now even obtain (in an admittedly somewhat artificial way) a fully metrized valuation by associating with each grade G_i a corresponding number

$g[G_i]$, doing so in such a way that

"G_i outranks G_j" entails "$g[G_i] > g[G_j]$"

For all that need be done to this end is to introduce the rule:

$\mu(x)$ FOR $g[\gamma(x)]$

In this way, any grading can be made to yield a fully metrized valuation, although the procedure by which this is accomplished is—at least in its full generality—somewhat contrived and artificial.

7.   THE METRIZATION OF INDIVIDUAL PREFERENCE

The question of the metrization of individual comparative preference poses crucial issues for the theory of value. Here we have to consider the means for effecting the step from

    1.   the purely qualitative or comparative grading in such terms as:

          bad $\longrightarrow$ indifferent $\longrightarrow$ good $\longrightarrow$ superlative

to

    2.   an actual metric valuation carried out in fully quantitative terms

How is evaluation to be carried out in terms of a numerical measurement? Here we had best seek guidance in the concept of *utility*, developed by the utilitarian school of value theorists, who above all have been concerned to promote value discussions within the context of a precise and mathematicized approach.

One of the principal objections to the application of the classical concepts and machinery of utilitarianism turns on various caveats, some urged on philosophical and some on economic grounds, regarding the idea of a measure of cardinal utilities. This project, it is argued, encounters virtually insuperable difficulties. Individual evaluations—it is agreed—cannot be compared inter-personally; we cannot compare the evaluations of individuals nor get an intersubjective utility measure to compare X's preference for oranges over apples with Y's preference for peaches over apricots. (Considerations of this sort have let modern welfare economists tend to abandon cardinal utilities, and to try to make do simply with the comparative *preferences* themselves.)

It can, however, be argued that the actual extent of the difficulties that lie in wait for a measure of cardinal utilities may have been exaggerated. We shall sketch an approach, or a point of view, from which the measurement of utilities can be placed upon a firm footing. The line of thought to be developed will be presented in two stages: the metrization of an individual's preferences and the interpersonalization of metrized individual preferences. The first of these problems will be dealt with in this chapter, the second being reserved for the next.

Consider the preferability comparisons that a person P may make within a set of three items x_1, x_2, x_3 (which may, at this stage of the discussion, be thought of as either particular commodities or as states of affairs). Say that he prefers x_3 to x_1, x_1 to x_2, and x_3 to x_2. This group of preferences, specifically,

$$x_2 < x_1 < x_3$$

actually tells us very little about P's views with respect to the items at issue, and in fact keeps us in the dark with respect to P's views regarding the items at issue (x_1, x_2, x_3) when considered by themselves. For consider such a valuation scale as:

Perfectly awful	Rather bad	Neutral (so-so)	Pretty good	Perfectly wonderful

If all that we know is that a person would group the items in the indicated preference order, we would be unable to distinguish between any of the following situations:

These situations obviously differ critically in regard to considerations which bear importantly upon the respective preferability of the items at issue.[2]

---

[2] This crude machinery is, for example, sufficient to exhibit the inadequacy of settling the matter of socially preferential choice by voting. For consider the case of such a choice between two alternatives, x_1 and x_2, where a majority would grade both x_1 and x_2 as neutral, but have a slight preference for x_1 over x_2, whereas a sizable minority grades x_2 as perfectly wonderful and x_1 as absolutely ghastly, and views the difference between them as a virtually life-and-death issue.

For a simple order-of-preference ranking is relatively uninformative—it does not tell us anything about:

1. *P*'s *absolute gradings* or valuations, assessing (qualitatively or quantitatively) the individual merits and demerits of the items.[3]
2. *P*'s *comparative assessment* of the extent to which one item is preferred to another (as in schemes IV through VI, although x_1 and x_3 are both preferred to x_2, whereas x_3 is preferred to x_1, the difference in the x_2–x_1 comparison is "as between night and day," whereas the difference in the x_3–x_1 comparison is "a trivial one").

It thus appears that preference orderings in themselves are weak and relatively inadequate instruments of evaluation.[4] The two factors that they neglect, as shown by these illustrations, are not only such as to be in general available, but are of obvious importance for preferability considerations.

Moreover, when these two items, viz., a *grading* (an at least rough and qualitative absolute valuation) and an (essentially quantitative) assessment of the *comparative extent of preference*, are brought upon the scene, the machinery for a metrization of individual preferences is at hand. Given a set of items $x_1, x_2, x_3, \ldots$, what we need to know with respect to an individual *P* is not only an answer to questions of the type

0. Which x_i's are in your view preferable to which x_j's?

but also the answers to questions of the types:

1. How do you grade the x_i with respect to their individual merits (ranging, say, from "perfectly awful" through "neutral" ("take it or leave it") to "perfectly wonderful"?
2. Given that you prefer x_i to x_j, just how would you describe the *extent* of this preference ("just a little," "quite a lot," or "all the difference in the world")?

When information of this sort can be elicited from *P*—and surely it will be available in many or most cases—we can proceed to construct on *P*'s behalf (even if *P* himself will not do so for us) a measure of *degree* of preference in order to capture and reflect with great fidelity the preference stance that *P* himself occupies vis-à-vis the x_i. Note that we do not *elicit* the measure from *P*, but rather *construct* it on the basis of information elicited from *P*, doing this in such a way that we do not *impose* any preference commitments upon him but rather simply reflect those which he affords us.

---

[3] *Commodities*, such as nails or cars, are graded on a scale ranging from the "*good-cum-superlative*" to the "*poor*" (of little or no value). States (especially those created by human action), on the other hand, are graded on a scale ranging from the "*good-cum-superlative*" to the "*bad*" (of disvalue). This makes for distinctions that we shall simply brush aside for the present. But we shall return to the topic below.

[4] The added detail required for a passage from an order-of-merit *ranking* and to a detailed *grading* by a suitable scale for assessment is familiar to any teacher who has evaluated a batch of student's essays.

It should also be noted in passing that certain obvious requirements of consistency (or "rationality"), of a sort strictly analogous to those needed for constructing an ordinal preference scale on the basis of an individual's preference indications, will have to be laid down for a cardinal preference measure also.[5] For example, we could not tolerate a grading of x_1 as good and x_2 as bad in the face of the claim that x_2 is preferable to x_1. The point is this: to obtain a set of ordinal preference evaluations from an individual, we need not proceed by asking him to hand it to us ready-made. We (i.e., a third person) can construct this for him, proceeding wholly on the basis of information elicited from him, but imposing the necessary requirements of consistency in the course of this construction. (The procedure is much the same as the "cleaning up" of the personal probability judgments elicited from someone to square with the consistency rules imposed by a theory of subjective probability.)

Supposing the problem of a quantified scheme for an individual's evaluations to be solved along some such lines as those discussed, we obtain for an individual P a measure of his "degree of preference" with respect to the alternatives $x_1, x_2, x_3, \ldots$, with the resulting schedule of (real number) values:

$$m(x_1), m(x_2), m(x_3), \ldots$$

Here we arrive at "evaluation" in its most robust and fully developed metric sense. This pretty much sums up the formal or structural aspects of the process of evaluation for an individual. The problem of *group* evaluation—of combining individual valuation into a social or collective valuation, and thus of resolving the difficulty of an interpersonal comparison of utilities—will be dealt with in Chapter VIII.

8. VALUATION AND VALUES

Whenever valuation takes place, in any of its diverse forms—comparative assessment grading or actual metric valuation—values must enter in. It is true that when somebody is grading apples, say, or peaches, he may never make overt reference to any values. But if the procedure were not guided by no doubt unspoken but nevertheless real involvement with such values as palatability and nourishability, we would be dealing with classification or measurement and not with grading and evaluation. It is a strictly semantical point, nonetheless reflecting a fact of real importance for our considerations, that in evaluation an indispensable recourse to underlying *values* is involved.

The process of evaluation can be described in somewhat general terms,

[5] Cf. R. D. Luce and H. Raiffa, *Games and Decisions* (New York, 1957), p. 35.

the concepts we have explicated being used as follows. Evaluation consists in bringing together two things: (1) an *object* to be evaluated, and (2) a *valuation*, providing the framework in terms of which evaluations can be made. The bringing together of these two is mediated by (3) a *criterion* of evaluation that embodies the standards in terms of which the standing of the object within the valuation framework is determined. [Note that (3) mediates a transition from "fact" to "value." It underwrites a move from the object's *de facto* possession of certain descriptive characteristics to its having certain value features. The presence or absence in an object of these characteristics whose possession endows it, according to the evaluative criterion, with a certain value, is a purely factual matter.]

This description of the procedure of evaluation brings out its substantial structural similarity to classification. In classification we have (1) an object to be classified, (2) a generic classificatory framework, and (3) a criterion of classification that specifies the classification of an object on the basis of its characteristics. Evaluation can in effect therefore be viewed as a mode of classification, viz., as classification in point of value considerations.

VII

Evaluation and
the Logic of Preference

1. THE PROBLEM OF A LOGIC
OF PREFERENCE

Traditionally, all attempts to develop an exact formal theory of evaluation have concentrated on the concept of preference. Philosophers, economists, and psychologists, however much they may have disagreed about the other aspects of the problem of value, have agreed in regarding the theory of preference as occupying a central part of the subject. And it is clear that there is an intimate connection between value and preference (in the sense of *rational* preference and objective preferability), and that preference will in general be based upon a comparative evaluation of the items at issue. Thus, in recent years especially, there have been many attempts by value theorists at constructing a formal systematization for the conception of preferability, a "logic of preference." The aim of the present chapter is to provide a picture of at least some of the important parts of this established terrain, and to make a positive, constructive contribution to the further development of such a logic of preference. (The reader to whose interests the treatment of these logical issues is irrelevant can skip this chapter without substantial loss to the continuity of development of the discussion.)

2. HISTORICAL INTRODUCTION

The founder of the "logic of preference" is the founding father of logic itself, Aristotle. Book III of the *Topics*, in which Aristotle is concerned with spelling out principles governing the concept of preferability hairetōteron, the worthier of choice, must be regarded as the inaugural treatment of the subject. The treatment there, however, is such that no adequate distinction is drawn between material and formal considerations. The bulk of the principles listed are of a strictly substantive, nonformal sort. For example:

> That which is more permanent or durable is preferable to that which is less so. (116a13–14)
> That which is to be chosen for its own sake is preferable to that which is to be chosen for the sake of another. (116a29–30)

Other principles given are of a more formal and logically more tractable sort. For example:

> The possible (practicable) is preferable to the impossible (impracticable). (316b27)
> That is preferable which is the more applicable on every occasion or on most occasions (for example, justice and self-control are preferable to courage, for the first two are always applicable, but courage only sometimes). (117a35–37)
> If A be absolutely better than (preferable to) B, then also the best specimen of A is better than (preferable to) B; e.g., if man is better than horse, then also the best man is better than the best horse. (117b33–35)

The study of preference principles acceptable upon abstract, formal, systematic grounds rather than upon any particular substantive theory of preferability determination is the task which the philosophically oriented "logic of preference," as we envisage it, is to set for itself.

In recent philosophy, this enterprise was revived in the orbit of influence of the school of Brentano, particularly by Hermann Schwarz and Max Scheler.[1] The relevant work of this school was carried forward by several continental investigators before World War II,[2] and since that time this line

---

[1] See *Schwarz* (1900) and *Scheler* (1913–14). For all citations of this sort see the bibliography at the end of the book.
[2] See *Katkov* (1937) and *Kraus* (1937).

of inquiry has flourished especially in Scandinavia.[3] Only recently has the subject begun to arouse interest in the United States—a phenomenon for which R. M. Martin and R. M. Chisholm have been largely responsible.[4]

Interest on the part of economists in the theory of preference as a special application of the concept of utility antedates this philosophical tradition. For the traditional theory, the reader should consult Chap. VI, "Value and Utility," of Alfred Marshall's classic *Principles of Economics*.[5] The recent formal development of this utility concept has primarily been in the direction of the mathematical theory of games.[6] The concept of valuation (and thus of preference) also plays a prominent and illuminating role in modern decision theory.[7]

It is a central part of the motivation of this paper to try to develop the logic of preference in such a way as to build a bridge connecting these traditions: the logico-philosophical on the one hand, and the mathematico-economic on the other.

3. MODES OF PREFERENCE

Two Modes of Goodness

The locutions "it is a good thing that *p*" or "*p*'s being the case is a good thing" involve a serious ambiguity in the notion of "good" at issue. Certain essential distinctions must be drawn if confusion is to be avoided. The need for these distinctions becomes manifest if we examine some specific illustrative situations. Consider, for example, the following case:

If it is the case that	*then one is to get*
p	+$1
not-*p*	(unspecified)

Here *p*'s being the case is a "good thing" in the precise sense that, supposing *p* to be so, a positive result ensues. (Locutions of the type "there is some-

---

[3] See *Halldén* (1957), *von Wright* (1963), and *Aqvist* (1963).

[4] See *Martin* (1963), *Chisholm* (1964), and *Chisholm and Sosa* (1966). It should be added that von Wright's influence has also been important in the U.S.A.

[5] London, 1890; 8th ed., 1920. For a helpful history of the recent history of economic utility theory see D. Braybrooke, "Farewell to the New Welfare Economics," *Review of Economic Studies*, Vol. 23 (1955), pp. 180–193.

[6] See R. D. Luce and H. Raiffa, *Games and Decisions* (New York, 1957), where a comprehensive bibliography is also given.

[7] See Richard Jeffrey, *The Logic of Decision* (New York, 1965).

thing in it for me" and "I am better off than I was before" come to be applicable.) The basis of comparison here is that between:

1. my situation *before* it eventuated that p was the case, and
2. my situation *after* the eventuation of p.

Correspondingly, by this standard of comparison, the p of the following situation

If it is the case that	*then one is to get*
p	$-\$1$
not-p	(unspecified)

is a bad thing, again in the precise sense that when p comes about "I stand to lose something" and "I am worse off than I was before."

Let us call this mode of goodness and badness, as based on a straightforward comparison of 1 and 2, *first-order* goodness and badness, choosing this qualification because the mode of "goodness" at issue turns on the value of the result of only one possible alternative in the situation in question (viz., p's being the case) to the exclusion of any concern with the result of the other alternative (viz., p's not being the case).[8]

That considerations over and above those involved in first-order goodness (or badness) must be introduced is readily established by the example of situations such as the following:

If it is the case that	*then one is to get*
p	$+\$1$
not-p	$+\$10$

By the standards of comparison 1 and 2 laid down above, it is clear that *both* p's and not-p's coming to be the case are first-order "good things." Nevertheless, it is also plain that one is entitled to regard p's happening as in some (different) sense a "bad thing" because p's happening of course precluded not-p's happening, and not-p's happening is—under the circumstances—a good thing of such a magnitude that one cannot but regard its preclusion as a "bad thing."

The contrast at issue here is brought out even more explicitly in the following situation:

---

[8] This conception would, we suppose, come reasonably close to capturing some aspects of the intent of the traditional notion of *intrinsic* goodness, but this idea has been used in such a variegated (and sometimes loose) way that it is pointless to employ it for our purposes.

If it is the case that	*then one is to get*
p	$-\$1$
not-p	$-\$100$

Neither p nor not-p are first-order "good things." Yet one cannot, under the circumstances, regard p's happening as other than a very "good thing" indeed, since it averts the minor catastrophe that ensues when not-p.

The contrast at issue in such cases, then, is not that between 1 and 2 as above, but that between:

2. my situation after the (assumed) eventuation of p, and
3. my situation after the (assumed) eventuation of not-p.

We shall call the type of goodness at issue here *differential goodness*. It is assessed by taking into *comparative* account—not just the situation under consideration but—the possible *alternatives* to the situation under consideration. As our examples have shown, it is clear that there is no inevitable correlation between first-order goodness (and badness) and differential goodness (and badness). First-order goods can be differential evils, and conversely.

The Two Corresponding Modes of Preference

As one would suspect, the distinction between *first-order* and *differential* goodness carries over into a parallel distinction between two corresponding modes of preference. This is again brought out most sharply by an examination of examples. Consider the following situation in which its coming-about-that-p and its coming-about-that-q are assumed to be independent events:

If it is the case that	*then one is to get*
p	$+\$10$
not-p	(unspecified)
q	$+\$1$
not-q	(unspecified)

Here one obviously prefers p's being the case to q's being the case, in the precise sense that the former conduces more to one's benefit (i.e., is such that one "stands to gain more by it"). This point can be made in the following terms: that the *extent* of p's first-order goodness (viz., a "gain" of \$10) is greater than the extent of q's first-order goodness (viz., a "gain" of \$1). We shall designate the mode of preferability at issue here as *first-order preference*. This mode of preference then is based upon a contrast of *the comparative extent of the first-order goodness* of the two items being compared.

Consider now the contrasting situation:

If it is the case that	then one is to get
p	+$2
not-*p*	+$2
q	+$1
not-*q*	−$100

The significant features to be noted with respect to this situation are: (1) There is no question that *p* is first-order preferable to *q* (the first-order goodness of *p* stands to that of *q* in a ratio of 2:1). Nevertheless (2), it is a matter of genuine indifference to oneself whether *p* is or is not the case— exactly the same result accrues either way. Moreover (3), it is highly important to one that *q* rather than not-*q* be the case (more than $100 being at stake with respect to these alternatives). In view of this—and despite the first-order preferability of *p* to *q*—there is a definite and important sense in which we prefer *q*'s being the case to that of *p*. This point can perhaps be sharpened by retabulating the alternatives as follows:

If it is the case that	then one is to get
p & *q*	+$ 3
p & ~*q*	−$98
~*p* & *q*	+$ 3
~*p* & ~*q*	−$98

Our intuitive preference for *q*'s being the case in contrast to *p*'s being the case is based on the impressive contrast between the facts that, as this tabulation renders palpable:

1. When *q* is the case, one cannot fail to gain $3 regardless of whether *p* is or is not the case.
2. When *p* is the case, then one either gains $3 or *loses* $98, depending upon whether *q* is or is not the case.

The sort of preference at issue here is clearly based upon a contrast of *the comparative extent of the differential goodness* of the two items being compared. Correspondingly, this type of preference will be designated as *differential preference*.

Our aim in this paper will be to lay the groundwork for a detailed study of the logical theory of preference relationships of this general sort: to elucidate what is involved in preference commitments of various types. The question of special interest to the economists, viz., how to *combine* the preference commitments of diverse individuals into one coherent interpersonal preferential scheme, lies outside the purview of our discussion.

4. SEMANTICAL MACHINERY

The Line of Approach

The basis for the semantical considerations we are attempting to develop is the concept of a propositional preference ordering. Presupposing a propositional logic of the familiar sort— and representing propositions by the metavariables α, β, γ, etc.—we introduce the propositional relationship P (for preferability) with the understanding that

$$\alpha P \beta$$

is to be understood as "α's being the case is preferred (preferable) to β's being the case." The only indispensable requirements we shall impose on the relationship P are:

1. That P be an ordering relation, i.e., that it be transitive, asymmetric, and irreflexive.
2. That P be an extensional relation among propositions, i.e., that it admit the substitution of provable equivalents.

Of course, in postulating, for example, transitivity we impose a certain limitation of rationality (consistency) on the kinds of preferences in question. (If *rational* preference were not at issue, it would make little sense to seek to systematize a normative "*logic* of preference.")

The exact interpretation of the sort of preference at issue in P is to be left open. Specifically, we shall not try to settle whether this is to be:

1. A matter of being *preferred* by a given individual (or group),

or

2. A matter of being *preferable* by some impersonal criterion.

Nor shall we make any specification about whether the preference at issue is a *synoptic* preference ("preferable when everything is taken into account") or an *aspectival* preference ("preferable in point of cost, or convenience, or the like"). However important these distinctions may be of themselves, they should be indifferent to the sort of abstract and "structural" considerations to which a *logic of preference* devotes itself.

A critical scrutiny of preferences is possible from two angles: (1) that of *rationality*, which looks to purely *formal* issues of logical consistency, and (2) that of *reasonableness*, which looks to *material* issues of appropriateness and correctness in application of substantive criteria and standards. The formal theory at issue in this chapter is concerned solely with considerations of the former type.

* * *

There are two alternative approaches to the development of a logic of preference: the *axiomatic* and the *semantic*. On the axiomatic approach, one lays down certain *basic formalized rules*, presumably underwritten by intuitive considerations, as a guiding basis for the formal development of a theory. From these basic rules the theory itself is then derived as a logical consequence. On the semantic approach one sets up a *criterion of acceptability* for such rules and includes in one's system all those rules classed as acceptable by the criterion. The former, axiomatic approach has to date been the standard for the logic of preference. The systematizations of von Wright, Halldén, Chisholm-Sosa, and Martin have all proceeded in its purview. The approach is, however, unsatisfactory because of the wide divergence among these pioneers about just what the "obviously acceptable" principles of a logic of preference are. (Only the irreflexivity, asymmetry, and transitivity of preference lie in the range of the clearly unproblematic.) We ourselves shall pursue various *alternative, but in principle reasonable*, possibilities along the line of the semantical approach. Here divergences are less harmful and issue not from outright inconsistencies of a system but from alternative plausible specifications of one intrinsically ambiguous idea. The approach is an experimental one: we do not seek to find "the correct" logic of preference but to explore some of the most promising systems that can be built up by way of tracing out various, of themselves plausible, conceptions of the nature of the preference relation. We hope in this way to be able to provide a *rationale* capable of explaining the divergencies between the several mutually incompatible axiomatizations that have been proposed for preference logic by various recent writers on the subject.

Formal Machinery of Analysis: Semantical Considerations

To develop the semantical groundwork for a theory that deserves the name of a "logic of preference," the sorts of considerations with which we have been dealing must be provided with a somewhat more systematic grounding.

Assume that we have a list

$$w_1, w_2, \ldots, w_n$$

of "possible worlds" (state descriptions in the sense of Carnap). Our starting point is provided by an *index of merit* measure $\#$ which assigns to each possible world w_1 a real-number value $\#(w_1)$. This measure, in effect, represents the entry point of *evaluation* into our considerations—it being clear that it plays an essential and fundamental role from the very outset in the theory of preference, since preference (i.e., *rational* preference) will in general be based upon evaluation. We shall not now enter upon a discussion of the specific substantive character of this measure, i.e., the specific respects in which it assesses the characteristics of the possible worlds, the sorts of considerations of which it takes account, and the relative importance with which it endows them. Considerations of this sort relate to the material side of the concrete application of the machinery and not to the formal side of the abstract logic of the matter, which alone concerns us at present.

Given this measure of merit or desirability for the possible worlds, we then assign to any proposition α that can be generated as a truth-functional compound of the w_1 the real-number value $\#(\alpha)$ to be the *average (arithmetical mean) of the $\#$-values of all the possible worlds w_1 within which α is true.*[9] [This leaves $\#(\alpha)$ undefined when α is a contradiction; a difficulty which we shall simply lay aside for the time being.][10]

We may construe $\#(\alpha)$ as measuring the extent of the first-order goodness of α (i.e., of the circumstance of α's being the case). In this case the corresponding mode of preference will obviously be represented by the definition:[11]

$$\alpha P^\# \beta \quad \text{for} \quad \#(\alpha) > \#(\beta)$$

Our $\#$ measure for first-order goodness is readily applied to a derivative measure for differential goodness—let it be represented by $*$:

$$*(\alpha) = \#(\alpha) - \#(\sim\alpha)$$

This measure has the interesting feature, which is of far-reaching significance, and whose counterpart emphatically does not hold for $\#$, that:

$$*(\sim\alpha) = -*(\alpha)$$

[9] An interesting variant of this approach would be to consider a distribution of probabilities across the possible worlds w_1 and then consider the correspondingly weighted average of the w_1, rather than their arithmetical mean. This approach is adopted as standard in R. Jeffrey's monograph [see *Jeffrey* (1965), Chap. 5], where, however, the propositional logic of the situation is not worked out. We shall return to the matter in footnote 16.

[10] The reader can, if he likes, remove this gap by thinking of $\#(\alpha)$ as fixed at 0 in this case.

[11] Note that we must throughout *exclude substitutions* that make α or β into *contradictions*, once we have left $\#$ undefined in this case.

The corresponding mode of preference will obviously be represented by the definition:

$$\alpha P^*\beta \quad \text{for} \quad *(\alpha) > *(\beta)$$

For the sake of an illustration of this group of ideas, consider the following:

Possible worlds	#-values
$w_1: p \,\&\, q$	a
$w_2: p \,\&\, \sim q$	b
$w_3: \sim p \,\&\, q$	c
$w_4: \sim p \,\&\, \sim q$	d

On this basis we may calculate, by way of illustration:

$$\#(p) = \frac{a+b}{2} \qquad\qquad *(p) = \frac{a+b}{2} - \frac{c+d}{2}$$

$$\#(\sim p) = \frac{c+d}{2} \qquad\qquad *(\sim p) = \frac{c+d}{2} - \frac{a+b}{2}$$

$$\#(q) = \frac{a+c}{2} \qquad\qquad *(q) = \frac{a+c}{2} - \frac{b+d}{2}$$

$$\#(\sim q) = \frac{b+d}{2} \qquad\qquad *(\sim q) = \frac{b+d}{2} - \frac{a+c}{2}$$

$$\#(p \lor q) = \frac{a+b+c}{3} \qquad\qquad *(p \lor q) = \frac{a+b+c}{3} - d$$

$$\#(p \,\&\, q) = a \qquad\qquad *(p \,\&\, q) = a - \frac{b+c+d}{3}$$

Thus, to say that $pP^{\#}q$ would be to have it that:

$$\frac{a+b}{2} > \frac{a+c}{2} \quad \text{or} \quad b > c$$

Or again, to say that $(p \lor q)P^*p$ would be to have it that:

$$\frac{a+b+c}{3} - d > \frac{a+b}{2} - \frac{c+d}{2} \quad \text{or} \quad 5c > a+b+3d$$

However, the salient difference between these two modes of preference is brought out by the fact that the principle

$$pPq \longrightarrow \sim qP \sim p$$

which fails in general for $P^{\#}$ does hold for P^*. [See the discussion of the principle (R1) on pp. 93–96 below.]

[A mode of preference with which it would also be interesting to deal is *preferability*, *other things being equal*, that is, a relation P' such that (say):

$pP'q$ iff (if and only if) $\#(p \,\&\, r) > \#(q \,\&\, r)$ obtains whenever r is independent of p and of q.

Although this sort of conception can be handled with the machinery here introduced, its treatment involves additional complications that militate against our dealing with it here. Compare, however, the treatment of the principle (W5) on pp. 95 ff. below.]

Viewed in somewhat general terms, our approach to the logic of preference thus proceeds in terms of a numerical criterion of merit. Given a proposition γ, we determine in some suitable way a numerical *measure of merit* $\mu(\gamma)$. Then we introduce a corresponding preference relation P^μ with the convention that:

$$\alpha P^\mu \beta \quad \text{for} \quad \mu(\alpha) > \mu(\beta)$$

A Purely Qualitative Alternative Approach

To the minds of some readers, the preceding quantitative line of approach might seem to have an air of unrealistic oversophistication. To assign to each possible world a specific real number as its "measure of merit" might appear a procedure that presupposes an unattainable differentiation in degrees of value. This line of criticism could, however, be accepted without vitiating the strategy of approach. We reply to the critic: "Have it your way—don't even try for precise distinctions! Grade possible worlds into (say) just three classes: desirable, undesirable, and neutral. You can still apply—and benefit from—the machinery here constructed."

The fact is clear that our entire procedure could be carried on in the setting of just three rough, individually undifferentiated entries of an index of merit measure. Merely let the w_i assume just one of three $\#$-values, as follows:

$+1$ favorable (desirable)

0 neutral

-1 unfavorable (undesirable)

The whole of the semantical machinery we shall construct now can be applied on the basis of such very rough and unsophisticated, purely qualitative, merit assessments—assessments so crude and rough-cut[12] that even the

---

[12] Our simplified approach, for example, fails entirely to distinguish different *degrees* of favorableness and unfavorableness. But, of course, to the extent that such distinctions are drawn we move away from the aspirations of our simplistic critic back toward our initial starting point.

reader favorably inclined to the sentiments of our hypothetical critic could hardly demur from following the direction of our quantitative method for so slight a distance. In any event, a device of this sort can certainly be used in the context of our present considerations to cut the Gordian knot that separates grading from actual evaluation.

It must, however, be made clear that our semantical approach to the logic of preference is not a *purely comparative* or *strictly ordinal* one based solely upon the conception of preferability as such, but an *evaluative* one in which preference relations are based derivatively upon an essentially *quantitative* approach, the assessment (measure) of the intrinsic merit (goodness) of the objects involved. We treat preference as being *derivative* from merit assessments and not as an ultimately self-contained comparison. To illustrate the distinction at issue, suppose that we are to deal with four possible worlds, w_1 through w_4, and suppose that we know them to be so listed in *order of . preference*. If this purely comparative preference information were all that we knew, we would be wholly unable to say (1) by *how much* w_1 (say) is preferred to w_2, let alone (2) what *the intrinsic merit* (goodness/badness) of w_1 (say) might be. This purely comparative basis would prove insufficient for the quality assessment (and thus essentially quantitative) processes that underlie the preferability comparison of our semantics.

These observations are important because it might otherwise seem that our approach has the somewhat unnatural feature of basing the theory of *preference* (a purely ordinal notion) upon a prior measure of merit (a cardinal notion). But this "putting the cart before the horse" is more apparent than real.

Relations Between the Two Modes of Preference

There is an interesting kinship between the two types of preference we have distinguished. Consider again the four possible worlds, w_1 through w_4, of the preceding section. Notice that

$$pP^{\#}q \text{ becomes } \frac{a+b}{2} > \frac{a+c}{2} \text{ or } b > c$$

and that

$$pP^{*}q \text{ becomes } \frac{a+b}{2} - \frac{c+d}{2} > \frac{a+c}{2} - \frac{b+d}{2} \text{ or } b > c$$

This suggests that $\#$-preference and $*$-preference are equivalent. But it is readily seen that this is not the case. For our procedure and our tabulations have to this point been based on the supposition that the variables involved

—'*p*', '*q*', etc.—represent *independent* propositions: propositions devoid of logical interconnections of such a kind that the #-value assigned to one must have a bearing upon that assigned to the other(s). *Only under this independence presupposition that '*p*', '*q*', etc. represent independent propositions do #-preference and *-preference come to coincide.* When this presupposition is not satisfied, the equivalence no longer obtains, as is shown by the following example. Consider:

$$pP(p \lor q)$$

First, let P represent #-preference, and let us go again to the four w_i of page 82. Then

$$pP^{\#}(p \lor q)$$

will represent

$$\frac{a+b}{2} > \frac{a+b+c}{3} \quad \text{or} \quad a+b > c$$

If, on the other hand, P represents *-preference, then

$$pP^*(p \lor q)$$

will represent

$$\frac{a+b}{2} - \frac{c+d}{2} > \frac{a+b+c}{3} - d \quad \text{or} \quad a+b+3d > 5c$$

and it is perfectly clear that these two inequalities are not equivalent. Thus it will be only in the special case of independent relata (essentially, those which do not share a common variable) that the two modes of preference will coincide.

The von Wrightean Semantics

We turn now to a variant approach to the semantics of preference logic which is designed to codify the approach of G. H. von Wright's recent monograph. We again suppose as starting point a series of possible worlds (state descriptions):

$$w_1, w_2, \ldots, w_n$$

We suppose that the propositions at issue are generated by truth-functional compoundings of the w_i. We suppose further a "ground floor" preference ordering of the w_i allowing the possibility of indifference, say, for example:

$$w_4 > w_3 \simeq w_5 > w_1 > w_2$$

(In such a list every possible world can occur just once, and a well ordering must result when $\simeq$-connected entries are identified.)

Let us now construe

$$\alpha P^w \beta$$

to mean:

> For every γ (independent of α and β)[13] we have it that every possible world w_1 in which $\begin{Bmatrix} \alpha \text{ true} \\ \beta \text{ false} \\ \gamma \text{ true} \end{Bmatrix}$ is $>$-preferable to all the corresponding possible world(s) w_j in which $\begin{Bmatrix} \alpha \text{ false} \\ \beta \text{ true} \\ \gamma \text{ true} \end{Bmatrix}$

Note that the condition on γ here plays the role of a requirement of "other things being equal."

This specification of a semantical interpretation of the P^w relationship corresponds closely to the system of von Wright's theory. It accords entirely with the motivations and explanations of his discussion and is such that all of his "basic principles" prove acceptable. (It does not, however, accord entirely with von Wright's elaborations of his ideas. This will be evident from an inspection of the table on page 92.)

Let us illustrate the working of this von Wrightean semantics in a numerical rather than merely comparative setting. Consider the following eight possible worlds:

World	p	q	r	$\#(w)_1$
w_1	$+$	$+$	$+$	z_1
w_2	$+$	$+$	$-$	z_2
w_3	$+$	$-$	$+$	z_3
w_4	$+$	$-$	$-$	z_4
w_5	$-$	$+$	$+$	z_5
w_6	$-$	$+$	$-$	z_6
w_7	$-$	$-$	$+$	z_7
w_8	$-$	$-$	$-$	z_8

Note now that on the von Wrightean semantics we have:

$$pP^wq \text{ iff } z_3 > z_5 \text{ and } z_4 > z_6$$

On the P^* semantics, on the other hand, we have

$$pP^*q \text{ iff } z_3 + z_4 > z_5 + z_6$$

---

[13] Actually, in realistic applications of this machinery, one would want to require here not merely logical independence alone, but causal independence as well.

It is thus obvious that P^w preferability entails $P*$ preferability, but not conversely, so that the former is significantly more restrictive than the latter. (Indeed, we shall shortly argue that there is good reason to think it to be actually too restrictive.) Again, by way of application of this machinery, note that "$(p \supset q)P^w p$" is a perfectly possible preference situation, which would prevail under the circumstance that both $[z_1, z_5, z_7] > z_3$ and $[z_2, z_6, z_8,] > z_4$.

Let us now develop the argument about the restrictiveness of P^w. Let the case with the possible worlds be as above, and let it be supposed that:

$z_3 = +1000$

$z_4 = 0$

$z_5 = -1000$

$z_6 = +0.0001$

Surely, in any intuitively plausible sense of the term, p is now "preferable" to q (for when p is true, we may gain as much as 1,000 but can lose no more than 0, whereas when q is true, we may lose as much as 1,000, but can gain no more than 0.0001). But on the (overly safe) construction of the von Wrightean semantics we cannot say that p is preferable to q because in one case (among potentially countless ones) we may lose a bit more by p than by q.

Despite the interpretative shortcoming brought out in such examples, the von Wrightean semantic does, however, enjoy one important systematic advantage. It proceeds simply and solely on the basis of an ordinal preference ordering of the possible worlds and does not call—as do the $P*$ and $P^{\#}$ relations—for an actual cardinal valuation of them. But actually this advantage is more seeming than real, since an ordering can always be transformed into a valuation by such devices as letting every possible world score one point for every other one that it excels in the rank ordering.

Preference Tautologies

On the basis of the semantical machinery developed above, we are able to introduce the concept of a *preference tautology*. Consider a preference principle of the type:

$pPq \rightarrow \sim(qPp)$

$pPq \rightarrow \sim qP \sim p$

$(pPq \,\&\, qPr) \rightarrow pPr$

Such a principle will be a $P^\#$ tautology (or a P^* tautology, respectively) if, when P is interpreted throughout as $P^\#$ (or P^*, respectively), the principle goes over into a truth, i.e., an arithmetical truth, with respect to every possible assignment of #-values to the possible worlds generated out of truth combinations of the variables that are involved.

For example, to see that the second principle of the preceding list is a #-tautology, we consider the #-value assignment:

Possible world	#-value
$w_1: p \And q$	a
$w_2: p \And \sim q$	b
$w_3: \sim p \And q$	c
$w_4: \sim p \And \sim q$	d

Now "$pP^\#q \longrightarrow \sim qP^\#\sim p$" amounts to

$$\frac{a+b}{2} > \frac{a+c}{2} \longrightarrow \frac{b+d}{2} > \frac{c+d}{2}$$

that is, to

$$b > c \longrightarrow b > c$$

which is an arithmetical truth.

On the other hand, it can be seen that the principle

$$pP^\#q \longrightarrow \sim qP^\#\sim p$$

breaks down under substitution for the variables involved. For if we substitute "$p \lor q$" for 'q', we obtain

$$pP^\#(p \lor q) \longrightarrow \sim(p \lor q)P^\#\sim p$$

which amounts to

$$\frac{a+b}{2} > \frac{a+b+c}{3} \longrightarrow d > \frac{c+d}{2}$$

that is, to

$$a + b > 2c \longrightarrow d > c$$

which is obviously falsifiable.

It is thus crucially important to distinguish between *unrestricted* preference tautologies such as

$$pP^\#q \longrightarrow \sim(qP^\#p)$$

which, as the reader can check, proves acceptable under *any and every* substitution of the variables involved, and *restricted* preference tautologies like

$$pP^{\#}q \longrightarrow \sim qP^{\#}\sim p$$

which has unacceptable substitution instances. On the other hand, it is readily shown that

$$pP^*q \longrightarrow \sim qP^*\sim p$$

is unrestrictedly acceptable.

It is an interesting fact, inherent in their "restricted equivalence," that despite their very great *conceptual* difference (*i.e.*, the very different meanings that attach to them), essentially the same preference theses obtain for $P^{\#}$ that do for P^*: the only differences that can arise between them are those growing out of substitution restrictions. The sorts of preference theses that can bring out on the side of formal acceptability the conceptual difference between the two concepts will be those that turn on substitution restrictions, such as

$$pP(p \vee q) \longrightarrow [\sim(p \vee q)]Pp$$

which is acceptable for P^* but not for $P^{\#}$.

The possession of a semantically viable concept of a *preference tautology* is of the utmost importance from the logical point of view. For with its guidance, the question of the axiomatization of preference logic can meaningfully be raised and fruitfully dealt with. Our interests here falling on the substantive, semantical rather than the formal, axiomatic side, we shall not pursue this prospect further on the present occasion.

Restricted and Unrestricted Quantification

To provide ourselves with a systematic formal mechanism for recording the (for our purposes) pivotal distinction between two different modes of quantifications, we shall introduce the unrestricted propositional quantifier $\forall$ with

$$(\forall p)(---p---)$$

to be construed as asserting that "$---p---$" holds with respect to *any and every* substitution for 'p', and the restricted propositional quantifier A with

$$(Ap)(---p---)$$

to be construed as asserting (only) that "$---p---$" holds for all those substitutions for 'p' which do not involve other variables that occur in "$---p---$".

Thus, for example, we would be in a position to assert the principle:

$$(\forall p)(\forall q)(pP^{\#}q \rightarrow \sim[qP^{\#}p])$$

On the other hand, it would not be correct to assert the principle

$$(\forall p)(\forall q)(pP^{\#}q \rightarrow \sim qP^{\#}\sim p)$$

although it would, by contrast, be correct to assert the principle

$$(\mathrm{A}p)(\mathrm{A}q)(pP^{\#}q \rightarrow \sim qP^{\#}\sim p)$$

The possibility is (of course) not to be excluded that in certain cases a mixture of these quantifiers is appropriate, so that one could assert a principle of the form

$$(\mathrm{A}p)(\forall q)(---p, q---)$$

claiming, in effect, that 'p' substitutions must be restricted, although 'q' substitutions can be made unrestrictedly.

The ideas and procedures at issue here are applied and illustrated in Appendix I. The logical characteristics of the nonstandard quantifiers that are at issue here have been explored in an interesting discussion by Alan Ross Anderson.[14]

5. AN EXAMINATION OF SOME PREFERENCE PRINCIPLES

The most extensive and doubtless the best-known treatment of preference logic is that of G. H. von Wright's book on *The Logic of Preference* (Edinburgh, 1963). Some brief suggestions are offered in Chap. II of R. M. Martin's book, *Intension and Decision* (Englewood Cliffs, N. J., 1963), and a suggestive discussion can also be found in an article by R. M. Chisholm and E. Sosa, "On the Logic of Intrinsically Better" (*American Philosophical Quarterly*, Vol. 3, 1966 pp. 244–249).[15] On the semantical side, these writers all proceed on the basis of intuitive, unformalized considerations. It is thus of interest to examine their preference-principles from the angle of their $P^{\#}$ and P^{*} tautologousness. The results of such an examination are tabulated on the opposite page.

[14] In his comments on a previous presentation of these ideas in N. Rescher (ed.), *The Logic of Decision and Action* (Pittsburgh, 1967), pp. 71–76.

[15] For a comprehensive survey of the literature of the subject see the bibliography at the end of the book.

Preference principle		$P\#$	$P*$
Von Wright			
(W1)	$pPq \longrightarrow \sim(qPp)$	+	+
(W2)	$(pPq \,\&\, qPr) \longrightarrow pPr$[16]	+	+
(W3)	$\begin{cases} pPq \longrightarrow (p \,\&\, \sim q)P(\sim p \,\&\, q) \\ (p \,\&\, \sim q)P(\sim p \,\&\, q) \longrightarrow pPq \end{cases}$	+ +	+ +
(W4)	$\begin{cases} [\sim(\sim p \,\&\, \sim q)P\sim(\sim r \,\&\, \sim s)] \longrightarrow [(p \,\&\, \sim r \,\&\, \sim s)P \\ \quad (\sim p \,\&\, \sim q \,\&\, r) \,\&\, (p \,\&\, \sim r \,\&\, \sim s)P(\sim p \,\&\, \sim q \,\&\, s) \\ \quad \&\, (q \,\&\, r \sim \,\&\, \sim s)P(\sim p \,\&\, q \,\&\, r) \,\&\, (q \,\&\, \sim r \,\&\, \sim s) \\ \quad P(\sim p \,\&\, \sim q \,\&\, s)] \\ [(p \,\&\, \sim r \,\&\, \sim s)P(\sim p \,\&\, \sim q \,\&\, r) \,\&\, (p \,\&\, \sim r \,\&\, \sim s)P \\ \quad (\sim p \,\&\, \sim q \,\&\, s) \,\&\, (q \,\&\, \sim r \,\&\, \sim s)P(\sim p \,\&\, \sim q \,\&\, r) \,\&\, \\ \quad (q \,\&\, \sim r \,\&\, \sim s)P(\sim p \,\&\, \sim q \,\&\, s)] \longrightarrow [\sim(\sim p \,\&\, \sim q) \\ \quad P \sim(\sim r \,\&\, \sim s)] \end{cases}$	$-$ $-$	$-$ $-$
(W5)	$\begin{cases} pPq \longrightarrow [(p \,\&\, r)P(q \,\&\, r) \,\&\, (p \,\&\, \sim r)P(q \,\&\, \sim r)] \\ [(p \,\&\, r)P(q \,\&\, r) \,\&\, (p \,\&\, \sim r)P(q \,\&\, \sim r)] \longrightarrow pPq \end{cases}$	$-$ $(+)$[1]	$-$ $(+)$[2]
Chisholm-Sosa		$P\#$	$P*$
(A1) = (W1)		+	+
(A2)	$[\sim pPq \,\&\, \sim(qPr)] \longrightarrow \sim(pPr)$	+	+
(A3)	$[\sim(pP \sim p) \,\&\, \sim(\sim pPp) \,\&\, \sim(qP \sim q) \,\&\, \sim(\sim qPq)] \longrightarrow$ $\quad [\sim(pPq) \,\&\, \sim(qPp)]$	+	+
(A4)	$[\sim(qP \sim q) \,\&\, \sim(\sim qPq) \,\&\, pPq] \longrightarrow pP \sim p$	+	+
(A5)	$[\sim(qP \sim q) \,\&\, \sim(\sim qPq) \,\&\, qP \sim p] \longrightarrow pP \sim p$	+	+

Key		Annotations
$-$	unacceptable	1. The appropriate quantifier prefix is $(\forall p)(\forall q)(Ar)$.
$+$	unrestrictedly acceptable	2. The appropriate quantifier prefix is $(Ap)(Aq)(Ar)$.
$(+)$	restrictedly acceptable	

R. M. Martin (*op. cit.*) accepts *inter alia* two principles whose status is as follows:

Preference principle		$P\#$	$P*$
(M1)	$(pPr \lor qPr) \longrightarrow (p \lor q)Pr$	$-$	
(M2)	$pP(q \lor r) \longrightarrow [pPq \,\&\, pPr]$	$-$	$-$

Moreover, the converses of these two principles also fail to obtain for both of our modes of preference:[17]

Preference principle		$P\#$	$P*$
(M3)	$(p \lor q)Pr \longrightarrow (pPr \lor qPr)$	$-$	$-$
(M4)	$(pPq \,\&\, pPr) \longrightarrow pP(q \lor r)$	$-$	$-$

[16] (W1) and (W2) represent the *antisymmetry* and the *transitivity* of the preference relation. [Between them they entail irreflexivity, viz: $\sim(pPp)$.] These are the minimal rules for "preferences" classically insisted upon in *all* treatments of the subject by logicians, economists, etc.

[17] Note, however, that this specific feature of these rules does not exclude them from a proper and positive role in the logic of preference viewed in a wider perspective. We shall return to this point below.

The same goes for various cognate rules, as may be seen from the tabulation:

THE STATUS OF VARIOUS PREFERENCE PRINCIPLES

Preference principle	Von Wright	Chisholm-Sosa	Martin	$P^{\#}$	P^{*}	P^{w}
1. $pPq \longrightarrow \sim(qPp)$	✓	✓	✓	+	+	+
2. $(pPq\ \&\ qPr) \longrightarrow pPr$	✓	✓	✓	+	+	+
3. $pPq \longrightarrow \sim qP \sim p$		x	✓	$(+)^1$	+	+
4. $\sim qP \sim p \longrightarrow pPq$		x	✓	$(+)^1$	+	+
5. $pPq \longrightarrow (p\ \&\ \sim q)P(\sim p\ \&\ q)$	✓	x		+	+	+
6. $(p\ \&\ \sim q)P(\sim p\ \&\ q) \longrightarrow pPq$	✓	x		+	+	+
7. $[\sim(pP \sim p)\ \&\ \sim(\sim pPp)\ \&\ \sim(qP \sim q)\ \&$ $\sim(\sim qPq)] \longrightarrow [\sim(pPq)\ \&\ \sim(qPp)]$	✓	✓		+	+	+
8. $[\sim(qP \sim q)\ \&\ \sim(\sim qPq)\ \&\ \sim pPp] \longrightarrow$ $pP \sim p$		✓		+	+	−
9. $[\sim(qP \sim q)\ \&\ \sim(\sim qPq)\ \&\ qP \sim p] \longrightarrow$ $pP \sim p$		✓		+	+	−
10. $pPq \longrightarrow [(p\ \&\ r)P(q\ \&\ r)\ \&\ (p\ \&\ \sim r)$ $P(q\ \&\ \sim r)]$	✓			−	−	+
11. $[(p\ \&\ r)P(q\ \&\ r)\ \&\ (p\ \&\ \sim r)P(q\ \&\ \sim r)]$ $\longrightarrow pPq$	✓			$(+)^2$	$(+)^3$	+
12. $[\sim(pPq)\ \&\ \sim(qPr)] \longrightarrow \sim(pPr)$		✓		+	+	−
13. $(pPr \lor qPr) \longrightarrow (p \lor q)Pr$			✓	−	−	−
14. $(p \lor q)Pr \longrightarrow [pPr\ \&\ qPr]$	✓			−	−	−
15. $[pPr\ \&\ qPr] \longrightarrow (p \lor q)Pr$	✓			−	−	−
16. $(p \lor q)Pr \longrightarrow (pPr \lor qPr)$				−	−	−
17. $pP(q \lor r) \longrightarrow (pPq\ \&\ pPr)$	✓		✓	−	−	−
18. $(pPq\ \&\ pPr) \longrightarrow pP(q \lor r)$	✓			−	−	−
19. $(pPr\ \&\ qPr) \longrightarrow (p\ \&\ q)Pr$				−	−	−
20. $(p\ \&\ q)Pr \longrightarrow (pPr\ \&\ qPr)$				−	−	−
21. $pP(q\ \&\ r) \longrightarrow (pPq\ \&\ pPr)$				−	−	−
22. $(pPq\ \&\ pPr) \longrightarrow pP(q\ \&\ r)$				−	−	−
23. $[\sim(\sim p\ \&\ \sim q)P \sim(\sim r\ \&\ \sim s)] \longrightarrow$ $[(p\ \&\ \sim r\ \&\ \sim s)P(\sim p\ \&\ \sim q\ \&\ r)\ \&$ $(p\ \&\ \sim r\ \&\ \sim s)P(\sim p\ \&\ \sim q\ \&\ s)\ \&$ $(q\ \&\ \sim r\ \&\ \sim s)P(\sim p\ \&\ \sim q\ \&\ r)\ \&$ $(q\ \&\ \sim r\ \&\ \sim s)P(\sim p\ \&\ \sim q\ \&\ s)$	✓			−	−	+
24. $[(p\ \&\ \sim r\ \&\ \sim s)P(\sim p\ \&\ \sim q\ \&\ r)\ \&$ $(p\ \&\ \sim r\ \&\ \sim s)P(\sim p\ \&\ \sim q\ \&\ s)\ \&$ $(q\ \&\ \sim r\ \&\ \sim s)P(\sim p\ \&\ \sim q\ \&\ r)\ \&$ $(q\ \&\ \sim r\ \&\ \sim s)P(\sim p\ \&\ \sim q\ \&\ s)]$ $\longrightarrow [\sim(\sim p\ \&\ \sim q)P \sim(\sim r\ \&\ \sim s)]$	✓			−	−	+

Key	*Annotations*
− unacceptable	
+ unrestrictedly acceptable	[1] The appropriate quantifier prefix is $(Ap)(Aq)$.
(+) restrictedly acceptable	[2] The appropriate quantifier prefix is $(\forall p)(\forall q)(Ar)$.
✓ explicitly accepted	[3] The appropriate quantifier prefix is $(Ap)(Aq)(Ar)$.
x explicitly rejected	

Several features of this tabulation warrant comment:

(i)   It is noteworthy that the only really uncontested principles are numbers 1 and 2 (i.e., irreflexivity and transitivity).[18]

(ii) It is striking that the various authorities are so seriously at odds with one another after going beyond the just-indicated point of common departure.

(iii) It is interesting that so few of the plausible-seeming principles listed after number 12 are acceptable on any of the three accounts of the matter here under consideration.

All this, we believe, goes far toward showing the undesirability of proceeding by intuition in the construction of an axiomatic theory for the rules of preference logic. The advantages of the semantical approach come strikingly to the fore.

We now have a guide to the selection of preference principles which safeguards us against the often paradoxical features of the deliverances of intuition. At the purely informal, intuitive level of understanding, a concept may well prove to be equivocal. In this case, it takes one form for which certain principles "obviously" hold, and also a second form for which other, equally "obvious" principles hold that are inconsistent with the former. The semantical approach protects us against this logically intolerable situation in which incompatible results confront us with equal plausibility.

Taking the semantical approach, we can say that "we know what we are doing" in a far more thoroughgoing way than is possible with any axiomatic treatment. Although serious problems doubtless still remain to be resolved, there can be little doubt that the *semantical*—in contrast to the *axiomatic*—approach affords the most promising prospects for the development of the logic of preference and that the best hopes for future progress in this field lie in this direction.

* * *

Chisholm and Sosa discuss two principles of the logic of preference which have been accepted by certain writers, but which they themselves reject. These principles are as follows:

Preference principle		$P\#$	$P*$
(R1)	$pPq \longrightarrow \sim qP \sim p$	(+)	+
	$\sim qP \sim p \longrightarrow pPq$	(+)	+
(R2)	$= $ (W3) above	+	+

---

[18] In this regard it deserves noting how matters fare with the preference measure $P\S$ based on the valuation of a proposition in terms of a probabilistically weighted mean of the possible worlds in which this proposition is true. (With $P\#$ all these weights are set equal. Cf. footnote 9 above.) Here principles (1) and (2) survive, but even such plausible principles as (3) through (6), acceptable for all the other modes of P preference, will fail to hold.

And the propositional #-valuations we would *then* derive—and thus the preferences that would be based upon them—would have a quite different structure, to wit:

Proposition	#-value
p	$+3.75$ units
$\sim p$	-0.25 units
q	$+2.50$ units
$\sim q$	$+1.00$ units

And on *this* basis of assessment it would have to be the case that, as we have shown, p's preferability to q guarantees not-q's preferability to not-p. In summary, the intuitive ideas operative in the Chisholm-Sosa concept of "intrinsic preferability" in no way conflict or involve incompatibilities with the procedures and results of our formal semantics.

Exactly the same line of analysis applies to the Chisholm-Sosa line of objection to von Wright's (W3):

$$pPq \leftrightarrow (p \, \& \sim q)P(\sim p \, \& \, q)$$

This counterexample is of the type:

If it is the case that	then one is to get
p	$+3$
$\sim p$	0
q	$+1$
$\sim q$	-2

Clearly one prefers p's happening to q's (i.e., prefers a three-unit gain to a one-unit gain). But one certainly does not prefer $(p \, \& \sim q)$'s happening (when one gets $+1$) to $(\sim p \, \& \, q)$'s happening (when one also gets exactly $+1$). But let us translate this "raw" valuation into our technical #-valuation via the consideration of the possible worlds:

Possible world	#-value
$w_1 \colon p \, \& \, q$	$+4$
$w_2 \colon p \, \& \sim q$	$+1$
$w_3 \colon \sim p \, \& \, q$	$+1$
$w_4 \colon \sim p \, \& \sim q$	-2

And now with respect to the derivative #-values, it is clear that we could not have

$$pP^{\#}q \quad \text{i.e.,} \quad \frac{\#(w_1) + \#(w_2)}{2} > \frac{\#(w_1) + \#(w_3)}{2} \quad \text{i.e.,} \quad \#(w_2) > \#(w_3)$$

without also concurrently having:

$$(p \ \& \ \sim q)P^{\#}(\sim p \ \& \ q) \quad \text{i.e.,} \quad \#(w_2) > \#(w_3)$$

* * *

The proscription of contradiction-generating substitutions with respect to the $\#$-measure requires further discussion. Consider, for example, the principle (acceptable both for $P^{\#}$ and P^*)

(W3) $\qquad pPq \longrightarrow (p \ \& \ \sim q)P(\sim p \ \& \ q)$

and let it be assumed that $\vdash p \longrightarrow q$, so that we have

(W4) $\qquad pPq \longrightarrow cP(\sim p \ \& \ q) \qquad c = $ a contradiction

Now take a concrete example, letting:

$p = $ Having \$12 (i.e., having at least \$12, that is, having \$12 or more)

$q = $ Having \$11 (i.e., having at least \$11, that is, having \$11 or more)

Note that *this p is preferable to this q* on any presystematic understanding of the matter and that, moreover, p entails q. Consequently, we would come to be committed by (W4) to:

cP(having exactly \$11)

This consequence is clearly absurd. But it is not, in fact, a valid consequence of our logic of preference, because one of the essential steps by which it was obtained involved a fallacious process of inference, to wit, a contradiction-generating substitution for the $\#$-measure.

It will be objected that the principle at issue (W3) holds not only for $\#$-preference, where we have insisted on excluding contradiction-generating substitutions, but also for $*$-preference, where this restriction has been dropped. Consequently, so goes the objection, the indicated way out is not available. This objection is correct, so far as it goes, but it fails to realize that, because of the *technical* character of $*$-preference, the entire difficulty at issue does not arise.

Let it be supposed, for the sake of simplicity, that \$20 is the maximum amount which, as a matter of the "practical politics" of the situation, is at issue (nothing would be affected if this were fixed at \$100 or \$1,000). Then we shall have it that:

$$\#(p) = \#(\$12 \text{ or more}) = \frac{12 + 13 + \cdots + 20}{9} = 16.0$$

$$\#(q) = \#(\$11 \text{ or more}) = \frac{11 + 12 + \cdots + 20}{10} = 15.5$$

$$\#(\sim p) = \#(\$11 \text{ or less}) = \frac{0 + 1 + 2 + \cdots + 11}{12} = 5.5$$

$$\#(\sim q) = \#(\$10 \text{ or less}) = \frac{0 + 1 + 2 + \cdots + 10}{11} = 5.0$$

As a consequence:

$$*(p) = 16.0 - 5.5 = 10.5$$
$$*(q) = 15.5 - 5.0 = 10.5$$

It is thus simply not the case with respect to the *technical* concept of $*$-preference now at issue, that p ("having \$12 or more") is preferable to q ("having \$11 or more"). The difficulty at issue falls to the ground because one of its essential premises fails to be true with respect to this specifically "differential" mode of preference.

6. A MEASURE-THEORETIC PERSPECTIVE UPON THE LOGIC OF PREFERENCE

It is useful to look at our quantitative approach to the logic of preference from a somewhat different perspective. Let it be supposed that we have a family of propositions represented by the meta-variables α, β, γ, etc. These proportions are assumed to range over the set S, assumed to be closed under the familiar truth-functional connectives. Let there be a real-value measure μ with

$$\mu(\alpha)$$

defined over the set S, subject to the stipulation that equivalent propositions obtain the same μ value, i.e., that:

If $\vdash \alpha \leftrightarrow \beta$, then $\mu(\alpha) = \mu(\beta)$

Moreover, let it be supposed that our μ measure is such as to satisfy the following additional condition:

$$\mu(\sim\alpha) = -\mu(\alpha)$$

[It should be observed that our measure $*(\alpha)$ is, whereas $\#(\alpha)$ is not, of such a kind as to meet this last-named condition.] It may be remarked, moreover, that this condition has the consequence that:

If $\mu(\alpha) = \mu(\sim\alpha)$, then $\mu(\alpha) = 0$

Now it is readily verified that if we stipulate a preference relation P^{μ} in such a way that

$$\alpha P^{\mu} \beta \quad \text{iff} \quad \mu(\alpha) > \mu(\beta)$$

then wherever the μ measure satisfies the aforementioned conditions, then P^μ must satisfy all of the Chisholm-Sosa axioms (as well as the first two von Wright axioms). It is also readily verified that, under the stipulated conditions, we must have it that P^μ must satisfy the Chisholm-Sosa rejected thesis:

$$\alpha P^\mu \beta \longleftrightarrow \sim\beta P^\mu \sim\alpha$$

This way of approaching the matter at once systematizes our previous group of findings with respect to P^*.

* * *

It is of interest to re-examine, in the light of our generalized measure-theoretic approach, some of the principles previously found unacceptable for $P^\#$ and P^*. By way of example, let us return to the axiom (in the style of R. M. Martin):

(M2) $pP^\mu(q \lor r) \longrightarrow (pP^\mu q \ \& \ pP^\mu r)$

This now becomes

$$\mu(p) > \mu(q \lor r) \longrightarrow \{[\mu(p) > \mu(q)] \ \& \ [\mu(p) > \mu(r)]\}$$

or equivalently,

$$\mu(q \lor r) \geqslant \max [\mu(q), \mu(r)]$$

Thus any μ measure that is a monotonically increasing function of its Boolean constituents will satisfy (M2). This condition, although unquestionably plausible for certain propositional measures (e.g., probability), is patently unsuitable for a measure of "goodness."

Again, consider the axiom:

(M1) $(pP^\mu r \lor qP^\mu r) > (p \lor q)P^\mu r$

This now becomes

$$\{[\mu(p) > \mu(r)] \lor [\mu(q) > \mu(r)]\} \longrightarrow \mu(p \lor q) > \mu(r)$$

or equivalently,

$$\mu(p \lor q) \geqslant \min [\mu(p), \mu(q)]$$

This, of course, would also be guaranteed immediately by the previous condition and—being substantially weaker—represents a more plausible requirement.

7. CONCLUSION

The main aim of this chapter has been to provide a systematically developed semantical theory for the logic of preference. Using as starting point the orthodox semantical notion of a "possible world," we have adopted the idea of a valuation measure for such worlds as a determinant of preferabilities. This apparatus has been applied to appraise the acceptability of various preference principles accepted on the basis of informal considerations by the several writers who have to date attempted to systematize the logic of preference. Our method has to some extent been able to reconcile the divergent approaches proposed in the literature. But in any case, sufficient evidence has, we trust, been provided to indicate the power and promise of the suggested line of approach.[19]

[19] This chapter draws extensively upon my paper, "Semantical Foundations for the Logic of Preference," in N. Rescher (ed.), *The Logic of Decision and Action* (Pittsburgh, 1967).

VIII

Individual Preference,
Social Choice, Welfare, and Value

1. THE PROBLEM OF A "SOCIAL PREFERENCE FUNCTION"

The combination of individual personal preferences into a social or group preference is an important issue for the theory of value. For this question indicates one of the most critical arenas in which conflicts of value come to be fought out. Such clashes need not even involve a contest between *different* values—one single value may be at issue. Values may represent a *common interest*, when their concurrent realization by different individuals is feasible (or even necessary), e.g., the "environmental beauty" of a given area or the "safety" of the road system. Contrastingly, other values are *competitive*, in that, like "power" or "status," they can be realized by some only at the expense of their nonrealization by others. In situations of the competitive type, people will have divergent preferences with respect to possible alternatives. It is one of the tasks for the *social* order embracing different individuals to find a means of resolving a unified result out of a mass of potentially divergent individual preferences.

99

Before we go on to a detailed consideration of this topic it is worth stressing that a rational social order should place great emphasis upon common-interest values. Justice, equality, and other supremely social values are of exactly this character. It is very much in the interest of a society to facilitate and implement values of this sort, and—to look at the other side of the coin—to temper the pursuit of competitive values and channel it into harmless, well-cushioned settings.

The problem of the socialization of individual preference can be posed in the following abstract terms. Suppose that we have a situation involving: (1) a group of people P_1, P_2, ..., P_n, (2) a set of alternatives x_1, x_2, ..., x_n, and (3) for each person P_i a specification of his ranking of the alternatives x_j,

$$k_{i,1}; k_{i,2}; \ldots ; k_{i,n}$$

where these $k_{i,j}$ exhaust all the integers up to some integer $m \leqslant n$, with two or more of the $k_{i,j}$ possibly the same. Thus if there are three persons and three objects we would obtain a ranking matrix of the type

	x_1	x_2	x_3
P_1	1	2	2
P_2	2	3	1
P_3	3	2	1

The numbers given in this tabulation indicate that:

1. P_1 prefers x_1 to the others, and is indifferent between x_2 and x_3 (i.e., x_2 and x_3 are tied for second place).
2. P_2 puts x_3 in first place, with x_1 next, and then x_2.
3. P_3 prefers x_3 to x_2, and x_2 to x_1.

The problem of the socialization of individual preferences can now be put simply:

> Given such a preference matrix for the n individuals P_1–P_n that constitute a society S, how is one to arrive at a combination preference ranking
>
> $$k_1, k_2, \ldots, k_n$$
>
> for the society as a whole?

Note that this matter of social preference cannot be settled by simply voting. For assume that we again have a 3×3 matrix, but this time as follows:

	x_1	x_2	x_3
P_1	1	2	3
P_2	3	1	2
P_3	2	3	1

Note that both P_1 and P_2 prefer x_2 to x_3, so we might be inclined to say that society prefers x_2 to x_3, and would certainly do so if the matter were settled by voting. Again both P_1 and P_3 prefer x_1 to x_2, so by parity of reasoning society prefers x_1 to x_2. Then we must seemingly have it (by transitivity of preference) that society prefers x_1 to x_3. But this is incompatible with the finding that both P_2 and P_3 prefer x_3 to x_1.

The problem of the socialization of individual preference is thus that of finding a plausible technique (given the failure of such methods as, e.g., voting) to distill a social preference ranking out of the matrix for the individual preference rankings.

2. THE ARROW BARRIER

The economist Kenneth Arrow has demonstrated in his important monograph on *Social Choice and Individual Values*[1] that the problem of a social preference function is insoluble if one lays down certain plausible requirements for such a function. These requirements that one postulates for the desired social preference function are as follows:

I. *Collective Rationality*
Given *any* set of individual preference rankings, a social preference ranking is determined.

II. *Citizens' Sovereignty*
For any pair of alternatives x and y, there is *some* set of individual preference rankings that leads to the result that society prefers x to y.

III. *Pareto Principle*
If alternative x is preferred to alternative y according to the preference rankings of *all* the individuals, then x will also be preferred to y by the social preference ranking.

IV. *Positive Association*
If for a given set of individual preference rankings, society—according to the preference function—prefers alternative x to alternative y, then this preferability will continue if the individual preference ratings are in some cases altered to x's advantage *vis-à-vis* other alternatives.

V. *Nondictatorship*
There is no individual with the property that whenever he prefers alternative x to y (for any alternatives x and y), then society does likewise, regardless of the preferences of the other individuals.

VI. *Irrelevance of Extraneous Alternatives*
Whenever two sets of social preference rankings are such that an individual's *pairwise* preference comparisons among two alternatives x and y are identical for both sets, then society's ranking of x versus y

[1] New York, 1951 (Cowles Commission Monograph, No. 12).

should be identical for both sets: it should not matter how the other alternatives "group around" the particular ones (x, y) that are at issue. (In other words, in determining society's preference between x and y we need look only at their pairwise ratings according to the individual preference rankings and can neglect all the other extraneous alternatives.)

Arrow demonstrated that these plausible-seeming requirements are mutually incompatible, so that there *cannot be any social welfare function that satisfies this group of requirements*. This blockage of the route to a reasonable method for blending individual preferences into a combined social preference may be called the *Arrow Barrier*.

The seriousness of this finding has been assessed differently by various writers. In the final analysis one's judgment of this matter will, of course, turn on one's assessment of the plausibility and acceptability of the specified requirements; if one is prepared to give one of them up, the impossibility result is avoided.

The most implausible member of this set of requirements, the one that represents the best candidate for rejection, is item VI, the Irrelevance of Extraneous Alternatives. (Arrow calls this postulate the Independence of Irrelevant Alternatives, but this very name begs the question at issue: are the extraneous alternatives actually irrelevant?) The questionability of this requirement is readily brought out by an example. Suppose that society consists of only two persons, who rank three alternatives x, y, z as follows:

(1, 2, 3)

(2, 3, 1)

Since both individuals prefer x to y, it is clear that society ought to prefer x to y. But note the two following facts: (1) in the x-z comparison, things are here pairwise the same as with the following set of rankings (since in both cases the first individual prefers x to z and the second z to x):

(1, 2, 3)

(3, 2, 1)

for which (by symmetry) society must be indifferent with regard to x and z. And (2) for the y-z comparison things are pairwise the same as with the following set of rankings (since in both cases the first individual prefers y to z and the second z to y):

(1, 2, 3)

(1, 3, 2)

for which (by symmetry) society must be indifferent with regard to y and z.

But from (2) and (3) it would then follow—by the transitivity of indifference —that society must be indifferent between x and y on the original set of preference rankings, and this result contradicts our initial preference finding.

This example[2] brings home the questionability of requiring the Irrelevance of Extraneous Alternatives. In turning to a consideration of ways of dealing with Arrow's finding of the "impossibility" of a social preference function, we shall suppose that this requirement may be dropped. (However, we shall retain all the other, apparently unexceptionable requirements.) The dropping of this requirement deserves one further comment. If the occurrence of z on a society's list of alternatives may "make a difference" to its preference as between x and y, then z's very presence on this list becomes an issue that has real consequences for social choice. Care must thus be taken in any *application* of the preference-combining machinery to insure that all the genuinely available alternatives do in fact figure on the list.

There are basically two ways to overcome, or, rather, to circumvent the Arrow Barrier. They are:

1. A process of group "consensus" in the determination of a social preference ranking that comes closest to meeting the rankings of the several individuals.
2. A process of "averaging out" the individual preferences on the basis of a quantification or metrization of preference.

We shall describe each of these procedures in turn.[3]

3. CONSENSUS DETERMINATION

In seeking to determine a "consensus" for a group of preferences, we attempt to seek out as the social preference relation that one of the logically possible

---

[2] Taken from R. D. Luce and H. Raiffa, *Games and Decisions* (New York, 1957), p. 338.

[3] For further discussion of the problems with which we have been dealing here, see Luce and Raiffa, *op. cit.*, especially Chap. 14, "Group Decision Making." A useful discussion from the economists' point of view is given in I. M. D. Little, *A Critique of Welfare Economics*, 2nd ed. (Oxford, 1957), pp. 32–37 and 52–54. The approach to the problem of metrizing individual preferences favored by Luce and Raiffa is the probabilized choice model exploited in J. von Neumann and D. Morgenstern's classic *Theory of Games and Economic Behavior* (Princeton, 1944; 2nd ed., 1947). Its advantages from the standpoint of the mathematical development of decision theory seem to me offset by difficulties on the side of application. Here the direct-comparison approach taken above seems to be significantly easier to implement. It may be mentioned here that nonprobabilistic measurement of utility has also been advocated by S. S. Stevens; see "Measurement Psychophysics, and Utility" in *Measurement: Definitions and Theories*, ed. by C. West Churchman and Philburn Ratoosh (New York and London, 1959).

relationships that best fits the indicated preferences. We may illustrate this procedure by a concrete example which is readily generalized.

Suppose that three objects are at issue. Then thirteen possible preference rankings can be conceived, as follows:

No.	Preference ranking	Degree
1	(1, 1, 1)	3
2	(1, 1, 2)	4
3	(1, 2, 1)	4
4	(2, 1, 1)	4
5	(1, 2, 2)	5
6	(2, 1, 2)	5
7	(2, 2, 1)	5
8	(1, 2, 3)	6
9	(1, 3, 2)	6
10	(2, 1, 3)	6
11	(2, 3, 1)	6
12	(3, 1, 2)	6
13	(3, 2, 1)	6

Whatever the social preference ranking may turn out to be, it will have (i.e., *logically* have) to be one of these. Consider now some specific cases. Suppose "society" consists of three individuals whose preference rankings are as follows:

(1, 2, 3)

(1, 2, 3)

(2, 1, 3)

Given such a set of individual preferences, we may take as our social preference ranking that one among the possible alternatives that has the best "fit" to the indicated preferences in the exact sense that *the sum total $\sum$ for all the individual preference rankings of the sum of the squares of the differences between their ranking numbers and those of this possible preference ranking is a minimum.* In the present case this will be the ranking (1, 2, 3) for which $\sum = 2$. [Note, for example, that for (1, 1, 2), $\sum$ would be 6.]

Again, if there were two individuals with preferences

(1, 2, 3)

(3, 2, 1)

the best-fit ranking would be

(2, 1, 2)

for which $\sum = 6$. [Note that (1, 2, 3), (3, 2, 1), and (1, 2, 1) would all have

$\sum = 8$.][4] Finally, consider a population of five individuals, with preferences:

(1, 2, 3)

(3, 2, 1)

(2, 1, 3)

(2, 3, 3)

(1, 3, 2)

The best-fit ranking is

(1, 3, 2)

with $\sum = 16$. [For comparison with that for (1, 2, 3) we have $\sum = 18$.]

There is, however, one minor difficulty on this approach. Consider the set of individual preferences:

(1, 1, 1)

(1, 1, 1)

(1, 1, 1)

(1, 2, 3)

The best-fit ranking is now (1, 1, 1), with $\sum = 5$. According to this result, society *must be indifferent* to the three alternatives. But this result is implausible. Since four of its population are individually *indifferent* among the three items, society might as well—indeed *ought* to—accommodate the fifth individual, who does have a distinct preference in our distribution-selection procedure. We would thus want to introduce the following amendment:

> If the "best-fit" ranking has places that are tied, then we are to modify it to resolve the tie in favor of one element if there is at least one gainer by this scheme, and otherwise every individual is either indifferent to this change or in favor of it.

Thus, given the preferences

(1, 2, 3)

(1, 2, 2)

(1, 1, 1)

we arrive at the best-fit ranking, (1, 2, 2). And the modified best-fit ranking is (1, 2, 3), a changeover which the first individual would favor, and the others view with indifference.

[4] In the example, considered above, of two individuals with preferences (1, 2, 3) (2, 3, 1), the best-fit ranking will be (1, 3, 2) with $\sum = 4$.

It might appear from the examples we have given that the social preference ranking could be determined simply by considering the column-sum of the individual preference ranking. This is not so. Consider the following set of five individual preferences:

(2, 1, 1)

(1, 2, 3)

(2, 2, 1)

(1, 1, 2)

(2, 2, 1)

Each column sums to 8, so that society would be indifferent according to the rule in question. But our own rule yields as the best-fit ranking (1, 1, 2) with $\sum = 10$ and not (1, 1, 1) with $\sum = 11$.

This completes our exposition of the process of consensus determination. It should be observed that this process satisfies all of Arrow's requirements for a social preference function except the last, the Irrelevance of Extraneous Alternatives. (Its failure is apparent from the example discussed at the end of Sec. 2 above.)

4. THE METRIZATION OF PREFERENCE

Given a solution to the problem of constructing a quantified scheme for an individual's evaluations along some such lines as those discussed in Chapter VI, we obtain for an individual P a measure of his rating of the alternatives $x_1, x_2, x_3, \ldots, x_n$ with the resulting schedule (real-number) values:

$m(x_1), \ m(x_2), \ m(x_3), \ldots, m(x_n)$

The question remains: How are we to *combine* such individual preference metrics into an interpersonal measure of preference, making possible the transition from *personal* to *social* valuation in the metrized case?

The relatively technical considerations by means of which a plausible answer to this question can be established are detailed in Appendix II. The upshot of the line of reasoning developed there is that we should take the social valuation measure m for the group of individuals to be defined as follows:

$m(x_j) = 1/n[m_1(x_j) + m_2(x_j) + \cdots + m_n(x_j)]$

That is, the plausible course is to let the social evaluation of an alternative be simply the *average* (over the entire "population" of that society) of the metrized individual evaluations of this alternative. This proposed metric solution, since it also represents a way of overcoming the Arrow Barrier, involves the violation of one of Arrow's requirements, again, the Independence of Irrelevant Alternatives.

Against this procedure of obtaining a social valuation m by simply averaging the individual m_i, the following line of objection could be developed.

Consider two items x_1 and x_2 valued by a group of ten individuals P_1 through P_{10} as shown by the following two "valuation vectors":

x_1: 1, 1, 1, 1, 1, 1, 1, 1, 1, 1

x_2: 10, 0, 0, 0, 0, 0, 0, 0, 0, 0

Now with respect to our social valuation measure m, we have it that:

$m(x_1) = m(x_2) = 1$

The society will thus be indifferent with regard to x_1 and x_2. But now suppose that x_1 and x_2 represent *commodities of exclusive possession*. Then the "realization" of x_1 in the society (i.e., its possession by someone) is worth exactly one unit. Each P_i would be willing to "pay," as it were, one unit for exclusive possession of x_1. The "social worth" of x_1 is now one unit per person *alternatively*. On the other hand, suppose P_1 is willing to "pay" ten units for x_2, and then make one unit available for all the other P_i: in short, as regards x_2, its "social worth" is now one unit per person *collectively*. It is clear, therefore, that it has been built into our approach that the items x_i at issue must be construed either as *complete social states* (involving everyone), or else as *commodities of public possession* (public assets or public facilities), but not as *commodities of exclusive possession*.

The (most important) point at issue here can perhaps be best brought out by an example. Let us suppose a single item x to be a commodity of exclusive possession valued among the three people of a (miniature) society P_1–P_3, as follows:

P_1 values a at 1 unit

P_2 values a at 1 unit

P_3 values a at 1 unit

This seems to give rise to the "valuation vector":

x: 1, 1, 1

But actually, from the *toti-comprising* perspective of our approach, we are dealing not with a single item a but with three alternative states:

x_1: P_1 has a, P_2 and P_3 do not

x_2: P_2 has a, P_1 and P_3 do not

x_3: P_3 has a, P_1 and P_2 do not

This leads us, not to a single valuation vector, but to the m measure of the valuation matrix:

	x_1	x_2	x_3
P_1	1	0	0
P_2	0	1	0
P_3	0	0	1

The resultant social valuation m that derives by our averaging procedure is given by the equations:

$$m(x_1) = m(x_2) = m(x_3) = \tfrac{1}{3}$$

Note that if the three members of our society were envious, but equally envious, the indicated matrix would change to:

	x_1	x_2	x_3
P_1	1	$-v$	$-v$
P_2	$-v$	1	$-v$
P_3	$-v$	$-v$	1

where $v > 0$

The social valuation would now be

$$m(x_1) = m(x_2) = m(x_3) = (1 - 2v)/3$$

which would—we rather expect it!—be uniformly less than $\tfrac{1}{3}$ and indeed would be negative when $v > \tfrac{1}{2}$. In a society of very envious people one man's gain is the group's misfortune.

It is worth exploring the possible desirability of modifying our definition of the social valuation measure m to include some principle of equity or consensus. Given the aforementioned valuation of items x_1 and x_2 by the ten P_i,

$$x_1 : 1, 1, 1, \ldots , 1$$

$$x_2 : 10, 0, 0, \ldots , 0$$

the society should, it might be argued, prefer x_1 to x_2 on account of its greater uniformity in the distribution of benefits. We should, perhaps, depress the social value of items to reflect unevennesses in the pattern of distribution of benefits. This suggests the merit of using not the average m, as above, but *the effective average*,

$$m^* = m - \tfrac{1}{2}\sigma$$

where σ is the standard deviation from the mean m of the several valuations $m_i(x_j)$. This conception of an effective average has been dealt with elsewhere at some length, and we shall not pursue the matter further here.[5] (Its adoption

[5] See N. Rescher, *Distributive Justice* (New York, 1966), Chap. 2.

means that of the four principles 1 through 4 of Appendix II, we can retain only the symmetry and uniformity conditions, 1 and 4, and will have to drop —or, rather, qualify—the scaling identity and linearity conditions 2 and 3.)

This section has set out a body of machinery for the interpersonalization of preference in such a way as to put this procedure into as promising and plausibly motivated a light as possible. In particular by breaking the problem apart into (1) that of the metrizing individual preferences and then (2) that of the combination of metrized individual preferences, we have been able to effect a "division of labor" according to which the bulk of the work is done by the former, seemingly less problematic, device.[6]

5. THE LIMITATIONS OF PREFERENCE AGGREGATION

Although preferences are important for the understanding of values, their proper place in the scheme of things must not be exaggerated, as economists above all are inclined to do. For example, when mooting the problem of *Social Choice and Individual Values*, it soon becomes apparent that by "individual values" Kenneth Arrow simply means *preferences* of the tea over coffee variety. This will not do: the road from preference to value is too long and winding. Values may—indeed, standardly do—provide an underpinning for the reasonable man's preferences, but that does not result in their mutual assimilation: preferences are therefore not to be identified with values. A person's preferences will in many, though by no means all, cases serve as indicators of his values, and, contrariwise, his values may be reflected in his preferences. But preference is too gross an instrument to capture the subtle nuances of value. Preferences may, to be sure, result from evaluations, but this relation is contingent, not necessary, and even here, as elsewhere, the effect may throw relatively little light upon the cause. If Jones prefers apples to oranges—be it in general or in point of, say, appearance or flavor—this does not go far to indicate what his values are. Values (as we have seen) are given stability and solidity by their essential relationship to benefits; preferences can be things of the fleeting moment, and at that, things which fly in the face of consciously reckoned benefits. Preferences are just that—preferences—and perfectly legitimate preferences need not be reasoned. But values are (so we have argued) invariable *instrumentalities for reasoning* about alternatives.

---

[6] This section draws upon the writer's paper "Notes on Preference, Utility, and Cost," *Synthese*, Vol. 16 (1966), pp. 332–343.

This is why the talk of some economists about preference-combining schemes in terms of "social *welfare* functions" rings a hollow note. Welfare is indeed an important consideration—but there is nothing sacred about preferences. Parents, physicians, and schoolmasters (among others) have long known that welfare is not to be extracted from preferences. Welfare has to do with our realization of genuine benefits and our achievement of what is in our real interests. What relates to welfare is objective and interpersonally debatable. But preferences frequently operate in the area of tastes, and fall within the purview of the classic maxim *de gustibus non est disputandum*. Thus to assign *central* importance to the project of distilling a conception of social *welfare* out of individual *preferences* is to espouse a highly questionable ideology in the economico-political sphere. (Nor will it do to follow some writers in seeking to equate *welfare* with "preference in the long run": no preestablished harmony is operative to assure that long-run preferences—any more than short-run ones—need conform with what is properly to be understood as "welfare.")

Democratic societies need not in fact—and surely ought not in theory—settle public issues in terms of such preference-pooling procedures as, for example, voting. Individual preferences do play an important role in the democratic process—but need not play a pervasive one. Most liberal democratic theorists see their principal use not in the making of decisions but in the choosing of decision makers. Apart from restricted categories of referendum issues, they are not used to resolve the administrative policy question of "Whether to do X or to do Y?", but rather to settle the *procedural issues posed in constitutional policy issues* of determining the methods for settling questions of the doing X vs. Y type. The question of the *modus operandi* for a well-ordered society's utilization of individual preferences in the conduct of its affairs poses significant social and political issues. Most democratic societies restrict the sphere of effective operation of individual preferences within a rather narrowly delimited area of procedural issues. Precisely because preferences need not automatically reflect interests and welfare there is nothing intrinsically objectionable about this.

IX

The Dynamics of
Value Change

1. MODES OF VALUE CHANGE:
A PRELIMINARY TYPOLOGY

This examination of value change will proceed within the framework of a group of basic concepts which must be explained at the outset. These concepts relate to the explication of what a "value change" is, distinguishing between the many different sorts of things that are at issue here.

Value acquisition and abandonment. When a person begins to subscribe to a value to which he did not previously give adherence, we may say that he has *acquired* this value. In the reverse case, when he gives up adherence to a value to which he previously subscribed, we shall say that he has *abandoned* this value. Value acquisition and abandonment are the most radical sorts of value "change" on the part of an individual or group with respect to a given value; it is not a matter of more or less and of degree, but rather turns on the yes-no issue of a given value's entering or exiting from that subscriber's set of accepted values. This is the sort of thing one thinks of in connection with a religious or ideological conversion.

Value redistribution. A given value is more or less widely distributed throughout a group according as a larger or smaller proportion of members of the group subscribe to it. We may speak of a *value redistribution* when there is a change in the extent or in the pattern of its distribution in the society. A very common way in which a value becomes a "value of a society" —that is, becomes successively more and more generally diffused (i.e., more and more extensively distributed) throughout this society in that most or virtually all of its members subscribe to it—is to start out as the value of some dedicated minority who successfully manage to promote its increasingly widespread acceptance. This has been the history of many widely held American values—e.g., "tolerance" (religious and racial).

Value emphasis and de-emphasis. A situation may develop in which a value, even when not affected by other modes of value change, may suddenly come to be emphasized (or de-emphasized), because changes in the life environment force it to our attention. If the value is securely established (like "economic security" in an affluent society), we need no longer pay it much heed— though of course we would if it were "threatened." The course of events renders some values operatively *topical*—having lain dormant before, they are now in the spotlight and are resource-demanding—while other values become more or less negligible (at any rate *pro tem.*).

Value rescaling. The set of values to which an individual or group sub-scribes can generally be compared on a value scale of higher and lower, and to some extent can even be arranged in a strict hierarchy.[1] This does not turn on the yes-no issue of whether a subscriber does or does not adhere to certain values, but on the *extent* of his commitment to them. The height of a value on the scale is determined by a multiplicity of factors, such as the tenacity of maintaining and preserving the value, preparedness to invest energy and resources in its realization and propagation, and the attachment of high sanctions to the value (i.e., how much compliance is expected and how much reproach heaped upon the transgressor). The reordering of such a value scale by mutual reranking of its components in a "revaluation of values" is among the most drastic varieties of value change. One finds this sort of thing, for example, where there is a widespread reorientation in the sources of identity and self-worth in a changing society (particularly in the wake of some extensive loss of social stability).

Value redeployment. A value is inevitably held in the context of a domain

[1] The ordering at issue here is not a strict but a *partial* ordering in the mathematicians' sense.

of application—the range of cases that are held to come within the purview of this value, that is, the objects or occasions for value-implementing action or appraisal. (Paradigm example: driving a car within the speed limit lies within the domain of application of the value "law abidingness.") The operative arena of the ideals of legal and political equality were gradually extended to include the American Negro and the American Indian, but this does not mean that these values as such were given a different or higher niche in the shrine of American values—simply that we began to apply them over an enlarged domain with changed boundaries. One of the most profound value changes in Roman history was the bringing of the provincials within the precincts of Roman citizenship; for the Roman politician and jurist this was clearly a matter of redeployment of existing values; rather than turning upon the acquisition of new values, it involved redefining the area of application of old ones. (Think also of Paul the Apostle's conception of some gentiles as being "circumcised of the spirit.") The education-for-social-adjustment cult in the United States in the 1920's to 1950's was moderately successful in promoting an enlargement in the domain of application of society's value requirement of "mature, socially responsible behavior" from young adult to teenager as starting point. (Part of the youth malaise of the 1960's may be seen in the light of a revolt against this conception.)

Value restandardization. A mode of value change that is particularly sensitive to and reflective of changes in the social, economic, and technological environment is a change in the *standard of implementation* of a value, the guide lines for assessing the extent to which a value is attained in particular cases within its domain of application. Here there are two possibilities: the changing of existing standards and the introduction of new ones. The airplane passenger has not changed the high importance he *places* upon the values of "safety," "speed," "reliability," and "comfort" with respect to his mode of transportation since the 1920's, but he expects these value desiderata to be realized in a heightened degree: he brings a different set of standards to bear in judging the degree of their attainment, especially in settling the question of whether they have been sufficiently or *minimally* realized.[2] (It is in this sense that we generally speak of the "raising" and "lowering" of standards.) A more dramatic example is that of the *standard of living*; a century ago economists thought of a worker's earning his "livelihood" in terms of *survival* for himself and his family; today we think of it in terms of a share in "the good life" which the economy makes possible for all and the

[2] It is useful to distinguish between *minimal standards* of this basic requirement on the one hand, and on the other, *optimal standards* of what one would ideally aspire to have.

society expects for everyone. This restandardization of the value of "public welfare" has been matched by a corresponding escalation of the value of "public health," which was formerly regarded in essentially negative terms (the absence of diseases and injuries) but has now come to be viewed in an essentially positive way (physical, mental, and social well-being, or even the optimal development of human potentialities). In an era of technological affluence one is no longer content to set value standards at the low point of catastrophe prevention. In such cases we have a restandardization of the value in question, a changed concept of the minimally acceptable degrees of their attainment. Also, new standards can be added, as in this age of pesticides we add standards of consumption safety to the usual standards of palatability in evaluating fruit.

With any value (such as "economic welfare" or "equality") is correlated a certain state of affairs (the poverty-free environment) corresponding to the idea of the *realization* of this value. But this realization state can obviously be attained in varying degrees. The extent to which the value subscriber sets the minimum extent of acceptable realization of the value may be specified as the *aspiration level* of his espousal of this value. (With a given individual, this aspiration level can, of course, vary over time, e.g., "having adequate means" for the rising man or "being physically fit" for the declining athlete.)

Value implementation retargeting. A value realization target is a specific goal or objective adopted by a value subscriber in the interests of making progress in the realization of the value at issue. For example, a person on whose value scale "the promotion of international understanding" rates high may in consequence set for himself the specific target of serving abroad in the Peace Corps. Now once he has done this—or found that he cannot do it—he may move on to adopt some other target for implementing the value at issue, and this is what we shall call value implementation retargeting. (Example: female suffrage, Negro suffrage, voter qualification age of 18, poll tax abolition, English literacy test abandonment, one-man–one-vote doctrine as targets for value of voting equality.) When a series of successive targets has been set as accepted for sequential attainment, we have a *priority schedule* in terms of the successive "orders of business" on the agenda of implementing the value at issue. The *revision* of such a list of priorities is a significant form of value change, albeit a mild one. An even milder version of this mode of value change is the resetting of a target date, the deadline for attaining the specific value target at issue. (Example: the Soviet Union and the ever-postponed transition from socialism to genuine communism.)

Upgrading/downgrading. We distinguish systematically between modes of upgrading and corresponding modes of downgrading in terms of the preceding varieties of value change, as follows:

Modes of upgrading		*Modes of downgrading*
value acquisition	1	value abandonment
increase redistribution	2	decrease redistribution
rescaling upward	3	rescaling downward
widening redeployment	4	narrowing redeployment
value emphasis	5	value de-emphasis
restandardization by a raising of standards	6	restandardization by a lowering of standards
retargeting by adding implementation targets or by giving higher priority to existing ones	7	retargeting by dropping implementation targets or by lowering priority to existing ones

The point is that the modes of upgrading represent very diverse ways in which heightened acceptances of or emphasis upon a given value can occur: the modes of upgrading all represent higher valuations of the value, and the modes of downgrading represent a devaluation of it.

2. SOME WAYS IN WHICH VALUE CHANGE CAN COME ABOUT IN A SOCIETY

When one talks of "the values" of a society, say American society, the question immediately arises: *Whose* values? Few societies are homogeneous, and American society certainly is not. For present purposes we shall focus upon the prevalent values of the society, those that are sufficiently pervasive and prominent throughout its fabric to be invoked by its major value spokesmen (politicians, newspaper editorialists, graduation-exercise speakers, sermonizers, etc.). The existence of subsocieties with divergent value schedules must, of course, be recognized (the Amish, the hip bohemians, etc.). Indeed, such subsocieties may well play an increasingly prominent role in the future.[3] But there unquestionably exists (and will continue to exist) a sufficiently prominent value consensus in America to underwrite a basis for proceeding with the discussion at the level of aggregation of a system of "generally accepted" values, without becoming enmeshed in the ramifications of social fragmentation.

The preceding section dealt with some of the principal modes or types

[3] For very different reasons than in the past, however. For in the past the opportunities for interaction were circumscribed, whereas in the future the relative desire for—or rather against—interaction may well be the key factor, as various groups "opt out" of the mainstream.

of value change from the *conceptual* angle and, in particular, classified these from the standpoint of (1) the person or group affected (e.g., in value redistribution) and of (2) the mode of affectation (e.g., the rescaling vs. the redeployment of a value). We now turn to a consideration of the sources in the sense of the *causal* origins of such changes. Our aim is to survey some of the most important causal factors which provide the motive power for the dynamical process of value change in persons and societies.

A value change can come about either *derivatively* or *directly*. It is derivative when, for example, the value at issue is *subsidiary* or subordinate to some other value and changes because this other value does so. For example, think of a complex value cluster (e.g., "economic justice") and a subordinate value that represents a constituent element of this cluster (say, "equality of opportunity"). Then a change in the fate of the one will generally involve a corresponding change in the fate of the other. A second important species of derivative value change exists in the context of a means value that is *instrumental* to some larger-scale end value. When one value (e.g., "cleanliness") is bound up with another ("health" or "godliness") in a strict means-end relation, then an upgrading or downgrading of one will call for a corresponding change in the status of the other.

A value change is direct (in contrast to derivative) when it comes about under the direct, immediate operation of causal factors, rather than coming about as the result of other value changes. Direct value changes are best classified according to the type of causal impetus that induces them. Here there are, of course, a vast number of alternatives. By way of explanation and illustration, let us consider a few examples.

(a) *Value change induced by a change of information.* Here the root cause of the change is of a purely cognitive character of the sort typified by value changes brought about by discoveries in the sciences. Suppose, for example, that Smith values A (say, "frugality") and values it instrumentally, i.e., largely or wholly because he believes it to be a means to B (say, "the economic prosperity of the country"). If something (the findings of economists) persuaded him of the incorrectness of this presumed means-end relationship, Smith would almost certainly downgrade the instrumental value in a corresponding way. (Something much of this sort seems to have happened in the 1960–1966 era to the "automation hysteria" that prevailed in the United States at the outset of the period.) Perhaps the most drastic way in which this sort of change could affect contemporary American values would be through the discovery of a supercivilization in a not-too-remote part of our galaxy. All of our values instrumental to human welfare and self-esteem would have to undergo an agonizing reappraisal.

(b) *Value change induced by ideological and political change.* Here the root cause is a matter of value indoctrination. There is a wide range of possibilities with respect to this source of value change. It can take the gradualistic form of conditioning, advertising, propaganda, and "promotion"; or it may take the form of an ideological steamroller as with Islam and the Bedouin in the eighth century or in the Evangelical movement in England in the last century. One of the most drastic ways in which this mode of change could come about in the America of the near future is by a collapse of the center in political life (erosion of consensus, a revolt against reason, upsurge of extremism) in response to disaffection as "rising expectations" outgrow the limits of the attainable, with an accompanying tendency to victory of extremism of the right or the left.

(c) *Value "erosion" induced by boredom, disillusionment, and reaction.* Here the root cause is one of a wide spectrum of sociological factors that are significantly operative in American society. The status of a value can be eroded away when, in the wake of its substantial realization in a society, the value "loses its savor" and comes to be downgraded by disenchantment and disillusionment. Some examples are "efficiency" in the era of automation, "progress" in our age of anxiety, "economic security" in a welfare state, and "national independence" for an "emerging" nation in socioeconomic chaos. Some erosion of the status of a value comes about through the mere passage of time in our evolution-minded and change-oriented society. It has been aptly noted that whereas "almost anywhere in the world outside the industrial areas, most types of change are considered undesirable," in our society change has, *per contra*, come to be regarded as almost a good in itself.[4] And this generic phenomenon of course affects values too. The very fact that a value has been accepted for some time is a point in its disfavor. Contrast the connotation of "of the past," "old-fashioned," "outmoded," "dated," and "passé" with that of "of the future," "new," "novel," "up to date," "recently introduced." (And note the demise in recent American usage of "newfangled" as a pejorative term and its lapse as an epithet of derogation.)

We turn now to a consideration of that causal source of value change that has greatest relevance for our investigation, to wit:

(d) *Value change induced by changes in the operating environment of a society.* By the "operating environment of a society" we understand the whole range of social, cultural, demographic, economic, and technological factors that comprise the way of life in that society. This brings us to the category

[4] E. M. Albert, "Conflict and Change in American Values," *Ethics*, Vol. 74 (1963), pp. 19–33; see p. 29.

of value changes of basic importance for our purposes and will form the central topic of the remaining parts of this chapter. It is clear that change in this operational sphere has enormous repercussions for values—providing tremendous opportunities for the enhancement of some of our traditional ideals and aspirations, and great threats to the realization of others.

It is appropriate to note one significant difference from the methodological point of view between this last item (d) and items (a) through (c), which preceded it. This is the inherently greater tractability to investigation of value changes that are rooted changes in the economic/technological/demographic sphere as contrasted with value changes stemming from some of the other sources we have considered. This has particularly important repercussions for the predication of value change. It is harder by at least an order of magnitude to forecast changes in information (scientific progress) and in the ideologico-political sphere than it is to predict changes that root in factors that (like those of the economic, technological, and demographic sphere) are of such a sort that their change is of a relatively gradualistic character, so that their forecasting turns in large measure on the extrapolation of existing trends and is less sensitive to the introduction of wholly new developments.

Values, though by no means totally unresponsive to environmental changes, are generally not highly sensitive to them. The pattern of concrete history is such that change in the status of values, though real, has usually been evolutionary rather than revolutionary. Moreover, it has been such that the *ethical* values of "honesty," "justice," etc., have been virtually immune from the influences of change: little short of a transformation of human nature or of a sensational alteration of the conditions of man's life on earth can happen to require a reevaluation of such values. Few things are immutable in human affairs, and man's values reflect this (itself abiding) circumstance. But there are, fortunately, at least some fundamental historic stabilities in the human condition, and it is preeminently these that are reflected in our adaptively well-established value systems.

3. A METHODOLOGICAL FRAMEWORK FOR ANALYZING INDUCED VALUE CHANGES

We must now examine in detail the basic question: How can a change in the operating environment (the economic/technological/demographic/etc. sector) of a society be expected to work to induce a change in its schedule of values? How is one to construct an analytical framework for the explanation of value changes?

One important key to this question lies in a consideration of the fact that values can come into conflict with one another, not, of course, in the abstract, but in the competing demands their realization and pursuit make upon man's finite resources of goods, time, effort, attention, etc. Thus when a change occurs in the operating rationale that constitutes the operative framework within which a value is pursued in a given society, we may expect a series of stresses upon our scale of values militating for a rescaling in their ordering or a change of the value standard, etc. But how is one to determine the character of this value response? Here key factors lie in two considerations: *cost* and *benefit*.

(a) *The cost of maintaining a value.* As was just said, pursuit of the realization of a value requires the investment of various resources. The extent of the requisite investment will be affected by changes in the environment: "cleanliness" comes cheaper in modern cities than in medieval ones, and the achievement of "privacy" costs more in urban environments than in rural ones. The maintenance of a value will obviously be influenced by its cost. When this becomes *very* low, we may tend to depreciate the value as such. When it becomes high, we may either depreciate the value in question as such (the "fox and the grapes" reaction), or—rather more commonly—simply settle for lower standards for its attainment. (Think here of "peace and quiet" in this era of jet screams, sonic booms, and auto sirens.)

(b) *The felt benefit of (or need for) maintaining a value.* Any society is likely to have a group of values that occupy a commanding position on its value scale. These are the values to which it is most fundamentally committed in the various relevant modes of commitment, such as the tenacity of maintaining and preserving the value, preparedness to invest energy and resources in its realization and propagation, the attachment of high sanctions to the value (i.e., how much compliance is expected, how much reproach heaped upon the transgressor, and the like). These most deeply held values are viewed as unchangeable and "beyond dispute."

In most modern, Westernized societies—and certainly in the United States—these dominant values prominently include: (1) the SURVIVAL of the society, (2) the WELFARE of the society, (3) the ADVANCEMENT of the society, and (4) the REALITY ADJUSTMENT of the society Here "survival" is, of course, not only a matter of the *mere* survival of the society, but also its survival as the sort of society it is; the holding of this value is thus a matter of a kind of homeostasis. We mean the "welfare" of the society to be concerned largely, in the manner of the economists, with the standard of living in the society, the set of goods and services available to its members, but also calling for a reasonable degree of attainment of its various (non-"materialistic") ideals. The third value, "progress," is primarily a matter of the improvement of the state of affairs obtaining under the two preceding heads. Finally, "reality adjustment" is a matter of accepting things as they are, and adjusting to them or changing them, rather than seeking security in myth or magic. If the pursuit of the realization of a value somehow becomes much more difficult or costly so that one must (*ex hypothesi*) "settle for less," one can either (1) adjust, or (2) keep the lamp of aspiration burning bright, possibly even giving this value a greater emphasis. A culture heavily committed to "reality adjustment" would by and large tend to the first mode of resolution, except where its dominant and basic values themselves are concerned.

Now when we speak of the "benefit of" or the "need for" maintaining a certain value in our society, we mean this to be thought of in terms of its inducing to realization of the four dominant values just indicated. Thus, for example, "pluralism," which plays such a prominent role in contemporary United States Catholic thought, answers to a "need" precisely because it conduces to the real interests of this group in helping it to operate effectively within the constraints of its environment. Again, "scientific and intellectual skill" and the various values bound up with this are of late coming to be upgraded on the American value scale precisely because of society's increased need for these skills in the interests of survival, welfare, and advancement under contemporary conditions. Much the same can be said for "innovation," as witness the really very modest degree of worker resistance to technological change in recent years.

* * *

The illustrations just given have got us ahead of our place; before turning to such items of concrete detail we must resume our topic of explanatory method. What we are proposing to do is to examine pressures upon a society's values in terms of the following line of methodological approach:

1. One begins with an environmental change in the operative context of a value represented by an economico-technological or a social or demographic change that increases the cost of pursuing the realization of a certain value.
2. One examines the nature of this increased cost to see what sorts of stresses and strains it imposes upon the pursuit of the value at issue.

3. One considers the likely resolution of the stresses and strains in the light of the needs of the society, construing "need" in terms of its continuing pursuit of its basic values.

One thus begins with a trend or tendency of economico-technological or social or demographic character that makes for changes in the costs of pursuing an existing scheme of values. Noting the difficulties or opportunities that such a cost change creates, one then examines how these difficulties are likely to be resolved (or opportunities capitalized on) effectively, assuming that certain basic values provide the relatively stable centers around which the resolution of value conflicts will pivot. Given a change in the pattern of the *costs* of the value pursuit, we pose the question: How most effectively can the society derive *benefits* therefrom—i.e., how best can "needs" of the society (construed in terms of an accommodation of its basic values) be accommodated?

This set of considerations provides an analytical framework for the explanation of value changes. The very substantial advantage of this pressure-resolving model is that it can be applied not only retrospectively in the explanation of past or current value changes but also prospectively to the prediction of future value changes.[5]

It should be stressed that certain quite significant technological changes may have very little effect upon values. For it is important to distinguish between a *value* as such on the one hand, and the means for its realization on the other. A technological change that affects the latter may leave the former substantially unaffected. (Think of the few relevant values affected by various items of significant technical progress, such as improvements in surgical techniques.)

4. AMERICAN VALUES IN THE FUTURE

The present discussion of future American values will focus upon those particular values that have featured explicitly and prominently in the first set of working papers of the working party on "values and rights" of the Commission on the Year 2000 of the American Academy of Arts and Sciences.[6]

[5] For an attempt along these lines see the writer's contribution in K. Baier and N. Rescher (eds.), *Values and the Future: Technological Change and American Values* (New York, 1968). The present chapter draws extensively upon this essay.

[6] *Working Papers of the Commission on the Year 2000 of the American Academy of Arts and Sciences*, Vol. 5 (Boston, 1966). Over half of these papers were published in *Daedalus: Journal of the American Academy of Arts and Sciences*, Summer 1967 issue.

In the deliberations comprising this document, the following values hold a place of prominence:

>Privacy
>Equality (legal, social, and economic)
>Personal integrity (vs. "depersonalization")
>Welfare (personal and social)
>Freedom (of choice and action)
>Law abidingness and public order
>Pleasantness of environment
>Social adjustment
>Efficiency and effectiveness in organizations
>Rationality (organizational and individual)
>Education and intelligence
>Ability and talent

These are the values which the authors of the document in question apparently regard as particularly affected by or involved in foreseeable future developments. This list will set the stage for our subsequent deliberations.

It is useful to observe that the "values" in this list can be sorted into three categories:

>   I. *Individual rights values*
>   "privacy," "equality," "personal integrity," "welfare," "freedom"
> II. *Life-setting values*
>   "public order," "pleasantness of environment"
> III. *Personal-characteristic values*
>   "efficiency," "rationality," "social adjustment," "education," "intelligence," "ability," "talent"

These three groupings would seem to provide a natural classification for the values of our basic list.

It is not difficult to supply by conjecture the (tacit) rationale by which the specific values of our basic list come to be accorded their place of eminence. Each of them falls into one of two groups when considered against the background of the major projectable demographic, social, economic, and technological trends. For the working of these trends is shaping a future society in which the value under consideration is either

>   1. markedly threatened, or
>   2. badly needed.

The first is the case in particular with the values of categories I and II (the indicated individual rights values and life-setting values), all of which are such that their realization is apt to be substantially more difficult in the America of the future. The second is the case in particular with the personal-characteristic values of category III, which are such that their espousal, maintenance, and realization will be especially important in the future society. The pair of indicated factors would thus appear to constitute a plausible rationale to explain why the values registered in the basic list figured in their prominent role in the document we have cited.

Two interestingly contrasting sets of considerations are operative here. In saying that a value is "threatened" by future developments, one takes one's footing upon the *current*, present-day value system. For it is to say that *they* (those future ones—and it is not, of course, to be precluded that we ourselves may be among them) will be under pressure to *downgrade* this value, that is, to be willing to "settle for less" in regard to it and give it less than its due. Indeed, describing the value as "threatened," we raise the specter of its abandonment. (There is, after all, the phenomenon of value obsolescence, when what was once, under certain conditions of life, a genuine and authentic value becomes outmoded under changed circumstances: "chivalry" and "noblesse oblige," for example.) By contrast, to say that a certain value will in the future be more badly needed, and so to suggest that they of the future will be under pressure to *upgrade* this value suggests nothing as to the proper place of the value according to the current value system. There is an asymmetry here. Saying that a value is "threatened" is necessarily to reflect the posture of the present value system in a way in which saying that a value is "underrated" is not.

An important feature of the strategy of value-change prediction should be noted in this connection. One of the key objects of the enterprise is obviously to identify threats to values, i.e., predictable developments that may exert a pressure upon the maintenance of a value in the society to the point where it becomes downgraded in the future. Such a prediction of a change regarding values can thus serve in an "early warning" role to trigger or facilitate preventive action to assure that the untoward foreseen consequences do not occur. The very prediction of a value downgrading may thus (hopefully) have a self-defeating effect, by being a causal factor in a chain of preventive developments.

Several further aspects of the basic list of values that seem likely to be affected by future developments deserve to be noted. One of the most interesting of these is the fact that the majority of these items are characteristically *social values*, in that they represent arrangements that his social environment affords to an individual (e.g., "equality," "privacy," "freedom," "public order"), and of the rest, the bulk consist in *virtues of ability* involving personal qualities that individuals prize, but over whose *possession*—albeit not whose *cultivation*—they have relatively little control (e.g., "rationality," "intelligence," "ability," and "talent"). Thus a striking feature of the list is the absence of the traditional *virtues of character*—in contrast with the virtues of ability—including such values as:

Honesty
Loyalty
Idealism
Friendliness
Truthfulness

What accounts for this gap? One is tempted to assume that the explanation of the absence of the character virtues from the basic list is implicit in the previously conjectured rationale of the list itself. For it was perhaps the view of the authors at issue that these specific values are neither particularly threatened by predictable trends shaping our future environment, nor that the degree to which they will be requisite in the future society is significantly greater than their present-day desirability. If this was indeed the view of these authors, then we should like to enter a sharp dissent from their position.

There can be little question that there are at least some values within the category of the "virtues of character" for which the crowded, depersonalized, and complex society of the year 2000 will have a yet greater need, however highly these values may have been prized heretofore. For example, one thinks here specifically of those values that are oriented toward service to others: "service to one's fellows," "a sense of responsibility," and "dedication to humanitarian ideals." American society has treasured these values throughout its history, but in the future they will very likely be markedly upgraded, as a social environment takes shape in which they are increasingly indispensable.

Over the past generation there has been a marked tendency in American life—one whose continuation and intensification can confidently be looked for—to a shift from the Protestant Ethic of "getting ahead in the world" to the Social Ethic of "service to one's fellows"—from the gospel of profit and devotion to Mammon to the gospel of service and devotion to Man. Many forces have produced this phenomenon—ranging from spiritual causes such as a decline of traditional Protestant Ethic on the one hand, to material causes such as the rise of the welfare state on the other ("God helps those who help themsevles" perhaps—but the state is not so exclusive about it, and so it is less urgent in our affluent society to "look out for oneself"). There has thus been in many sectors of our national life, including the industrial, a distinct elevation of the historic American value of public service. This is a trend that will certainly continue and possibly intensify. However, this will presumably happen in such a way that the present tendency to the institutionalization of these social-service values (e.g., the Peace Corps and Vista) will continue and perhaps intensify.

This contention that *certain* of the virtues of character will be upgraded in the America of the year 2000 must not be inflated beyond intended limits, however. Some of these traditional values seem very definitely on the decline. A trend toward the welfare state, for example, will very likely add "charity" to the roster of outmoded values. Again, "compassion" may well become downgraded in an environment in which violence is an increasingly familiar phenomenon. (One thinks with dismay of incidents like the murder of a young lady on Long Island in the midst of some two-score unbudging witnesses.)

* * *

Yet another negative feature of the basic list deserves to be noted: the absence of aesthetic values. Increasing affluence and leisure—and the growing worldiness and sophistication that come in their wake—promise to give a definitely more prominent place to the ornamental aspects of life. Specifically, there is every reason to think that the aesthetic dimension will play a vastly more significant role in American life in the year 2000. Moreover, one need not dwell upon the unpleasing aspects of a graphic picture of the degradation in the quality of life that will come to realization if our response to the needs of the future for housing, for transportation, etc., are dictated by considerations of economy and efficiency alone, without due heed of "human considerations," prominently including aesthetic factors. The probable upgrading of the aesthetic element is something that an examination of American values of the year 2000 cannot afford to overlook.

* * *

The crowding of the avenues of action in modern life increasingly puts the individual into a position not so much of interacting with others as individual agents, but of reacting to them as a mass comprising a complex "system." Many of the things that go wrong are best looked at—at any rate from the standpoint of their victims—as system *malfunctions*. It seems probable in this context that we will less and less treat such failures as matters of individual accountability. If X cheats, burgles, or inflicts motor vehicle damage upon Y, the view will increasingly prevail that Y should not have to look to X for recovery from loss but to a depersonalized source—viz., some agency of the society. We will not improbably move increasingly toward the concept of a "Veteran's Administration" for the victims of the ordinary hazards of life in our society. Individual responsibility and personal accountability has suffered some depreciation in American life over the past two decades, but it seems likely that in the years ahead social accountability will become an increasingly prominent ideal.

This illustrates a rather more general tendency with respect to future values: it would appear on the basis of present trends and predictable developments that we can look for a significant upgrading of institutional values.

Although America has in the past been able to achieve prodigies of progress on the basis of a large measure of individual effort and individual initiative, the value of organization in common effort for the public good has been recognized since the days of Benjamin Franklin as a natural channel for constructive individual effort. The value of common action through association and institutionalization has always been accepted—despite a strong strain of independence of the "No thanks, I'll go my own way" type. But in days ahead with an increasing dependence on and need for (and thus augmented—though at first, no doubt, ambivalent—respect for) institutions we may reasonably expect an increased respect for institutions and an upgrading of institutional values and the social ethic generally. The decline of independence remarked on above may be looked upon to undermine the traditional individualistic (and even anarchic) strain in American life with its concomitant ambivalence toward laws, rules, and law-abidingness. Our increasing reliance on institutions will increasingly emphasize and strengthen institutional values. The present-day "revolt" of the Negro, for example, is perhaps not so much a rebellion against American institutions as such as a protest on the part of those who look on themselves as outsiders excluded from them. Note that the current remedies to the exclusion problem (e.g., the "War on Poverty" and the Job Corps) are of a strictly institutional character. So are various of the means to solve the problem of youth anomie by creating institutional means for helping the young to find the "meaning of life" in socially useful service (e.g., the Peace Corps). (Such ventures represent an institutionalization of idealism—they involve a scaling down in individual ambition, a shift from playing a part on the big stage oneself to being a small cog in a big venture.)

Such a predictable upsurge of institutional values and the social ethic is an important trend in future American values whose workings would not be suspected on the basis of even a careful scrutiny of the basic list.

Considerations such as these underline the fact that it is critically important for the viability of our future society that people *have values of a socially beneficent sort*, that they be persons of the type one characterizes as being "dedicated to sound values" and as having a "good sense of values." The need of society for such people raises the question of where they are to come from—of how people are to be trained in this way.

This question brings vast difficulties to the fore. With the decline of religious commitment in American life, the churches are losing their traditional effectiveness as value inculcators. The weakening of the family undermines many of its roles, definitely including that of a center for value teaching. Nor in this "post-ideological" age are politico-economic doctrines a potent force for value propagation. The question of the *teaching* of values—especially of their transmission to the younger generation in the operative environment of the future—would seem to constitute one of the large problem issues in the public-policy domain of the (nonremote) future.

This problem has been rendered the more difficult to grapple with by a significant social development of relatively recent vintage. This relates to the importance not merely of *having* socially desirable values in the weak sense of according them verbal recognition and adherence, but in the significantly stronger sense of actually *acting* upon them. The present "revolt" of a sector of American youth against the mainstream of adult thought and behavior is in fact largely based on an *acceptance* (rather than rejection) of mainstream values. The disaffected young do not advocate an abandonment or transvaluation of the traditional values—rather, they accuse those who have succeeded in the mainstream of American life of a *betrayal* of these values (a sort of *trahison des arrivistes*). In the eyes of disaffected youth, adult society is not *misguided* in holding the "wrong" values but *hypocritical* in not acting on the "correct" values it overtly holds and professes. American society is "sick" in the eyes of its youthful critics because it *fails to implement its own values* in an appropriate way: the society's actions distort its own value scale (e.g., in giving low priority to "personal aggrandizement" and "success" and "material welfare" in the value teaching of the middle class, in contrast with their intensive pursuit in practice; or at the national level in propagandizing the ideals of a great society at home and good neighborliness abroad while expending a vastly greater share of the national budget on the space race than on foreign aid, on military preparedness than on domestic welfare). The cynicism about our values created by such developments will greatly complicate the intrinsic difficulties of value teaching in the days ahead.

Here lies one of the great gaps in our knowledge in this sphere: How to generate adherence to values? Precious little is known about many key empirical aspects of values, despite the monumental labors of Clyde Kluckhohn and his school in the area of sociological value studies. And no part of this knowledge gap is more notable than that relating to the *teaching* of values, nor more acute in an era when the historic media of value transmission are losing much of their traditional effectiveness.

X

The Critical Assessment
of Values

1. THE NATURE AND IMPORTANCE OF
THE PROBLEM OF VALUE EVALUATION

In the systematic study of the value system of persons or groups, three
diverse but interrelated tasks have primary importance: (1) the *analytic*
task of characterizing, classifying, and explicating the concepts of the
various "values" that are at issue, (2) the *descriptive* task of applying the
value concepts so clarified to the specific, concrete setting of the person or
group of persons at issue, and (3) the *normative* task of evaluating this specific
pattern of value subscription. The second, descriptive task is obviously a
matter for empirical inquiry, and presents work for psychologists, historians,
social psychologists, and sociologists. The first, analytic task lies on ground
common to these sciences on the one hand and philosophical value theory on
the other. The third item, that of the normative *evaluation of values*, is one
of the tasks, characteristic of their discipline, to which philosophers have
addressed themselves throughout the ages. (The social scientists in the cognate

areas have often quite deliberately sought to put it aside.) It is with this task
that we shall here be concerned.

The methodology for the critique of the values to which people subscribe
—the procedural aspects of the endorsement of some values and rejection
of others, and of the reasoned recommendation for change: in short, the
"critical assessment of values"—will form our object of study in the present
chapter. Such criticism is obviously of great importance for the rational
scrutiny of policies in individual and collective action. It is our present aim
to clarify, from the methodological standpoint, how such criticism becomes
possible—to pinpoint as exactly as possible the bases upon which a reasoned
evaluation of values can proceed.

2. CORRECT AND INCORRECT EVALUATION

One point regarding evaluation—unquestionably a controversial point—has
been much stressed by philosophers concerned about value as it relates to
"what is really important." It is this: there is a tenable distinction between
valuing that that is *right* or *correct* and valuing that that is *wrong* or *incorrect*.
This relates to a conception that is present throughout the axiological
tradition, but is perhaps clearest in Aristotle and Brentano.

This thesis is uncontroversial and unproblematic in the case of means
values. There is no fundamental problem about applying the concepts of
correctness and incorrectness in the case of valuing things as means. Smith's
valuing "dissolute living" as a means to "bad health" is correct if dissolute
living produces bad health and incorrect otherwise. (To be sure, there is still
room for disagreement here. For example, is Smith's valuing dissolute living
correct only if such a life generally leads to bad health, for *anyone* who lives
this way, or would it suffice that the relationship should hold in Smith's case
alone? But such points are unimportant—people who disagree on them could
easily come together.) Again, there is no issue of principle in the case of
valuing things according to a certain given standard. Whether or not, say,
a certain measure would conduce to "the material advantage of the country"
is, in the final analysis, a simply technical question, contentions about which
can in principle always be resolved by strictly factual considerations. The
pivotal question is whether the issue of correctness vs. incorrectness applies
to valuing things intrinsically, as ultimate ends.

The Aristotle-Brentano position can most effectively be set forth by
a quotation from the former:

What affirmation and negation are in thinking, pursuit and avoidance are in desire; so that since moral virtue is a state of character concerned with choice, and choice is deliberate desire, therefore both the reasoning must be true and the desire right, if the choice is to be good, and the latter must pursue just what the former asserts. Now this kind of intellect and of truth is practical; of the intellect which is contemplative, not practical nor productive, the good and the bad state are truth and falsity respectively (for this is the work of everything intellectual); while of the part which is practical and intellectual the good state is truth in agreement with right desire.[1]

To appreciate what Aristotle and Brentano had in mind, one must pursue Aristotle's analogy of "correct" and "incorrect" as applicable to *belief* or *judgment* on the one hand, and to *desire* and *valuing* upon the other. Consider the correspondences:

belief	valuing or desire
correctness of belief	correctness of valuing or desire
believed to be true	valued or desired
actually true	valuable or desirable

An analogy can be based on this correspondence: Take whatever you would regard as a plausible thesis with respect to the familiar left-hand column. [For example: "With respect to belief, we may characterize belief as correct if the item (viz., proposition) which is the object of that belief is actually true."] Then use the correspondence to translate this thesis into the language of the right-hand column. The result will be a thesis that is also plausible— and indeed correct on the Aristotle-Brentano view. [In the example: "With respect to desire, we may characterize a desire as correct if the item (viz., thing) which is the object of that desire is actually of value."] It is along this line of analogy that Brentano, following Aristotle, elaborates a theory of the correctness of desire and valuation.[2]

The distinction between, not only correct and incorrect valuing, but between correct and incorrect *values*, between perverse or misguided values and genuine and authentic ones, can be developed in general terms along the lines of the Aristotle-Brentano doctrine. But upon what material foundation can this formal distinction rest; what is the substantive aspect of the issue; what factors render certain values correct (genuine, authentic)? In short, upon what basis is a criticism of values possible?

[1] *Nicomachean Ethics*, VI, 2; 1139a 20–31 (Oxford tr.).
[2] For further details see R. M. Chisholm, "Brentano's Theory of Correct and Incorrect Emotion," *Révue Internationale de Philosophie*, Vol. 78 (1966), pp. 395–415.

3. THE ABSTRACT CRITICISM
OF VALUES

When one speaks of the "evaluation of values," one can think of this in
two ways. One can have in mind the evaluation of the entire complex of
a person's values, i.e., the pattern of his *attachment* to values—as when one
says such things as "He is a shallow type—without any attachment to values"
or "He lives for the moment only—the prudential values mean nothing to
him." Or one can have in mind the impersonal evaluation of a single value
such as "self-aggrandizement" or "chivalry." It is this second type of value
evaluation that is the primary target of the present discussion. But the former
type is far from irrelevant—for these two sorts of value evaluation are, as
we shall see, intimately interconnected.

The locution "*v* is one of *N*'s values" ("The discomfort of his neighbors
is one of Smith's values") does not carry any implication whatever regarding
the *actual* value of *v*. In saying that something is valued we speak descriptively
rather than normatively; we do not concede that this item *has value*. But
when we simply speak of something as "being a value" *tout court*, without
the "for *N*" attribution to some particular valuing subject, we do ourselves
thereby accord it recognition as a *genuine* value. There can be little doubt
that a positive value bias is built into the very concept of "a value" with
which we commonly operate. This is clearly brought out by distinguishing
between valuing something (e.g., money) and valuing *the valuing of that thing*
(viz., avarice). It is part of the logical grammar of the concept that a genuine
value is *always reputable*. In recognizing something as authentically a value,
we view it as being of such a sort that (like *intelligence* or *justice*) we would
count upon its espousal as itself being valued by the person who holds the
value at issue. We would, in fact, not be prepared to class as *a value* unqualifiedly and pure and simple those "disreputable values" (like avarice or self-
aggrandizement) the espousal of which we would ordinarily expect the person
of whom we say that "he has this value" to gainsay.

It is thus in the nature of things that when something is classed as *a value*
it is placed within the category of putatively "good things," because its promotion and realization is viewed as inherently beneficial. This consideration
points to one important way in which values can be criticized *abstractly*
and on their own account. For here we can look to exactly what sorts of goods

and benefits would accrue from the realization of the value.[3] Such an assessment of value realization on the side of the resulting benefits alone (without any reference to the various costs involved in this realization) provides a basis for the criticism of values *in the abstract*. On the basis of such a cost-ignoring "evaluation of values" we would be able to arrive at such abstract comparative judgments as those, e.g., between higher and lower values. Such grading judgments about values are an important result of the abstract—or, as it might perhaps be better called, the *acircumstantial*—criticism of values. However, in the context of certain specific circumstances, it may be ill-advised (foolish, wrong-headed, conceivably even perverse) to act on a value so thoroughly established and reputable as to seem "above criticism," say, one's value of devotion to duty (bravery, love of beauty, etc.) We must now turn to the issue of the circumstantial criticism of values, which takes account of the operative costs exacted by efforts to realize the benefits that result from acting to attain those conditions whose realization an espousal of the value urges upon us.

4. COST/BENEFIT ANALYSIS OF THE IMPLEMENTATION OF VALUES

In saying that v is one of N's values ("Patriotism is one of Smith's values") we underwrite, *inter alia*, the inference to two conclusions:

1. N is prepared to devote some of his resources (money, time, effort, discomfort, etc.) to the implementation of v—i.e., in furthering the extent of its realization in the world.
2. He does so *in the belief*—and indeed *for the reason*—that the increased realization of v will benefit ("prove advantageous for," "promote the interests of") certain individuals—either N himself or others to whose interest he is attached.

A brief comment on each of these points is in order.

First consider point 1. When we unqualifiedly say (seriously and committally) that v is one of N's values we must be prepared to claim that N would take v into due account in making relevant choices, with the result that the outcome of these choices, viz., N's actions, significantly reflect N's commitment to v. Thus we may view N's investment of resources (money, time, etc.) in those of his actions explicable in terms of his espousal of v as an indispensable part of this acceptance of v. Authentic adherence to a value

---

[3] Actually, one should think here of estimating the resulting *balance* of benefits over disadvantages.

implies *some* commitment to the pursuit of its realization, and this, in turn, calls for at least some investment of resources (advocacy and verbal support at the very minimum). The extent of this requisite investment will be dependent upon—and will be affected by changes in—the operating environment: *cleanliness* comes cheaper in modern cities than medieval ones, and the achievement of *privacy* costs more in urban environments than in rural ones.

As regards point 2, it is of the essence of v's serving in the role of *a value* for N that he views the realization of v as potentially beneficial (for someone, not necessarily himself). Moreover, these benefits at issue will have to be of such a kind as to be a benefit ("a thing of positive value") from N's own point of view. Some benefits will be more fundamental than other, subsidiary benefits, and the most basic and fundamental ones will be those associated with dominant values (including survival, security, health, and pleasure in the case of individuals, and survival, security, welfare, and progress in that of societies). Of course, there are many different types of benefits, just as there are many different kinds of investments of resources or *costs* (e.g., money time, effort, discomfort). And different people can assess these benefits differently—just as they can assess different costs differently. However, complexities of this sort need not concern us for the moment. The key fact is that values are inherently benefit-oriented. A man's values are factors in what the economists refer to as his *welfare function*. We measure the extent of our state of welfare in large measure via the question of the extent to which our values have been realized, so that values come to be intimately linked up with benefits.

The rational criticism of values is possible because (in our view) values are inherently benefit-oriented. The whole structure of value rests ultimately on what is beneficial to man. The dual aspect of costs and benefits thus provides the key in the rational evaluation of values. The critical assessment of values— of their "correctness" or the reverse—is thus possible in a rational way.

This dual aspect of costs and benefits provides the key to the single most important type of critical assessment of values. For it renders them susceptible to an evaluation procedure of the cost-benefit type familiar from economic analysis. In the case of any value we can make a kind of balance sheet of (1) the balance of benefits—i.e., advantages over disadvantages[4]—inherent in its realization, as contrasted with (2) the various sorts of costs that would be entailed by the endeavor to bring this realization about. The following

[4] If the upshot of its realization were not such that, on balance, the resultant advantages overshadow the disadvantages, then the value could hardly be maintained as such, i.e., as a *value*. For it would then be open to decisive criticism of the sort we have characterized above as *abstract*.

possibilities obviously arise in the context of a cost-benefit analysis of this sort. In the circumstances of a given operating environment:

1. N may "oversubscribe" to v (the value at issue) either because (a) he has an exaggerated conception of the benefits involved, and accordingly "invests" too much in the value, or (b) he has a correct conception of the benefits involved, but nevertheless makes a larger than proportionate investment toward securing these benefits (i.e., "overpays" for them).
2. N may "undersubscribe" to v (the value at issue) either because (a) he has an unduly deflated conception of the benefits involved, and accordingly "invests" too little in the value, or (b) he has a correct conception of the benefits involved, but nevertheless makes a less than proportionate investment toward securing these benefits.

This description clearly shows the results of such a critical review of a value can be positive as well as negative so far as the significance of this value is concerned. A survey of possibilities of this sort indicates the type of considerations that bear upon a criticism of values from the direction of a cost-benefit approach. Such criticism is not, of course, one of abstract values as such, but rather is a criticism of the value subscriptions made under specific circumstances.

There is a striking parallelism between this view of values and Aristotle's doctrine of the "mean." Take money, for instance: The avaricious man "overvalues" it (we can say that "money is one of his values"), and the improvident man "undervalues" it (we can speak of him as "recklessly indifferent to money"). Both of these "value extremes" are, plainly, conceived of against the backdrop of what is—under the assumed circumstances—a certain neutrally "normal" involvement with money. This illustrates the largely Aristotelian perspective of our view of value assessment. For in the case of most sorts of values, there can be undervaluing and overvaluing: even as a man can act too much or too little prudently, so he can assign an inordinately high or low place to prudence in his system of values.

Put in a nutshell, the proposed method of value "criticism" is an extension into the area of value studies of the cost-benefit or cost-effectiveness approach of economic analysis.[5] To adopt a value is to espouse principles of policy in the expenditure of resources, and the mode of value evaluation with which we are now concerned is predicated on the somewhat hard-

---

[5] A very similar general position regarding the possibilities of an evaluation of values is taken—without, however, any recourse to an economic point of view—in Chap. V ("Principles of Criticism of Value") cf. Dewitt H. Parker. *Human Values* (New York, 1931). In particular, Parker's invocation of a "principle of success" for values resonates with our concerns.

headed standpoint of the question of whether, how, and to what extent such expenditures are worthwhile.

To be clear about the sorts of considerations that are at issue here, consider the following situations:

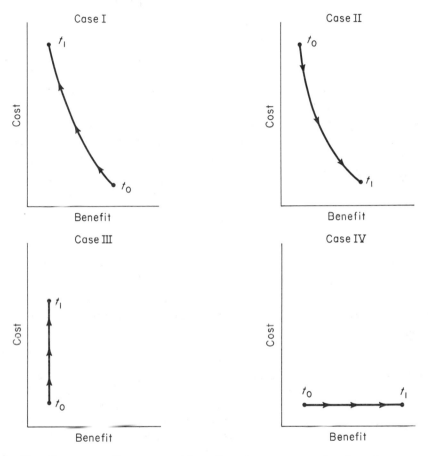

In Case I we move from a great benefit at low cost to a low benefit at great cost, and in Case II from a low benefit at great cost to a great benefit at low cost. An increased emphasis upon values of the second type is clearly warranted. In Case III we confront an increasing cost for a fixed benefit, and in Case IV derive an increasing benefit at fixed cost. Clearly a situation of the former type warrants a relative de-emphasis on the value, other things being anything like equal.

Such consideration of the cost-benefit status of an *isolated* value is only a first step. The question of the merits of a given expenditure of cost for obtaining a specific benefit can be settled only by examining the context of alternative cost investments yielding their several benefits. What is at issue, then, is not simply the cost-benefit situation with regard to one fixed value, but a complex *value economy* that embraces many values. We shall shortly return to this idea.

5.   MUST VALUE BE BENEFIT-ORIENTED?

Our conception of the matter is that values are inherently benefit-oriented. We have repeatedly insisted that acceptability of the claim that "patriotism is one of Smith's values" requires that Smith believes that the exercise of patriotism will "benefit," "prove advantageous for," or "conduce to the best interests of," certain individuals. From this standpoint, it is maintained that all rational evaluation will be benefit-oriented, since any such evaluation, being based on values, must ultimately involve a reckoning of benefits.

Now this position conflicts with what many philosophers have held. For example, G. E. Moore in his *Principia Ethica*[6] proposed his celebrated "method of absolute isolation" (§§ 50, 55, 57, 112–113), which invites us to make comparative evaluations of two hypothetical worlds supposed to be alike in all relevant respects except that in one of them some factor is exhibited which is lacking in the other. Thus Moore contends for the intrinsic value of natural beauty (i.e., its value even apart from human contemplation) by the argument:

> [A hypothetical] beautiful world would be better still, if there were human beings in it to contemplate and enjoy its beauty. But that admission makes nothing against my point. If it be once admitted that the beautiful world *in itself* is better than the ugly, then it follows, that however many beings may enjoy it, and however much better their enjoyment may be than it is itself, yet its mere existence adds something to the goodness of the whole: it is not only a means to our end, but also itself a part thereof (*op. cit.*, § 50).

Moore's position is, on the surface of it, squarely opposed to Henry Sidwick's thesis that: "If we consider carefully such permanent results as are commonly judged to be good, other than qualities of human beings, we can find nothing that, on reflection, appears to possess this quality of goodness out of relation to human existence, or at least to some [presumably animal] consciousness of feeling."[7]

Our own position is that this seeming conflict of views is not a real conflict.

[6] Cambridge, 1903.
[7] *Methods of Ethics*, I, ix, § 4.

Let the correctness of Moore's position be granted. Let it be that the world is better for the existence of a beautiful sunset even if no one sees it, and no one benefits by it. Still the *potential* benefit remains in the hypothetical thesis: *If* someone were suitably placed into such a world, he *would* be able to appreciate and enjoy this sunset. That is, the unseen sunset has aesthetic value because of the potential benefits it affords— though they are, *ex hypothesi*, unactualized in an unpopulated world.[8]

Nor does the benefit-oriented concept of values abolish the idea of intrinsic value, of that which is valued "for itself." In holding, say, knowledge to be intrinsically valuable, the advocate of intrinsic value asserts no more than that the possession of knowledge is not to be prized as a means to some knowledge-remote benefit such as impressing one's associates or advancing in one's career. It is surely not maintained that knowledge-proximate benefits do not accrue benefits and satisfactions that are inherent in the possession of knowledge as such. The benefit-oriented conception of value is not inherently inimical to a doctrine of intrinsic value, but can accommodate itself to such a doctrine by drawing a suitable distinction about the *way* in which values involve benefits.

6. THE IDEA OF A "VALUE ECONOMY" OF A LIFE

The pivotal ideas of resources and benefits as they relate to the espousal of values provide the basis for a quasi-economic critique of values. The main concept is that of a proper balance among the different sorts of benefits toward the attainment of which values serve as a guide.

The consideration of a person's *system* of values points one towards the conception of an *ideal*. Consider various life-history ideals and character ideals as defined in a reasonably specific way in our cultural tradition (the statesman, the inventive genius, the successful businessman, the champion athlete), all suggestive of a certain plan of life, a *curriculum vitae* (or at least a part thereof), in which they unfold over time in the guiding light of a governing commitment to certain values.[9] Here we always expect to find a constellation of values in some degree of rational balance in the deployment of resources (in "budgets" of time and effort) toward the attainment of

[8] For a discussion of value at this metaphysical level of evaluation see N. Rescher, "The Dimensions of Metaphysics" in *Idem, Essays in Philosophical Analysis* (Pittsburgh, 1968).

[9] But of course the opposite can happen also: the ideals can be too modest rather than too ambitious as concerns their inherent values.

specifiable benefits for self and others.[10] We can criticize such ideals—among various other ways of criticizing—in the light of the constellation of values implicit within them. For these may involve what, in the particular operative setting, requires an exorbitant or inappropriate investment of resources for the attainment of the relevant complex of benefits. Values being inherently benefit-oriented, the value holder may expend too much or too little on the pursuit of the benefits at issue. We thus arrive at the conception of imbalances in a value economy.

7. IMBALANCES IN A VALUE ECONOMY

When we consider the constellation of value commitments of a person (or a society), the soundness of a value can be assessed, not abstractly, but *in context*. One can test the value economy at issue against the background of the concept of a spectrum of well-ordered modes of life, each one of which is characterized by an appropriate and viable balance of value commitments and each of which carries its characteristic pattern of rewards. In extreme instances, the entire value economy that is built into the framework of a life-history ideal can become obsolete by becoming infeasible under changed circumstances (e.g., the knight-errant, the master craftsman).

This brings out the contextual nature of this mode of value criticism—its dependence on the setting of a complex of value commitments held under certain specific conditions and circumstances. It is clear that value criticisms of this sort would never result in the verdict that a certain value (i.e., genuine value) is wrong or improper as such. But it could maintain that a person, leading his life in a certain particular setting, oversubscribes or undersubscribes to a given value, given the nature of this setting. Such criticism, then, does not address itself to values directly and abstractly, but rather to the holding—and consequent concrete action upon—certain values under specifiable conditions.

When we concern ourselves not merely with the assessment of individual values but with the criticism of value systems or complexes, of course yet another line of critical approach becomes possible, viz., that of coherence or consistency. The presence on a person's value schedule of such "contrary" values as liberality/frugality, selflessness/prudence, or pride/humility lays

---

[10] On our economic line of approach we can, for example, introduce the idea of the "marginal significance" of a value (i.e., the infinitesimal ratio of added benefit per added cost investment), using this idea to depict the fact that, in the circumstances, some values yield a larger return on a given investment.

the basis for an obvious tactic for criticism. This too would be a matter of contextual analysis—of application rather than theory.

* * *

It is important to notice that social and technological change in a life environment can centrally affect the assessment of values from this cost-benefit point of view. For on the one hand, such change can alter the costs involved in realizing a value (either downward, as with air-travel "safety" in recent years, or upward, as with urban "privacy"). And on the other hand, such changes in the life environment can also alter the benefits derivable from realizing a value (as the benefits to be derived from wealth decline in an affluent society).

This perspective highlights the idea of the *relevance* of values to the specific life environment that provides the operative setting within which a value is espoused. For with a change in this setting, a certain value may be greatly more or less *deserving* of emphasis, depending on the changes in the nature and extent of the corresponding benefits in the altered circumstances. Or again, the value may be greatly more or less demanding of emphasis depending on changes in the cost of its realization in a given degree. In extreme cases, a value can become *irrelevant* when the life setting has become such that the historically associated benefits are no longer available (e.g., "knight-errantry," "chivalry," and, perhaps, "noblesse oblige"), or it can even become malign when action on it comes to produce more harm than good (as with certain forms of "charity"). Some values are such that this very status as values is vulnerable to changes in the social or technological (etc.) circumstances of life.

8. EVALUATIVE LABELS FOR VALUES

This chapter has contended that a cost–benefit evaluation of values can in principle be achieved within the context of the value-economy of a way of life. In this connection, considerable importance attaches to the distinction between *true* and *false* values. A *false* value—like a *false* friend—is "false" in the sense of *deception*: it seems to be what it is not. (Note that although we can speak of "correct" and "incorrect" *evaluation*, viz., evaluation that conforms or fails to conform to the appropriate standards, we cannot unproblematically speak of correct and incorrect *values*: an explanatory gloss is in general required here.)

It is important to distinguish between strictly *descriptive* labels that can be attached to values (e.g., "treasured," "neglected," "prized," "unheeded"), and more emphatically *evaluative* labels such as *real* and *authentic*—or, with greater variety at the negative pole of the spectrum, as *false, outmoded,* or even *perverse.* On the view we have argued, labels of this negative sort can come to be correctly applied to values in consequence of a critical assessment of the kind described. When this happens— when changes in the conditions of life are such as to cast from the pedestal of the *true* and *genuine* some heretofore accepted value that once belonged there, there lies before us a (Nietzsche-reminiscent) "transvaluation" of values. But of course to say this is not to deny that it is unlikely to the point of inconceivability that many of our historic social or personal values—"justice," "intelligence," and "kindness," to give just three examples—could ever, under any realistically foreseeable circumstances, lie open to valid negative criticism.

I

Restricted vs.
Unrestricted Quantification

It was noted in Chapter VI that when one considers the tautologousness of
a preference principle such as

$$pPq \longrightarrow \sim qP \sim p$$

for a specific construction of the preference relationship P, such as $P^{\#}$ or
P^*, one must inquire into the style of universal quantifier that is to govern
the propositional variables here. The purpose of this appendix is to explain
and illustrate the sort of checking procedure involved in the tautology test-
ing here at issue.

Let us first consider the $P^{\#}$ interpretation of P:

    1. $pP^{\#}q \longrightarrow \sim qP^{\#} \sim p$

And let us begin by understanding this principle as asserted with respect to
weak (i.e., restricted) quantification:

    1(a) $(\mathrm{A}p)(\mathrm{A}q)[pP^{\#}q \longrightarrow \sim qP^{\#} \sim p]$

Consider now an (arbitrary) index-of-merit measure # for the relevant possible worlds w_i, as follows:

Possible worlds	#-values
w_1: p & q	a
w_2: p & $\sim q$	b
w_3: $\sim p$ & q	c
w_4: $\sim p$ & $\sim q$	d

Given our canonical interpretation of $P^\#$, thesis 1 is now rendered as a relationship between arithmetical inequalities as follows

$$\left(\frac{a+b}{2} > \frac{a+c}{2}\right) \to \left(\frac{b+d}{2} > \frac{c+d}{2}\right)$$

or equivalently,

$$(b > c) \to (b > c)$$

The acceptability of this, its arithmetical transform, at once establishes the acceptability of thesis 1 when construed as 1(a).

Let us next consider whether we can strengthen this to

1(b) $(\forall p)(\mathsf{A}q)[pP^\#q \to \sim qP^\# \sim p]$

that is, let us ask whether we can make arbitrary substitutions for 'p', putting for 'p' also formulas involving 'q'. We must in particular examine the result of putting in place of 'p' such replacements as:

$q, \sim q, p \,\&\, q, p \,\&\, \sim q, p \lor q, p \lor \sim q$

(In fact, this list must prove sufficient.) But now, when we put "$p \,\&\, q$" for 'p' in thesis 1, we obtain

2. $(p \,\&\, q)P^\#q \to \sim qP^\# \sim (p \,\&\, q)$

whose arithmetical transform is

$$\left(\frac{b+c+d}{3} > \frac{b+d}{2}\right) \to \left(\frac{a+c}{2} > a\right)$$

Since this is not a truth of arithmetic, we see that thesis 2 is not a #-tautology and therefore have it that 1(a) cannot be strengthened to 1(b).

But, on the other hand, can 1(a) be strengthened to

1(c) $(\mathsf{A}p)(\forall q)(pP^\#q \to \sim qP^\# \sim p)$?

Again let us examine the result of 'q'-substitutions. Consider putting "$p \lor q$" for 'q':

3. $pP^\#(p \lor q) \to \sim (p \lor q)P^\# \sim p$

The arithmetical transform of this $P^\#$ principle is

$$\left(\frac{a+b}{2} > \frac{a+b+c}{3}\right) \rightarrow d > \frac{c+d}{2}$$

which is clearly not a truth of arithmetic. Thus thesis 3 is not a $P^\#$ tautology, and consequently we cannot strengthen 1(a) to 1(c). In the face of these findings, it now goes without saying that 1(a) cannot be strengthened to:

1(d) $(\forall p)(\forall q)(pP^\# q \rightarrow \sim qP^\# \sim p)$

Let us turn now to the P^* interpretation of our initial preference principle:

4. $pP^* q \rightarrow \sim qP^* \sim p$

Again, let us begin by understanding this principle as asserted with respect to weak (i.e., restricted) quantification:

4(a) $(Ap)(Aq)(pP^* q \rightarrow \sim qP^* \sim p)$

This version of the principle yields the arithmetical transform

$$[*(p) > *(q)] \rightarrow [*(\sim q) > *(\sim p)]$$

which, by the definition of the $*$-measure, amounts to

$$([\#(p) - \#(\sim p)] > [\#(q) - \#(\sim q)]) \rightarrow \{[\#(\sim q) - \#(q)] > [\#(\sim p) - \#(p)]\}$$

which, being of the form

$$(x > y) \rightarrow (-y > -x)$$

is a truth of arithmetic.

It remains to be seen whether 4(a) can actually be strengthened to

4(b) $(\forall p)(\forall q)[pP^* q \rightarrow \sim qP^* \sim p]$

Let us try the effect of some particular substitution, say "$p \& q$" for 'p'. Then 4(b) yields

5. $(p \& q)P^* q \rightarrow \sim qP^* \sim (p \& q)$

whose arithmetical transform is

$$\left[\left(a - \frac{b+c+d}{3}\right) > \left(\frac{a+c}{2} - \frac{b+d}{2}\right)\right] \rightarrow$$
$$\left[\left(\frac{b+d}{2} - \frac{a+c}{2}\right) > \left(\frac{b+c+d}{3} - a\right)\right]$$

which, being of the form

$$(x > y) \rightarrow (-y > -x)$$

is again a truth of arithmetic. So far so good. Moreover, the general fact that all substitution instances of

$$pP^*q \rightarrow \sim qP^* \sim p$$

are P^* tautologies is readily established—as follows: Regardless of the substitutions made in thesis 4, the result will take the form

$$\alpha P^*\beta \rightarrow \sim \beta P^* \sim \alpha$$

whose arithmetical transform will be

$$\{[\#(\alpha) - \#(\sim\alpha)] > [\#(\beta) - \#(\sim\beta)]\}$$
$$\{[\#(\sim\beta) - \#(\beta)] > [\#(\sim\alpha) - \#(\alpha)]\}$$

which is readily seen—on analogy with the preceding—to be a truth of arithmetic,

It is thus clear that the preference principle we have selected for examination,

$$pPq \rightarrow \sim qP \sim p$$

is unrestrictedly tautologous for P^*, but is only a restricted tautology for $P^{\#}$, the restrictions being such as we have chosen to indicate by means of the two different styles of general quantification.[1]

---

[1] For an interesting attempt to systematize the formal logical theory of the two styles of quantification here at issue the reader is referred to Alan Ross Anderson's discussion of an earlier version of Chapter VI in N. Rescher (ed.), *The Logic of Decisions and Action* (Pittsburgh, 1967), pp. 63–70.

The Social Fusion
of Personal Evaluations

In Chapter VIII the problem of combining personal, individual evaluations into a transpersonal, social evaluation is mooted. The aim of this appendix is to set out the somewhat technical considerations by means of which a relatively simple solution can be found for this seemingly complicated problem.

If we assume the persons involved to be $P_1, P_2, P_3, \ldots, P_n$, our starting point then is a tabulation (matrix) of the following sort, specifying for each person and each alternative his individual, personal metrized evaluation of its merits:

	x_1	x_2	x_3	$\cdots$	x_j	$\cdots$	x_n
P_1	$m_1(x_1)$	$m_1(x_2)$	$m_1(x_3)$	$\cdots$	$m_1(x_j)$	$\cdots$	$m_1(x_n)$
P_2	$m_2(x_1)$	$m_2(x_2)$	$m_2(x_3)$	$\cdots$	$m_2(x_j)$	$\cdots$	$m_2(x_n)$
P_3	$m_3(x_1)$	$m_3(x_2)$	$m_3(x_3)$	$\cdots$	$m_3(x_j)$	$\cdots$	$m_3(x_n)$
$\vdots$	$\vdots$	$\vdots$	$\vdots$	$\vdots$	$\vdots$	$\vdots$	$\vdots$
P_i	$m_i(x_1)$	$m_i(x_2)$	$m_i(x_3)$	$\cdots$	$m_i(x_j)$	$\cdots$	$m_i(x_n)$
$\vdots$	$\vdots$	$\vdots$	$\vdots$	$\vdots$	$\vdots$	$\vdots$	$\vdots$
P_k	$m_k(x_1)$	$m_k(x_2)$	$m_k(x_3)$	$\cdots$	$m_k(x_j)$	$\cdots$	$m_k(x_n)$

We thus assume as our starting point that the issue of Chapter VI, the metrization of individual preferences, has been resolved. The problem now is to find a function of combination F to define an interpersonalized, social measure $m(x_j)$ on the basis of the evaluation of x_j by the different individuals at issue:

$$m(x_j) = F[m_1(x_j), m_2(x_j), m_3(x_j), \ldots, m_k(x_n)]$$

How are we to determine such a combination function F?[1] Let us first consider what can be said about the general nature of this function.

One general feature we must stipulate for F is that of *symmetry*:

> 1. $F(\ldots, x, \ldots, y, \ldots) = F(\ldots, y, \ldots, x, \ldots)$

The best light in which to view 1 is as a principle of equity, or of indifference (of persons), asserting that F takes account of the preference ratings of the different individuals of the social group in exactly the same way.

A second feature that could plausibly be stipulated for F is the (closely related) thesis of *person-to-person indifference of an increment*:

> 2. $F(\ldots, x, \ldots, y + \xi, \ldots) = F(\ldots, x + \xi, \ldots, y, \ldots)$,
>   identically in ξ

This second stipulation in effect claims that the different m_i measure the preferences of their respective P_i in the same manner on essentially the same scale. (So that, say, we do not measure P's preferences on a scale ranging from $-\infty$ to $+\infty$ and Q's on a scale ranging from -100 to $+100$ and R's on one from -1 to $+1$.) There must be, so to speak, a one-to-one correspondence between the various preference scales—their end points must be the same (e.g., we, the society, must view P's *bad* as "just as bad" as Q's *bad*), and increments must also be viewed as corresponding (e.g., we must view P's *just a very little bit better* as "just as much better" as Q's *just a very little bit better*). The stipulation formalizes the idea that, in the construction of a social preference valuation each person is to count for one. So regarded, this principle provides for an *identity of scaling* in the construction of the various individual preference functions. It has it that the evaluations of dif-

---

[1] This way of posing the problem is based on its presentation in R. D. Luce and H. Raiffa, *Games and Decisions* (New York, 1957). Our general approach to its solution is closely akin to the line of procedure adopted in L. A. Goodman and H. Markowitz, *Social Welfare Functions Based on Rankings* (Cowles Commission Discussion Paper, Economics, No. 2017), 1951. (Cf. Luce and Raiffa, pp. 345–353.) Our approach has, however, bypassed their somewhat dubious reliance on the use of the concept of just-noticeable differences for preference determination, borrowed by Goodman and Markowitz from the area of the psychology of sensation.

ferent individuals are to be indicated on one and the same common scale of mensuration.

This second principle is readily seen to have the consequence that

$$F(x, y, \ldots, z) = F(x + y + \cdots + z, 0, 0, \ldots, 0)$$

so that F is in fact a function simply of the *sum* of its parameters. The *simplest* assumption with respect to such a function is to suppose it to be linear, so that F satisfies the *linearity condition*:

3. $F(x, y, \ldots, z) = a(x + y + \cdots + z) + b$

Another look at the linearity assumption of the preceding paragraph is warranted. What this amounts to is the thesis of *marginal indifference of an increment*:

3.′ $F(\ldots, x + \xi, \ldots) - F(\ldots, x, \ldots) \equiv F(\ldots, u + \xi, \ldots)$
$\quad - F(\ldots, u, \ldots)$, identically in ξ

The "marginal value" of a fixed increment is thus held to be constant. Our linearity assumption thus does no more than provide a group-relativized counterpart to the fact that the individualized m_i valuations are to be construed as measures of *utility*, i.e., of valuation of constant marginal worth, rather than one of decreasing marginal worth, such as money. This is a feature inherent in our construction of the m_i, but its interpersonalized reflection in the linearity of F does represent an added assumption.

There is yet another light in which this linearity assumption can be viewed. Let us rewrite 3′ as:

3.″ $F(\ldots, x + \xi, \ldots) - F(\ldots, u + \xi, \ldots)$
$\quad \equiv F(\ldots, x, \ldots) - F(\ldots, u, \ldots)$, identically in ξ

According to this, any linear transformation of the individual preference metrization

$$m_i'(x_j) = m_i(x_j) + c; \quad c \text{ constant}$$

that is, any systematic resetting of the orgin of an individual's preference valuation, will leave the differences in the social metrization of the alternatives unaffected. Individual preference differences of a given size make for social preference differences of a fixed size, regardless of where these individual preference differences happen to fall on the scale. From this angle, the linearity assumption 3 can be viewed in the guise of a stipulation of scaling invariance.

Let us now impose one further, very plausible restriction, namely, the *uniformity condition*

    4. $F(x, x, \ldots, x) = x$

where there are n entries (all of them x) in $F(\ldots)$. That is, if everyone agrees in valuing something in a given degree, then so does the society as a whole also value it in the same degree. Setting $x = 0$, we at once obtain that $b = 0$ in principle 3 above. Therefore in general we have that

    $F(x, x, \ldots, x) = a(n \cdot x) = x$

so that $a = 1/n$. This establishes the desired combination function F to be simply *the average* (arithmetical mean) of its parameters.

Bibliography on
the Theory of Value

The aim of this list of references is not to give a comprehensive bibliography of the subject but rather to provide a *bibliographic introduction* to the study of values in both the philosophical and the scientific sectors of the domain. Something approaching completeness has been attempted only in certain special categories, to wit: I, III.A.1.b, III.C.3, IV.C.5, IV.D, and V. The listing is organized topically, and most topics have been treated in a highly selective way, items being selected for inclusion sometimes because of their own importance as contributions to this domain, sometimes because they furnish a good introduction to its problems and above all to its *literature*. The reader who wishes to probe more deeply into value problems within the area at issue will find helpful guidance by consulting these works and will also find help in the reference works listed in the section on *Bibliographies*. A newly founded quarterly, *The Journal of Value Inquiry*, whose first issue appeared in the spring of 1967, should prove of substantial value to students and workers in this field.

CONTENTS OF BIBLIOGRAPHY

BIBLIOGRAPHY

I. Historical accounts

BAMBERGER, FRITZ, *Untersuchungen zur Entstehung des Wertproblemes in der Philosophie des 19. Jahrhunderts, I: Lotze* (Halle, 1924).

CHAKRAVARTI, APALA, *The Idealist Theory of Value* (Calcutta, 1966).

EATON, H. O., *The Austrian Philosophy of Values* (Norman, 1930).

EDEL, ABRAHAM, "The Concept of Values in Contemporary Philosophical Value Theory." *Philosophy of Science*, vol. 20 (1953), pp. 198–207.

EISLER, ROBERT, *Studien der Werttheorie* (Leipzig, 1902). Article "Wert" in *idem, Wörterbuch der philosophischen Begriffe* (3rd ed., Berlin, 1910), pp. 1764–1773.

FERRATER MORA, JOSÉ, Article "Valor" in *idem, Diccionario de Filosofia*, vol. II (5th ed., Buenos Aires, 1965), pp. 867–872.

FRONDIZI, RISIERI, *What is Value? An Introduction to Axiology* (La Salle, 1963).

JAENSCH, ERICH, *Wirklichkeit und Wert in der Philosophie und Kultur der Neuzeit* (Berlin, 1929).

JOHNSON, J. PRESCOTT, "The Fact-Value Question in Early Modern Value Theory." *The Journal of Value Inquiry*, vol. 1 (1967), pp. 64–71.

KAULLA, RUDOLF, *Die geschichtliche Entwicklung der modernen Werttheorie* (Tübingen, 1904).

KRAUS, OSKAR, *Die Werttheorien: Geschichte und Kritik* (Brünn, 1937). [A comprehensive critical history of value theory from antiquity onward, with emphasis —as regards recent developments—on Brentano and his school.]

KRUSÉ, CORNELIUS, "Western Theories of Value," in C. A. Moore (ed.), *Essays in East-West Philosophy* (Honolulu, 1951), pp. 383–397.

VON MERING, OTTO, *A Grammar of Human Values* (Pittsburgh, 1961).

MESSER, AUGUST, *Deutsche Wertphilosophie der Gegenwart* (Leipzig, 1926). *Wertphilosophie in der Gegenwart* (Berlin, 1930; Forschungsberichte, No. 4).

PEPPER, STEPHEN C., "A Brief History of General Theory of Value," in V. Ferm (ed.), *A History of Philosophical Systems* (New York, 1950), pp. 493–503.

POLIN, RAYMOND, "The Philosophy of Value in France," in M. Farber (ed.), *Philosophic Thought in France and the United States* (Buffalo, 1950), pp. 203–218.

VON RINTELEN, FRITZ-JOACHIM, *Das philosophische Wertproblem—Der Wertgedanke in der europäischen Geistesentwicklung; I. Altertum und Mittelalter* (Halle, 1932).

ROTTER, FRIEDERICH, *Die Erkenntnislehre der Wertphilosophie* (Gemersheim, 1926). [On the Baden School.]

SCHILLER, F. C. S., Article "Value" in Hastings' *Encyclopedia of Religion and Ethics*, vol. 12 (New York, 1922), pp. 584–589.

STERN, ALFRED, *La philosophie des valeurs: Regards sur ses tendences actuelles en Allemagne* (Paris, 1936).

URBAN, WILBUR MARSHALL, Article on "Axiology" in D. Runes (ed.), *Twentieth Century Philosophy* (New York, 1943).

WARD, LEO RICHARD, *Philosophy of Value* (New York, 1930).

II. Methodological issues
A. Methods of value inquiry

ALBERT, ETHEL M., "Value Sentences and Empirical Research." *Philosophy and Phenomenological Research*, vol. 17 (1957), pp. 331–338.

BAIER, KURT, "The Concept of Value," in K. Baier and N. Rescher (eds.), *Values and the Future* (New York, 1968).

BARTON, ALLEN, "Measuring the Values of Individuals." *Review of Recent Research Bearing on Religious and Character Formation* (Research Supplement to *Religious Education*, July/August, 1962). *Organizational Measurement* (New York, 1961).

BAYLIS, CHARLES A., "The Confirmation of Value Judgments." *The Philosophical Review*, vol. 61 (1952), pp. 50–58.

BERELSON, BERNARD, *Content Analysis* (Glencoe, 1952).

VON EHRENFELS, CHRISTIAN, *System der Werttheorie*. 2 vols. (Leipzig, 1897; 1898). [An extensive study of valuation based on the concept of value as degree of "desirability." See also the other references given in Sec. III. A.1.b.]

HARTMAN, ROBERT S., *The Structure of Value* (Carbondale, 1967).

HULL, CLARK L., "Value, Valuation, and Natural Science Methodology." *Philosophy of Science*, vol. 4 (1944), pp. 125–141.

KLUCKHOHN, CLYDE, "The Scientific Study of Values," in *idem*, *Three Lectures* (Toronto, 1959), pp. 25–54. "The Study of Values," in D. N. Barett (ed.), *Values in America* (Notre Dame, 1961). "Values and Value Orientations in the Theory of Action," in T. Parsons and E. Shils (eds.), *Towards a General Theory of Action* (Cambridge, Mass., 1951), pp. 388–433.

KLUCKHOHN, FLORENCE R., and F. L. STRODBECK, *Variations in Value Orientations* (Evanston, 1961).

KOFFKA, KURT, "The Ontological Status of Value," in H. M. Kallen and S. Hook (eds.), *American Philosophy Today and Tomorrow* (New York, 1935).

KÖHLER, WOLFGANG, *The Place of Value in a World of Fact* (New York, 1938).

LEDDEN, J. E., "On the Logical Status of Value." *The Philosophical Review*, vol. 59 (1950), pp. 354–369.

LEE, HARALD NEWTON, *Essays on the Theory of Value and Valuation*, ed. by H. N. Lee (Minneapolis, 1935). "Methodology of Value Theory," in R. Lepley (ed.), *Value; A Cooperative Inquiry* (New York, 1949).

LEPLEY, ROY, *The Verifiability of Value* (New York, 1944). *Value: A Cooperative Inquiry*, ed. by Roy Lepley (New York, 1949). *The Language of Value*, ed. by Roy Lepley (New York, 1957).

LEWIS, CLARENCE IRVING, *An Analysis of Knowledge and Valuation* (La Salle, 1946). *The Ground and Nature of the Right* (New York, 1955).

MEINONG, ALEXIUS, *Psychologisch-ethische Untersuchungen Zur Werttheorie* (Graz, 1894). [See also the other references given in Sec. III. A.1.b.]

PERRY, O. L., "The Logic of Moral Valuation." *Mind*, vol. 66 (1957), pp. 42–62.

PICKARD-CAMBRIDGE, SIR ARTHUR WALLACE, "On Our Knowledge of Value." *Proceedings of the Aristotelian Society*, vol. 17 (1917), pp. 216–255.

SCRIVEN, MICHAEL, *The Methodology of Evaluation*. Publication 110 of the Social Science Education Consortium (1966).

TAYLOR, PAUL W., *Normative Discourse* (New York, 1961).

URBAN, WILBUR MARSHALL, "Value Propositions and Verifiability." *The Journal of Philosophy*, vol. 34 (1937), pp. 589–602.

WHITE, RALPH K., *Value Analysis: The Nature and the Use of Its Methods* (Glen Gardner, N. J., 1951).

B. Models for value description
(See also parts IIA and IV of this bibliography.)

1. Empirical models

ALLPORT, GORDON W., PHILIP E. VERNON, and GARDNER LINDSEY, *A Study of Values* (Boston, 1951, revised edition). *Manual for the Study of Values* (Boston, 1960).

BARTON, ALLEN, "Measuring the Values of Individuals." *Review of Recent Research Bearing on Religious and Character Formation* (Research Supplement to *Religious Education*, July/August, 1962). *Organizational Measurement* (New York, 1961).

CARTER, ROY E., "An Experiment in Value Measurement." *American Sociological Review*, vol. 21 (1956), pp. 156–163.

FALLDING, HAROLD, "A Proposal for the Empirical Study of Values." *American Sociological Review*, vol. 30 (1965), pp. 223–233.

GRAHAM, JAMES L., "Some Attitudes Towards Values." *Journal of Social Psychology*, vol. 12 (1940), pp. 405–414.

LEPLEY, ROY, *The Verifiability of Value* (New York, 1944).

PODELL, LAWRENCE, "An Interviewing Problem in Values Research." *Social Science Research*, vol. 41 (1956), pp. 121–126.

SCOTT, WILLIAM A., "Empirical Assessment of Values and Ideologies." *American Sociological Review*, vol. 24 (1959), pp. 299–310.

STREFFRE, BUFORD, "Concurrent Validity of the Vocational Values Inventory." *Journal of Educational Research*, vol. 52 (1959), pp. 339–341.

VAN DUSEN, A. C., S. WIMBERLY, and C. I. MOISIER, "Standardization of a Values Inventory." *Journal of Educational Psychology*, vol. 30 (1939), pp. 53–62.

WILKENING, E. A., "Techniques of Assessing Form Family Values." *Rural Sociology*, vol. 19, (1959), pp. 39–49.

2. Formal models

ACKOFF, RUSSELL L., "On a Science of Ethics." *Philosophy and Phenomenological Research*, vol. 9 (1949), pp. 663–672.

ANDERSON, ALAN ROSS, "The Logic of Norms," *Logique et Analyse*, vol. 1 (1958), pp. 84–91. "Logic, Norms and Roles," *Ratio*, vol. 4 (1962), pp. 36–49. "The Formal Analysis of Normative Systems," in N. Rescher (ed.), *The Logic of Decision and Action* (Pittsburgh, 1967), pp. 147–213.

AYRES, CLARENCE E., "The Value Economy," in R. Lepley (ed.), *Value: A Cooperative Inquiry* (New York, 1949), pp. 43–63.

BOULDING, KENNETH E., "Some Contributions of Economics to the General Theory of Value." *Philosophy of Science*, vol. 23 (1956), pp. 1–14.

CHURCHMAN, C. WEST, *Prediction and Optimal Decision: Philosophical Issues of a Science of Values* (Englewood Cliffs, 1961).

CHURCHMAN, C. WEST, and RUSSELL L. ACKOFF, "An Approximate Measure of Value." *Operations Research*, vol. 2 (1954), pp. 172–187.

DAVIDSON, DONALD, J. C. C. McKINSEY, and PATRICK SUPPES, "Outline of a Formal Theory of Value." *Philosophy of Science*, vol. 22 (1955), pp. 140–160.

HARE, RICHARD M., *The Language of Morals* (Oxford, 1952).

MORRIS, CHARLES W., "Axiology as the Science of Preferential Behavior," in Roy Lepley (ed.), *Value: A Cooperative Inquiry* (New York, 1949), pp. 211–222. *Varieties of Human Value* (Chicago, 1956).

PERRY, DAVID L., "What Things Can Be Evaluated?" *The Journal of Philosophy*, vol. 61 (1964), pp. 186–192.

SMITH, NICHOLAS M., JR., "The Theory of Value and the Science of Decision—A Summary," ed. by Nicholas M. Smith, Jr., *Journal of the Operations Research Society of America*, vol. 1 (1953), pp. 103–113. "A Calculus for Ethics; A Theory of the Structure of Value," *Behavioral Sciences*, vol. 1 (1956), Pt. I, pp. 111–142; Pt. II, pp. 186–211.

C. Values and science

BAIN, READ, "The Scientist and his Values." *Social Forces*, vol. 31 (1952), pp. 106–109.

BENNE, KENNETH, and G. E. SWANSON, "Values and the Social Scientist," ed. by Kenneth Benne and G. E. Swanson, *The Journal of Social Issues*, vol. 6 (1950), pp. 2–7.

BENOIT-SMULLYAN, E., "Value Judgments and the Social Sciences." *The Journal of Philosophy*, vol. 42 (1945), pp. 197–210.

BOWMAN, CLAUDE C., "Evaluations and Values Consistent with the Scientific Study of Society." *American Sociological Review*, vol. 10 (1945), pp. 709–715. "Is Sociology Too Detached?", *American Sociological Review*, vol. 21 (1956), pp. 563–568.

BRONOWSKI, JACOB, *Science and Human Values* (New York, 1958).

CAWS, PETER, *Science and the Theory of Value* (New York, 1967).

COHEN, MORRIS R., "Values, Norms, and Science," in *A Preface to Logic* (New York, 1964), pp. 155–178.

EDEL, ABRAHAM, *Ethical Judgment: The Uses of Science in Ethics* (Glencoe, 1955).

HALL, EVERETT W., *Modern Science and Human Values* (Princeton, 1957).

HOLLS, WILLIAM L., "The Impingement of Moral Values on Sociology." *Sociological Problems*, vol. 2 (1954), pp. 66–70.

IRVING, JOHN A., *Science and Values* (Toronto, 1952).

JEFFREY, RICHARD C., "Valuation and Acceptance of Scientific Hypotheses." *Philosophy of Science*, vol. 23 (1956), pp. 237–246.

KNIGHT, FRANK H., "Fact and Value in Social Science," in R. Aushen (ed.) *Science and Man* (New York, 1942).

KÖHLER, WOLFGANG, *The Place of Value in a World of Facts* (New York, 1938; paperback ed.). "Value and Fact," *The Journal of Philosophy*, vol. 41 (1944), pp. 197–212.

LIPPITT, RONALD, "Action Research and the Values of the Social Scientist." *The Journal of Social Issues*, vol. 6 (1950), pp. 50–55.

LUNDBERG, GEORGE A., "Science, Scientists, and Values." *Social Forces*, vol. 30 (1952), pp. 373–379.

MITCHELL, WESLEY C., "Facts and Values in Economics." *The Journal of Philosophy*, vol. 41 (1949), pp. 212–219.

MYRDAL, GUNNAR, *Value and Social Theory* (New York, 1958).

NAGEL, ERNEST, "Methodological Problems in the Social Sciences," in *idem, The Structure of Science* (New York, 1961).

NORTHROP, FILMER S. C., *Logic of the Sciences and the Humanities* (New York, 1947). "The Physical Sciences, Philosophy, and Human Values," in E. M. Wigner (ed.), *Physical Science and Human Values* (Princeton, 1947).

POLANYI, MICHAEL, *Science, Faith and Society* (London, 1946).

RESCHER, NICHOLAS, "The Ethical Dimension of Scientific Research," in R. Colodny (ed.), *Beyond the Edge of Certainty* (Pittsburgh, 1965) pp. 261–276.

RIEMER, SVEND, "Values and Standards in Research." *American Journal of Sociology*, vol. 55 (1949), pp. 131–136.

RUDNER, RICHARD, "The Scientist *Qua* Scientist Makes Value Judgments." *Philosophy of Science*, vol. 20 (1953), pp. 1–6.

SCHOECK, H., and J. W. WIGGINS (eds.), *Scientism and Values* (Princeton, 1960).

SCHUMPETER, JOSEPH A., "Science and Ideology." *American Economic Review*, vol. 39 (1949), pp. 345–369.

SHERRINGTON, SIR CHARLES, "An Essay in the Relation of Science to Human Values," in D. P. Geddes (ed.), *An Analysis of the Kinsey Reports on Sexual Behavior in the Human Male and Female* (New York, 1954).

SNOW, C. P., *Two Cultures and the Scientific Revolution* (New York, 1959).

THORNDIKE, EDWARD C., "Science and Values." *Science*, vol. 83 (1936), pp. 1–8.

URBAN, WILBUR M., "Science and Value." *Ethics*, vol. 51 (1941), pp. 291–306.

WALDO, DWIGHT, "'Values' in Political Science," in R. Young (ed.), *Approaches to the Study of Politics* (Evanston, 1958), pp. 96–111.

WEBER, MAX, *The Methodology of the Social Sciences*, tr. by E. A. Shils and H. A. Finch (Glencoe, 1949).

WIGNER, EUGENE, *Physical Science and Human Values*, ed. by E. Wigner (Princeton, 1947).

ZNANIECKI, FLORIAN, "Should Sociologists Be Also Philosophers of Values?" *Sociology and Social Research*, vol. 37 (1952), pp. 79–84.

III. **Philosophical approaches to value**
   A. **General value theory**
      1. **Axiology and the theory of value in general**
         a. **The Baden school of neo-Kantians and its congeners**

LOTZE, HERMANN (1817–1881)

Works by Lotze

Mikrokosmos (3 vols., Leipzig, 1857–1864). English tr. as *Microcosmus* by E. Hamilton and E. E. C. Jones (2 vols., Edinburgh, 4th ed., 1885).

Grundzüge der praktischen Philosophie (Leipzig, 1882). *Logik* (Leipzig, 1874) and *Metaphysik* (Leipzig, 1879), tr. by B. Bosanquet as *Lotze's System of Philosophy*, (Oxford, 1884; 2nd. ed., 1887).

Works about Lotze

MAXSEIN, A., "Die Begriffe der Geltung bei Lotze." *Philosophisches Jahrbuch*, vol. 51 (1938), pp. 457–470.

WINDELBAND, WILHELM (1848–1915)

Works by Windelband

Präludien: Aufsätze und Reden zur Einführung in die Philosophie. 2 vols. (Freiburg im Breisgau, 1884; 9th ed., Tübingen, 1924).

Einleitung in die Philosophie (Tübingen, 1914), tr. by J. McCabe as *An Introduction to Philosophy* (New York, 1921).

Works about Windelband

GRONAU, GOTTHARD, "Die Kultur und Wertphilosophie Wilhelm Windelbands," in *idem, Die Philosophie der Gegenwart* (Langensalze, 1922).

HOFFMAN, ARTHUR, *Das Systemprogram der Philosophie der Werte: Eine Würdigung der Axiologie W. Windelbands* (Erfurt, 1922).

MÜNSTERBERG, HUGO (1863–1916), *Philosophie der Werte: Grundzüge einer Weltanschauung* (Leipzig, 1908; 2nd. ed., 1921).

RICKERT, HEINRICH, *W. Windelband* (Tübingen, 1915; 2nd ed., 1925).

RICKERT, HEINRICH (1863–1936)

Works by Rickert

"Lebenswerte und Kulturwerte: Vom System der Werte." *Logos*, vol. 3 (1912), and vol. 4 (1913), pp. 295–327.

Kulturwissenschaft und Naturwissenschaft (Tübingen, 1899; 5th ed., Tübingen, 1921).

Die Probleme der Geschichts-philosophie (Heidelberg, 1905; 3rd ed., Heidelberg, 1924).

"Psychologie der Weltanschauungen und Philosophie der Werte." *Logos*, vol. 9 (1920), pp. 1–42.

Die Grenzen der naturwissenschaftlichen Begriffsbildung. 3 vols. (Tübingen and Leipzig, 1896, 1902; 5th ed., 1929).

Works about Rickert

FREDERICI, FEDERICO, *La Filosofia dei valori de H. Rickert* (Florence, 1933).

GURVITCH, GEORGES, "La Théorie des valeurs de Heinrich Rickert." *Révue Philosophique*, vol. 124 (1937), pp. 80–85.

b. The school of Brentano ("second Austrian school") and its congeners and successors

Note: A general account of the work of this school, including extensive bibliographical references, can be found in Howard O. Eaton, *The Austrian Philosophy of Values* (Norman, 1930).

BRENTANO, FRANZ (1838–1917)

Works by Brentano

Grundlegung und Aufbau der Ethik, ed. by F. Mayer-Hillebrand (Bern, 1952).

Grundzüge der Asthetik, ed. by F. Mayer-Hillebrand (Bern, 1959).

Psychologie vom empirischen Standpunkt, vol. 1 (Leipzig, 1874). Second edition, edited with Introduction and Notes, by Oskar Kraus. 3 vols. (Leipzig, Meiner, 1924, 1925, 1928).

Von Ursprung sittlicher Erkenntnis (Leipzig, 1889). English translation, with biographical note, by Cecil Hague, *The Origin of the Knowledge of Right and Wrong* (Westminister, 1902). Second edition, edited with introduction and notes, by Oskar Kraus, and containing theretofore unpublished material (Leipzig, Meiner, 1921); 4th ed., 1955. New English translation by R. M. Chisholm and E. Schneewind, *The Origin of Our Knowledge of Right and Wrong* (London, 1968).

Works about Brentano

CHISHOLM, RODERICK M., "Brentano's Theory of Correct and Incorrect Emotion." *Révue Internationale de Philosophie*, vol. 78 (1966), pp. 397–415. [The entire issue in which this article appeared is devoted to Brentano.]

KASTIL, ALFRED, *Die Philosophie Franz Brentanos: eine Einführung in seine Lehre* ed. by F. Mayer-Hillebrand (Bern, 1951).

KRAUS, OSKAR, *Franz Brentano: zur Kenntnis seines Lebens und seiner Lehre, Mit Beiträgen von Carl Stumpf und Edmund Husserl* (Munich, Beck, 1919). *Die Werttheorien: Geschichte und Kritik* (Brünn, 1937).

MARTY, ANTON (1847–1914)

Works by Marty

Gesammelte Schriften, ed. by J. Eisenmeir, A. Kastil, and O. Kraus., 2 vols. (Halle, 1916, 1920).

Nachgelassene Schriften, ed. by O. Funke (Bern, 1940–1950).

Works about Marty

KRAUS, OSKAR, *Anton Marty: sein Leben und seine Werke* (Halle, 1916). *Die Werttheorien: Geschichte und Kritik* (Brünn, 1937).

MEINONG, ALEXIUS (1853–1920)

Works by Meinong

Psychologisch-ethische Untersuchungen zur Werttheorie (Graz, Leuschner u. Lubensky, 1894).

"Uber Werthalten und Wert." *Archiv für systematische Philosophie*, vol. 1 (Berlin, 1895), pp. 327–346.

"Über Urtheilsgefühle, was sie sind und was sie nicht sind." *Archiv für die gesammte Psychologie*, vol. 4 (1906), pp. 21–58.

"Für die Psychologie und gegen den Psychologismus in der allgemeinen Werttheorie." *Logos*, vol. 3 (1912), pp. 1–14.

"Über emotionale Präsentation." *Sitzungsberichte der kaiserlichen Akademie der Wissenschaften zu Wien* (phil.-hist. Klasse), vol. 183 (1917).

Zur Grundlegung der Allgemeinen Werttheorie, ed. E. Mally (Graz, 1923).

Works about Meinong

FINDLAY, JOHN NIEMEYER, *Meinong's Theory of Objects and Values* (London, 1963, 2nd ed.).

VON EHRENFELS, CHRISTIAN (1859–1932)

"Über Fühlen und Wollen." *Sitzungsberichte der kaiserlichen Akademie der Wissenschaften zu Wien* (phil.-hist. Klasse), vol. 114 (1887), pp. 523–636.

"Werttheorie und Ethik." *Vierteljahrschrift für wissenschaftliche Philosophie*, vol. 17 (Leipzig, 1893–1894), pp. 76–110, 200–206, 321–363, 413–475, and vol. 18, pp. 77–97.

"Von der Wertdefinition zum Motivationsgesetz." *Archiv für systematische Philosophie*, vol. 2 (Berlin, 1896), pp. 103–122.

System der Werttheorie, 2 vols. (Leipzig, Reisland, 1897–1898).

Grundbegriffe der Ethik (Wiesbaden, Reigmann, 1907).

SCHWARTZ, HERMAN (1864–1951)

Psychologie des Willens: Zur Grundlegung der Ethik (Leipzig, 1900).
Das Ungegebene: Eine Religions und Wertphilosophie (Tübingen, 1921).
Ethik (Breslau, 1925).

KRAUS, OSKAR (1872–1942)

Zur Theorie des Wertes: eine Bentham-Studie (Halle, 1901).
"Die Grundlagen der Werttheorie." *Jahrbücher der Philosophie*, vol. 2 (1914).
Franz Brentano: zur Kenntnis seines Lebens und seiner Lehre (Munich, Beck, 1919.)
Die Werttheorien: Geschichte und Kritik (Brünn, 1937).

FISHER, RUDOLF (1873–1926)

Studien zur Werttheorie (Leipzig, 1902).

SCHELER, MAX (1874–1928)

Zur Phänomenologie und Theorie der Sympathie-gefühle und von Liebe und Hass (Halle, 1913).
Abhandlungen und Aufsätze (Leipzig, 1915).
Vom Umsturz der Werte. 2 vols. (Bern, 1915, 1925).
Der Formalismus in der Ethik und die materiale Wertethik. 2 vols. (Halle, 1913, 1916; 4th ed., Bern, 1954).
Über Ressentiment und moralisches Werturtheil (Leipzig, 1912). Tr. by W. W. Holdheim as *Resentiment* (New York, 1960).

HARTMANN, NICOLAI (1882–1950)

Ethik (Berlin, 1926; 2nd ed., 1935). Tr. by S. Coit as *Ethics*. 3 vols. (London, 1932). [Vol. II, "Moral Values," is especially germane to our purposes.]

MENGER, KARL (1840–1921)

Grundlagen zur Logik der Sitten. 4 vols. (Wien, 1934). Vol. IV contains the essay "Moral, Wille, und Weltgestaltung."

c. Anglo-American writers

AIKEN, HENRY D., "Definitions of Value and the Moral Ideal." *The Journal of Philosophy*, vol. 42 (1945), pp. 337–352.

ALEXANDER, SAMUEL, "The Idea of Value," *Mind*, vol. 1 (1892), pp. 32–55. *Beauty and Other Forms of Value* (London, 1933).

AYER, ALFRED JULIUS, *Language, Truth and Logic* (London, 1953).

BLANSHARD, BRAND, *Reason and Goodness* (London, 1961).

BOSANQUET, BERNARD, *The Principle of Individuality and Value* (London, 1912).

BRANDT, RICHARD B., "Some Puzzles for Attitude Theories of Value," in R. Lepley (ed.), *The Language of Value* (New York, 1957), pp. 153–171.

BRIGHTMAN, E. S., *Nature and Values* (New York, 1945).

BROGAN, ALBERT P., "The Fundamental Value Universal," *The Journal of Philosophy*, vol. 16 (1919), pp. 96–104. "Urban's Axiological System," *The Journal of Philosophy*, vol. 18 (1921), pp. 197–209. "Philosophy and the Problems of Value," *The Philosophical Review*, vol. 42 (1933), pp. 105–129.

CAMPBELL, C. A., "Moral and Non-Moral Values: A Study in the First Principles of Axiology." *Mind*, vol. 44 (1935), pp. 273–299.

CERF, WALTER, "Value Decisions." *Philosophy of Science*, vol. 18 (1951), pp. 26–34.

DASHIELL, J. FREDERIC, *The Philosophic Status of Values* (New York, 1913).

DEWEY, JOHN, "The Problem of Value," *The Journal of Philosophy*, vol. 10 (1913), pp. 268–269. "Values, Liking, and Thought," *The Journal of Philosophy*, vol. 20 (1923), pp. 617–622. "The Meaning of Value," *The Journal of Philosophy*, vol. 23 (1924), pp. 126–133. "Some Questions About Value," *The Journal of Philosophy*, vol. 41 (1944), pp. 449–455. "Theory of Valuation," in *International Encyclopedia of Unified Science* (Chicago, 1939, reprinted 1952).

EVANS, DANIEL LUTHER, *The Status of Value in New Realism: A Study of New Realism from the Standpoint of Axiology* (Columbus, Ohio, 1923).

FEIBLEMANN, JAMES K., "Towards an Analysis of the Basic Value System." *American Anthropologist*, vol. 56 (1954), pp. 421–432.

FEIGL, HERBERT, "The Difference Between Knowledge and Valuation," in K. Benne and G. E. Swanson (eds.), "Values and the Social Scientist," *The Journal of Social Issues*, vol. 6 (1950), pp. 39–44. "Valuation and Vindication: An Analysis of the Nature and the Limits of Ethical Arguments," in W. Sellars and J. Hospers (eds.), *Readings in Ethical Theory* (Appleton, 1952).

FINDLAY, J. N., *Values and Intentions* (London, 1961).

FISHER, D. WARREN, "Professor Urban's Value-Theory." *The Journal of Philosophy*, vol. 17 (1920), pp. 570–582.

GARNETT, ARTHUR CAMPBELL, *Reality and Value: An Introduction to Metaphysics and an Essay on the Theory of Value* (London, 1937). *Reality and Value* (New Haven, 1937).

GOLIGHTLY, CORNELIUS L., "Value as a Scientific Concept." *The Journal of Philosophy*, vol. 53 (1956), pp. 233–245.

GOTSHALK, DILMAN W., "Value Science." *Philosophy of Science*, vol. 19 (1952), pp. 183–192.

GRAHAM, ANGUS CHARLES, *The Problem of Value* (London, 1961).

GRUBER, FREDERICK C., *Aspects of Value*, ed. by F. C. Gruber (Philadelphia, 1959).

HAHN, LEWIS E., "A Contextualist Looks at Values," in R. Lepley (ed.), *Value: A Cooperative Inquiry* (New York, 1949), pp. 112–124.

HALL, EVERETT W., "A Categorical Analysis of Value," *Philosophy of Science*, vol. 14 (1947), pp. 333–344. *What is Value?—An Essay in Philosophical Analysis* (New York, 1952).

HANDY, ROLLO, "Philosophy's Neglect of the Social Sciences." *Philosophy of Science*, vol. 25 (1958), pp. 117–124.

HARE, R. M., *The Language of Morals* (Oxford, 1952). *Freedom and Reason* (Oxford, 1963).

HART, SAMUEL L., *A Treatise on Value* (New York, 1949).

HARTMAN, ROBERT S., *The Structure of Value* (Carbondale, 1967).

HILLIARD, ALBERT LEROY, *The Forms of Value: The Extension of a Hedonistic Axiology* (New York, 1950).

HOOK, SYDNEY, *Nature and Values* (New York, 1945).

JESSUP, BERTRAM E., *Relational Value Meanings* (Eugene, 1943).

JURY, G. S., *Value and Ethical Objectivity* (London, 1937).

KECSKEMETI, PAUL, *Meaning, Communication, and Value* (Chicago, 1952).

KRUSÉ, CORNELIUS, "Cognition and Value Reexamined." *The Journal of Philosophy*, vol. 34 (1937), pp. 225–234.

KUHN, HELMUT, "Fact and Value in Ethics." *Philosophy and Phenomenological Research*, vol. 2 (1942), pp. 501–510.

KURTZ, PAUL W., "Human Nature, Homeostasis, and Value." *Philosophy and Phenomenological Research*, vol. 17 (1956), pp. 36–55.

LADD, JOHN, "Value Judgments, Emotive Meaning, and Attitudes." *The Journal of Philosophy*, vol. 46 (1949), pp. 119–128.

LAIRD, JOHN, *The Idea of Value* (Cambridge, 1929).

LAMONT, WILLIAM DAWSON, *The Value Judgment* (Edinburgh, 1955).

LEPLEY, ROY, "The Dawn of Value Theory," *The Journal of Philosophy*, vol. 34 (1937), pp. 365–372. "The Verifiability of Different Kinds of Facts and Values," *Philosophy of Science*, vol. 7 (1940), pp. 464–475.

LEWIS, CLARENCE IRVING, *An Analysis of Knowledge and Valuation* (La Salle, 1946). *The Ground and Nature of the Right* (New York, 1955).

LEYS, WAYNE A. R., "Human Values in the Atomic Age." *Annals of the American Academy of Political and Social Science*, vol. 290 (1953), pp. 127–133.

LOSSKI, N. O., *Valeur et être* (London, 1936).

MACKENZIE, JOHN STUART, *Ultimate Values* (London, 1924). "Spiritual Values," *International Journal of Ethics*, vol. 33 (1923), pp. 248f. "Notes on the Theory of Value," *Mind*, N. S., vol. 4 (1895), pp. 425–449.

MARGENAU, HENRY, "The Scientific Basis of Value Theory," in A. H. Maslow (ed.), *New Knowledge in Human Values* (New York, 1958).

McCRACKEN, D. J., *Thinking and Valuing* (New York, 1950).

McGREAL, IAN, "A Naturalistic Analysis of Value Terms." *Philosophy and Phenomenological Research*, vol. 10 (1949), pp. 73–84.

McINTYRE, JAMES LEWIS, "Value Feelings and Judgments of Value." *Proceedings of the Aristotelian Society*, 1904–1905 (1905), pp. 53–73.

McKEON, RICHARD, "Conflicts of Values in a Community of Cultures." *The Journal of Philosophy*, vol. 47 (1950), pp. 197–210.

MONTAGUE, WILLIAM PEPPERILL, "The True, the Good, and the Beautiful from a Pragmatic Standpoint." *The Journal of Philosophy*, vol. 6 (1909), pp. 233–238.

MOORE, GEORGE EDWARD, *Principia Ethica* (Cambridge, 1903). "The Conception of Intrinsic Value," in *Philosophical Studies*, (London, 1922), pp. 253–275.

MORRIS, CHARLES W., "Axiology as the Science of Preferential Behavior," in R. Lepley (ed.), *Value: A Cooperative Inquiry* (New York, 1949), pp. 211–222. *Varieties of Human Value* (Chicago, 1956).

MORRIS, CHARLES W., and LYLE V. JONES, "Value Scales and Dimensions." *Journal of Abnormal and Social Psychology*, vol. 51 (1955), pp. 523–535.

NORTHROP, FILMER S. C., "Conflicts of Values in a Community of Cultures," *The Journal of Philosophy*, vol. 47 (1950), pp. 197–210. "Cultural Values," in A. L. Kroeber (ed.), *Anthropology Today*, (Chicago, 1952), pp. 668–681. "The Physical Sciences, Philosophy, and Human Values," in E. M. Wigner (ed.), *Physical Science and Human Values* (Princeton, 1947), pp. 78–113.

OSBORNE, HAROLD, *Foundations of the Philosophy of Value: An Examination of Value and Value Theories* (Cambridge, 1933).

PARKER, DEWITT H., "The Notion of Value," *The Philosophical Review*, vol. 38 (1929), pp. 303–325. "Value as Any Object of Any Interest," *Ethics*, vol. 40 (1930), pp. 465–495. *Human Values* (New York, 1931). "Reflections of the Crisis in Theory of Value. Part I: Mostly Critical," *Ethics*, vol. 56 (1946), pp. 193–207. *The Philosophy of Value* (Ann Arbor, 1957).

PAP, ARTHUR, "The Verifiability of Value Judgments." *Ethics*, vol. 56 (1946), pp. 178–185.

PARSONS, TALCOTT, and EDWARD A. SHILS, *Toward a General Theory of Action*, ed. by T. Parsons and E. A. Shils (Cambridge, Mass., 1951).

PEIRCE, CHARLES S., *Values in a Universe of Chance* (Stanford, 1958).

PEPPER, STEPHEN C., *The Equivocation of Value* (Berkeley, 1923; University of California Publications in Philosophy, vol. 4). *A Digest of Purposive Values* (Berkeley, 1947). *The Sources of Value* (Berkeley, 1958).

PERRY, CHARNER M., "Some Difficulties in Current Value Theory," *The Journal of Philosophy*, vol. 25 (1928), pp. 281–287. "Principles of Value and the Problem of Ethics," *Révue Internationale de Philosophie*, vol. 1 (1939), pp. 666–683.

PERRY, RALPH BARTON, "The Definition of Value," *The Journal of Philosophy*, vol. 11 (1914), pp. 141–162. "Religious Values," *The American Journal of Theology*, vol. 19 (1915), pp. 1–16. *General Theory of Value* (New York, 1926). "Value as an Objective Predicate," *The Journal of Philosophy*, vol. 28 (1931), pp. 477–484. *Realms of Value: A Critique of Human Civilization* (Cambridge, 1954).

PRALL, DAVID WRIGHT, *A Study in the Theory of Value* (California, 1921; University of California Publications in Philosophy, vol. 3, no. 2). "The Present Status of the Theory of Value," in G. Adams and J. Lowenberg (eds.), *Issues and Tendencies in Contemporary Philosophy* (Berkeley, 1923), pp. 77–103.

RASHDALL, HASTINGS, *The Theory of Good and Evil*. 2 vols. (Oxford, 1924).

REID, JOHN R., *A Theory of Value* (New York, 1938).

RICE, PHILIP BLAIR, "Toward a Syntax of Evaluation " *The Journal of Philosophy*, vol. 71 (1944), pp. 309–320.

ROSE, M. C., "Value Experience and the Means-Ends Continuum." *Ethics*, vol. 65 (1954), pp. 44–54.

ROSS, WILLIAM DAVID, *The Right and the Good* (Oxford, 1930).

SCHILLER, F. S. C., "Truth, Value, and Biology." *The Journal of Philosophy*, vol. 17 (1920), pp. 36–44.

SCHNEIDER, HERBERT W., "The Theory of Value." *The Journal of Philosophy*, vol. 14 (1917), pp. 141–157.

SCHUSTER, CYNTHIA A., "Rapprochement in Value Theory." *The Journal of Philosophy*, vol. 50 (1953), pp. 653–662.

SHELDON, WILLIAM HENRY, "An Empirical Definition of Value." *The Journal of Philosophy*, vol. 11 (1914), pp. 113–124.

SMITH, JAMES WARD, "Should the General Theory of Value Be Abandoned?" *Ethics*, vol. 57 (1947), pp. 274–288.

SORLEY, WILLIAM RITCHIE, "Value and Reality," in J. H. Muirhead (ed.), *Contemporary British Philosophy* (London, 1925).

STACE, WALTER TERENCE, *What Are Our Values?* (Lincoln, 1950). "Values in General," "Democratic Values," and "Why Do We Fail," in *Man Against Darkness, and Other Essays* (Pittsburgh, 1967).

STEVENSON, CHARLES L., "The Emotive Meaning of Ethical Terms," *Mind*, vol. 46

(1937), pp. 14–31. *Ethics and Language* (New Haven, 1944). *Facts and Values* (New Haven, 1963).

STORER, THOMAS, "The Logic of Value Imperatives." *Philosophy of Science*, vol. 13 (1946), pp. 25–40.

TAYLOR, HENRY OSBORN, *Human Values and Virtues* (New York, 1928).

TAYLOR, PAUL W., *Normative Discourse* (Englewood Cliffs, 1961).

URBAN, WILBUR M., "Definition and Analysis of the Conscienceness of Value," *Psychological Review*, vol. 14 (1907), pp. 1–36, 92–121. "The Individual and the Social Value Series," *The Philosophical Review*, vol. 11 (1902), pp. 125–138, 249–263. "What Is the Function of a General Theory of Value?", *The Philosophical Review*, vol. 17 (1908), pp. 42–62. *Valuation: Its Nature and Laws* (New York, 1909). "Knowledge of Value and the Value Judgment," *The Journal of Philosophy*, vol. 13 (1916), pp. 673–687. "Appreciation and Description and the Psychology of Values," *The Philosophical Review*, vol. 14 (1905), pp. 645–668. "Value and Existence," *The Journal of Philosophy*, vol. 13 (1916), pp. 449–465. "The Pragmatic Theory of Value," *The Journal of Philosophy*, vol. 14 (1917), pp. 701–706. "Ontological Problems of Value," *The Journal of Philosophy*, vol. 14 (1917), pp. 309–327. "Value Theory and Esthetics," *Philosophy Today* (Chicago and London, 1928), pp. 54–75. "The Present Situation in Axiology," *Révue Internationale de Philosophie*, vol. 1 (1939), pp. 609–621.

WARD, LEO RICHARD, *Philosophy of Value: An Essay in Constructive Criticism* (New York, 1930).

WELLS, DONALD A., "Phenomenology and Value Theory." *The Journal of Philosophy*, vol. 52 (1955), pp. 64–70.

WERKMEISTER, WILLIAM HENRY, "Problems of Value Theory," *Philosophy and Phenomenological Research*, vol. 12 (1952), pp. 495–512. "Prolegomena to Value Theory," *Philosophy and Phenomenological Research*, vol. 14 (1954), pp. 239–308.

WHITE, MORTON G., "Value and Obligation in Dewey and Lewis." *The Philosophical Review*, vol. 58 (1949), pp. 321–329.

WOOD, LEDGER, "Cognition and Moral Value." *The Journal of Philosophy*, vol. 34 (1937), pp. 234–239.

d. Other writers

ACKENHEIL, F., *Sollen, Werten, und Wollen* (Berlin, 1912).

ALTMANN, ALEXANDER, *Die Grundlagen der Wertethik* (Berlin, 1931).

ARÉVALO, JUAN JOSÉ, *La filosofia de los valores en la pedagogica* (Buenos Aires, 1939).

BEHN, SIGFRIED, *Philosophie der Werte* (Munich, 1930).

BENÉZÉ, GEORGES, *Valeur: Essai d'une théorie générale* (Paris, 1936).

BETTERMANN, ALBRECHT C., *Psychologie und Psychopathologie des Wertens* (Meisenheim am Glan, 1949).

CÉSARI, PAUL, *La Valeur* (Paris, 1957).

COHN, JONAS, *Wertwissenschaft*. 5 vols. (Stuttgart, 1932).

CROCE, BENEDETTO, "Über die sogenannten Werturtheile." *Logos*, vol. 1 (1910), pp. 71–82.

DUPRÉEL, EUGÈNE, *Equisse d'une philosophie des valeurs* (Paris, 1939).

EBERHARD, MARGARETE, *Das Werten: Der Nachweis einer höchsten Richtungsweisers als Lösung des Wertproblems* (Hamburg, 1950).

FRONDIZI, RISIERI, *What is Value? An Introduction to Axiology* (La Salle, 1963).

GOBLOT, EDMOND, *La Logique des jugements de valeur* (Paris, 1927).

GOEDECKE, PAUL, *Wahrheit und Wert* (Hildburghausen, 1927).

GOLDSCHEID, RUDOLF, *Entwicklungswerttheorie* (Leipzig, 1908).

GROOS, KARL, *Zur Psychologie und Metaphysik des Werterlebens* (Berlin, 1932).

GRUEHN, W., *Neuere Untersuchungen zum Wertproblem* (Dorpat, 1920).

GRÜHN, L. WERNER, *Das Werterlebnis* (Leipzig, 1924).

GUTWENGER, ENGELBERT (S. J.), *Wertphilosophie* (Innsbruck, 1952).

HESSEN, JOHANNES, *Wertphilosophie* (Paderbornn, 1937). *Lehrbuch der Philosophie*, vol. II, "Wertlehre" (Munich, 1948).

HEYDE, JOHANNES ERICH, *Grundlegung der Wertlehre* (Leipzig, 1916). *Wert: Eine philosophische Grundlegung* (Erfurt, 1926).

HONECKER, MARTIN, "Versuch einer gegenstands-theoretischen Grundlegung der allgemeinen Werttheorie." *Philosophische Jahrbücher*, vol. 36 (1923), pp. 125–131.

KERLER, HEINRICH DIETRICH, *Weltwille und Wertwille* (Leipzig, 1925).

KRAFT, VICTOR, *Die Grundlagen einer wissenschaftlichen Wertlehre* (Vienna, 1937; 2nd ed., 1951).

KREIBIG, J. C., *Psychologische Grundlegung eines Systems der Werttheorie* (Wien, 1902).

KRÜGER, FELIX, *Der Begriff des absolut Wertvollen als Grundbegriff der Moralphilosophie* (Leipzig, 1898).

LALANDE, ANDRÉ, *La Psychologie des jugements de valeur* (Cairo, 1929).

LARROYO, FRANCIS, *La filosofia de los valores* (Mexico City, 1942).

LAVELLE, LOUIS, *Traité des valeurs*. 2 vols. (Paris, 1951, 1955).

LESSING, THEODOR, *Studien zur Wertaxiomatik* (Berlin, 1908).

LORING, L. M., *Two Kinds of Values* (New York, 1966).

LUDEMANN, D. H., *Das Erkennen und die Werturteile* (Leipzig, 1909).

METZGER, WILHELM, "Objektwert und Subjektwert." *Logos*, vol. 4 (1913), pp. 85–99.

MÜLLER, MAX, *Über die Grundbegriffe der philosophische Wertlehre: Logische Studien über Wertbewusstsein und Wertgegenständlichkeit* (Halle, 1932).

MÜLLER-FREIENFELS, RICHARD, "Grundzüge einer neuen Wertlehre." *Annalen der Philosophie*, vol. 1 (1919), pp. 319–381.

NIETZSCHE, FRIEDERICH, *The Will to Power* (Subtitled "Versuch einer Umwertung aller Werte"). (Several translations and numerous editions.) *Beyond Good and Evil* and *The Genealogy of Morals* in W. Kaufmann (ed.), *Basic Writings of Nietzsche* (New York, 1966).

OFSTAD, HARALD, "Objectivity of Norms and Value-Judgments According to Recent Scandanavian Philosophy." *Philosophy and Phenomenological Research*, vol. 12 (1951), pp. 42–68.

ORESTANO, FRANCESCO, *I Valori Umani* (Milano, 1909).

ORTEGAY GASSET, JOSÉ, "Qué son los valores?" *Revista de Occidente*, vol. 4 (1913), pp. 39–70.

OSTWALD, WILHELM, *Die Philosophie der Werte* (Leipzig, 1913).

PICARD, MAY, *Values, Immediate and Contributory* (New York, 1920).

POLIN, RAYMOND, *La Création des valeurs* (Paris, 1944). *La Compréhension des valeurs* (Paris, 1945). *Du Lait, du mal du faux* (Paris, 1948).

PUCELLE, JEAN, *Études sur la valeur*. 3 vols. (Paris, 1957, 1959).

REDING, MARCEL, *Metaphysik der sittlichen Werte* (Düsseldorf, 1949).

RITSCHL, OTTO, *Über Werturtheile* (Freiburg im Breisgau and Leipzig, 1895).

RODHE, SVEN EDVARD, *Über die Möglichkeit einer Werteinteilung* (Lund, 1937).

ROMANO, PIETRO, *Ontologia del Valore* (Padova, 1949).

RUYER, RAYMOND, *La Monde des valeurs* (Paris, 1948). *La Philosophie de la valeur* (Paris, 1952).

SACHELLI, CALOGERO ANGELO, *Atto e Valore* (Firenze, 1938).

SCHWARZ, ERNEST, *Über den Wert, das Soll, und das richtige Werthalten* (Graz, 1934).

STERN, WILHELM, *Wertphilosophie* (Leipzig, 1924).

STÖRRIŃG, GUSTAV E., *Die Moderne ethische Wertphilosophie* (Leipzig, 1935).

TEGEN, EINAR, "The Basic Problem in the Theory of Value." *Theoria*, vol. 10 (1944), pp. 28–52.

THIELEN, DOROTHEA, *Kritik der Werttheorien* (Hamburg, 1937).

THYSSEN, JOHANNES, "Vom Ort der Werte." *Logos*, vol. 15 (1926), p. 309.

WEISS, KARL FRIEDERICH, *Studien zur allgemeinen Theorie des Wertes* (Tübingen, 1913).

WIDMER, G.-PH., *Les valeurs et leur signification* (Neuchatel, 1950). "La conscience des valeurs." *Studia Philosophica*, vol. 13 (1953), pp. 135–156.

WIEDERHOLD, KONRAD, *Wertbegriff und Wertphilosophie* (Berlin, 1920; Ergänzungsheft to Kanstudien).

2. Dimensions of value and value classification

ALBERT, ETHEL M., "The Classification of Values: A Method and Illustration." *American Anthropologist*, vol. 58 (1956), pp. 221–248.

DODD, STUART A., "On Classifying Human Values." *American Sociological Review*, vol. 16 (1951), pp. 645–653.

HILLIARD, ALBERT LEROY, *The Forms of Value—The Extension of a Hedonistic Axiology* (New York, 1950).

VON MERING, OTTO, *A Grammar of Human Values* (Pittsburgh, 1961).

MORRIS, CHARLES W., *Varieties of Human Value* (Chicago, 1956).

PEPPER, STEPHEN C., *A Digest of Purposive Values* (Berkeley, 1947). *The Sources of Value* (Berkeley, 1958).

PERRY, RALPH BARTON, *Realms of Value: A Critique of Human Civilization* (Cambridge, Mass.; 1959).

POLIN, RAYMOND, *Du Lait, du mal du faux* (Paris, 1948).

RICKERT, HEINRICH, *Lebenswerte und Kulturwerte: Vom System der Werte* in *Logos*, vol. 3 (1912) and vol. 4 (1913).

RODHE, SVEN EDVARD, *Über die Möglichkeit einer Werteinteilung* (Lund, 1937).

SPARSHOTT, F. E., *An Inquiry into Goodness* (Toronto, 1958).

TAYLOR, PAUL W., *Normative Discourse* (Englewood Cliffs, 1961).

VON WRIGHT, GEORG HENRIK, *The Varieties of Goodness* (London, 1963).

3. Rules of valuation and the measurement of value
(See also part IV.B.)

BAYLIS, CHARLES A., "Grading, Values, and Choice." *Mind*, vol. 67 (1958), pp. 485–501.

CARTER, ROY E., JR., "An Experiment in Value Measurement." *American Sociological Review*, vol. 21 (1956), pp. 156–163.

CLARKE, MARY E., *A Study in the Logic of Value* (London, 1929).

DODD, STUART C., "How to Measure Values." *University of Washington Research Studies*, vol. 18 (1950), pp. 163–168.

FRIEDMAN, BERTHA B., *Foundations of the Measurement of Values* (New York, 1946).

LAIRD, JOHN, *The Idea of Value* (Cambridge, 1929).

LESSING, THEODOR, "Studien zue Wertaxiomatik." *Archiv für Systematische Philosophie*, vol. 14 (1908).

RATHS, LOUIS, "Approaches to the Measurement of Values." *Educational Research Bulletin*, vol. 19 (1940), pp. 275–282, 309.

RESCHER, NICHOLAS, *Distributive Justice* (New York, 1966).

THURSTONE, LEWIS LEON, *The Measurement of Values* (Chicago, 1959).

URMSON, JOHN O., "On Grading." *Mind*, vol. 59 (1950), pp. 145–169.

WEINBERG, ALFRED, "Value Interpretation: The Methodological Formulation of a Psychological Discipline." *Ethics*, vol. 38 (1922–1928), pp. 44–57.

4. Value as qualitative or relational (Are values properties?)

BROAD, CHARLES D., "Is 'Goodness' the Name of a Simple, Non-Natural Quality?" *Proceedings of the Aristotelian Society*, vol. 34 (1933–34), pp. 249–268.

VON EHRENFELS, CHRISTIAN, "Von der Wertdefinition zum Motivationsgesetz." *Archiv für systematische Philosophie*, vol. 2 (1896), pp. 103–122.

HALL, EVERETT W., *What is Value?—An Essay in Philosophical Analysis* (New York, 1952).

HARTMANN, NICOLAI, *Ethics*, 3 vols. (London, 1932).

LAIRD, JOHN, *The Idea of Value* (Cambridge, 1929).

LEWIS, CLARENCE IRVING, *An Analysis of Knowledge and Valuation* (La Salle, 1946).

MOORE, GEORGE EDWARD, "The Conception of Intrinsic Value," in *Philosophical Studies* (London, 1922). *Principia Ethica* (Cambridge, 1903).

PERRY, RALPH BARTON, *General Theory of Value* (New York, 1926). "Value as an Objective Predicate," *The Journal of Philosophy*, vol. 28 (1931), pp. 477–484. *Realms of Value* (Cambridge, 1954).

ROSS, WILLIAM DAVID, *The Right and the Good* (Oxford, 1930). *The Foundations of Ethics* (Oxford, 1939).

SCHELER, MAX, "Der Formalisimus in der Ethik und die materiale Wertethik." *Jahrbuch für Philosophie und Phänomenologische Forschung*, vol. 1 (1913), vol. 2 (1916, 4th ed., Bern, 1954).

STEVENSON, CHARLES L., "The Emotive Meaning of Ethical Terms," *Mind*, vol. 44 (1937) pp. 14–31. *Ethics and Language* (New Haven, 1944). *Fact and Value* (New Haven, 1963).

TOULMIN, STEPHEN, *An Examination of The Place of Reason in Ethics* (Cambridge, 1958).

5. Value as objective or subjective (Are values relative?)

AYER, ALFRED JULIUS, *Language, Truth and Logic* (London, 1962). [*Against* objectivity of values.]

BAIER, KURT, *The Moral Point of View* (Ithaca, 1958).

Durkheim, Émile, "Jugements de valeur et jugements de réalité." *Révue de metaphysique et de morale*, vol. 19 (1911), pp. 437–453. [*Against* objectivity of values.]

von Ehrenfels, Christian., For references to the works in which Ehrenfels develops his position against the objectivity of values see Sec. III.A.1.b.

Ewing, A. C., "Subjectivism and Naturalism in Ethics." *Mind*, vol. 53 (1944), pp. 120–141.

von Fritz, Kurt, "Relative and Absolute Values," in R. N. Anshen (ed.), *Moral Principles of Action* (New York, 1952), pp. 94–121.

Frondizi, Risieri, *What is Value?—An Introduction to Axiology* (La Salle, 1963).

Hall, Everett W., *Our Knowledge of Fact and Value* (Chapel Hill, 1961).

Hare, Richard M., *The Language of Morals* (Oxford, 1952). [*Against* objectivity of values.]

Hartmann, Nicolai, *Ethics*, 3 vols., tr. by S. Coit (London, 1932). [*For* objectivity of values.]

Hilliard, Albert Leroy, *The Forms of Value—The Extension of a Hedonistic Axiology* (New York, 1950). [*Against* objectivity of values.]

Laird, John, *The Idea of Value* (Cambridge, 1929). [*For* objectivity of values.]

Meinong, Alexius. For references to the works in which Meinong develops his position for the objectivity of values see Sec. III.A.1.b.

Moore, George Edward, *Principia Ethica* (Cambridge, 1903). [*For* objectivity of values.]

Morris, Charles W., *Varieties of Human Value* (Chicago, 1956).

Parker, DeWitt H., *The Philosophy of Value* (Ann Arbor, 1957).

Perry, Ralph Barton. For references to the works in which Perry develops his position against the objectivity of values, see Sec. III.A.1.c.

Rapoport, Anatol, "How Relative are Values?" *Etc.*, vol. 8 (1951), pp. 180–192.

Scheler, Max, "Der Formalismus in der Ethik und die materiale Wertethik." *Jahrbuch für Philosophie und Phänomenologische Forschung*, vol. 1 (1913), vol. 2 (1916). [*For* objectivity of values.]

Smith, James Ward, "Senses of Subjectivism in Value Theory." *The Journal of Philosophy*, vol. 65 (1948), pp. 393–405.

Stevenson, Charles L., *Ethics and Language* (New Haven, 1944). [*Against* objectivity of values.]

Taylor, Paul W., *Normative Discourse* (Englewood Cliffs, 1961).

Urmson, John O., "On Grading." *Mind*, vol. 59 (1950), pp. 145–169. [*Against* objectivity of values.]

Westermarck, Edward, *Ethical Relativity* (New York, 1932). [*Against* objectivity of ethical values.]

B. Special spheres of value

1. Ethics

Note: This list concentrates upon works that provide bibliographic aids.

Abelson, Raziel, *Ethics and Metaethics* (New York, 1963).

Albert, Ethel M., and Clyde Kluckhohn, *A Selected Bibliography on Value, Ethics, and Esthetics* (Illinois, 1959).

Bagolini, Luigi, "Value Judgments in Ethics and in Law." *The Philosophical Quarterly*, vol. 1 (1951), pp. 423–432.

BROAD, CHARLES D., *Five Types of Ethical Theory* (London, 1930).

BRANDT, RICHARD B., *Ethical Theory* (Englewood Cliffs, 1959). [Furnishes many bibliographical data.]

EDWARDS, PAUL, *The Logic of Moral Discourse* (Glencoe, 1955).

EVERETT, WALTER GOODNOW, *Moral Values: A Study of the Principles of Conduct* (New York, 1918). *Moral Values* (New York, 1928).

FRANKENA, WILLIAM K., "Ethical Theory," in R. M. Chisholm, et al., *Philosophy*, (New York, 1964). [A survey of American work in ethics and value theory during 1930–1960. Includes a comprehensive bibliography.]

GARVIN, LUCIUS, *A Modern Introduction to Ethics* (New York, 1953).

HARTMANN, NICOLAI, *Ethics*, tr. by S. Coit, 3 vols. (London, 1932).

HILL, THOMAS ENGLISH, *Contemporary Ethical Theories* (New York, 1950). [Already somewhat behind the times as regards current developments, but useful for the bibliography of its period.]

HOSPERS, JOHN, *Human Conduct: An Introduction to the Problems of Ethics* (New York, 1961).

HOURANI, GEORGE F., *Ethical Value* (Ann Arbor, 1956).

KURTZ, PAUL W., *The Problems of Value Theory* (New York, 1952).

MARGOLIS, JOSEPH, *Contemporary Ethical Theory* (New York, 1966).

MELDEN, ABRAHAM IRVING, *Ethical Theories* (Englewood Cliffs, 1959).

MORRIS, CHARLES, *Paths of Life* (New York, 1956).

REININGER, ROBERT, *Wertphilosophie und Ethik* (Leipzig, 1939).

SELLARS, WILFRID, and JOHN HOSPERS, *Readings in Ethical Theory* (New York, 1952).

SESONSKE, ALEXANDER, *Value and Obligation: The Foundations of an Empiricist Ethical Theory* (Berkeley, 1957; University of California Publications in Philosophy, vol. 31, no. 1).

STOFER, HELLMUTH, *Über das Sittliche Werturtheil* (Basel, 1955).

STÖRRING, GUSTAV, *Die moderne ethische Wertphilosophie* (Leipzig, 1935).

2. Aesthetics

Note: This list focuses narrowly upon works that provide bibliographic aids. For the older literature of the subject see:

HAMMOND, WILLIAM A., *A Bibliography of Aesthetics and the Philosophy of the Fine Arts from 1900 to 1932* (New York, 1934).

ALBERT, ETHEL M., and CLYDE KLUCKHOHN, *A Select Bibliography on Values, Ethics, and Esthetics* (Illinois, 1959).

BEARDSLEY, MONROE C., *Aesthetics: Problems in the Philosophy of Criticism* (New York, 1958). [A textbook that has a good bibliography.]

COLEMAN, FRANCIS J., *Contemporary Studies in Aesthetics*, ed. by F. J. Coleman (New York, 1967).

ELTON, WILLIAM, *Aesthetics and Language*, ed. by W. Elton (Oxford, 1954).

HOSPERS, JOHN, *Meaning and Truth in the Arts* (Chapel Hill, 1946).

MARGOLIS, JOSEPH, *Philosophy Looks at the Arts*, ed. by J. Margolis (New York, 1962). "Recent Work in Aesthetics," *American Philosophical Quarterly*, vol. 2 (1965), pp. 182–192. [A survey with a good bibliography.] *The Language of Art and Art Criticism* (Detroit, 1965).

PEPPER, STEPHEN, *The Work of Art* (Bloomington, Indiana, 1955).

PRALL, DAVID, *Aesthetic Analysis* (New York, 1936).

STOLNITZ, JEROME, *Aesthetics and Philosophy of Art Criticism* (Cambridge, Mass., 1960).

URBAN, WILBUR M., "Value Theory and Esthetics," in E. L. Schaub (ed.), *Philosophy Today* (Chicago and London, 1928), pp. 54–75. Cf. two papers of the same title in *The Monist*, vol. 36 (1936), pp. 605–626.

WARD, LEO RICHARD, *Philosophy of Value: An Essay in Constructive Criticism* (New York, 1930).

WEISS, PAUL, *The World of Art* (Carbondale, Illinois, 1961).

WEITZ, MORRIS, *Philosophy of the Arts* (Cambridge, Mass., 1950).

WHITMORE, CHARLES H., "The Scale of Esthetic Values." *The Journal of Philosophy*, vol. 21 (1924), pp. 617–631.

3. Social and political theory

Note: For a somewhat more extensive bibliography of this area see:

ALBERT, ETHEL M., and CLYDE KLUCKHOHN, *A Bibliography on Values, Ethics, and Esthetics* (Glencoe, 1959).

ADLER, MORTIMER, *The Idea of Freedom* (Garden City, 1958).

BARKER, ERNEST, *Principles of Social and Political Theory* (New York, 1951).

BAYLIFF, RUSSELL E. et al., *Values and Policy in American Society* (Dubuque, 1954).

BERN, S. I., and R. S. PETERS, *Social Principles and the Democratic State* (London, 1959).

BRANDT, RICHARD, *Social Justice* (Englewood Cliffs, 1962).

BRAYBROOKE, DAVID, "Let Needs Diminish that Preferences May Prosper," in *Studies in Moral Philosophy* (Oxford, 1968), *American Philosophical Quarterly*, Monograph No. 1.

BRAYBROOKE, DAVID, and CHARLES E. LINDBLOM, *A Strategy of Decision* (New York, 1963).

BUCHANAN, J. M., and G. TULLOCH, *The Calculus of Consent* (Ann Arbor, 1962).

CARRITT, E. F., *Ethical and Political Thinking* (Oxford, 1947). *Morals and Politics* (Oxford, 1958).

CARVER, THOMAS NIXON, *Essays in Social Justice* (Cambridge, Mass., 1915).

COOK, THOMAS I., "Politics, Sociology and Values." *Journal of Social Philosophy*, vol. 6 (1940), pp. 35–46.

DAHL, ROBERT A., and CHARLES E. LINDBLOM, *Politics, Economics, and Welfare* (New York, 1953).

DEXTER, LEWIS A., "Political Processes and Judgments of Value." *American Political Science Review*, vol. 40 (1946), pp. 294–301.

DIETZE, GOTTFRIED, *In Defense of Property* (Chicago, 1963).

DROR, YEHESHIL, "Values and the Law." *Antioch Review*, vol. 17 (1957–58), pp. 440–454.

FAIDHERBE, A. J., *La Justice distributive* (Paris, 1934).

FRIEDRICH, CARL J., *The Public Interest*, Nomos V, ed. by Carl Friedrich (New York, 1962). *Justice*, Nomos VI, ed. by Carl Friedrich (New York, 1963).

GALBRAITH, JOHN KENNETH, *The Affluent Society* (New York, 1958).

HOBHOUSE, L. T., *The Elements of Social Justice* (New York, 1922).

HOBSON, JOHN A., *Economics and Ethics: A Study in Social Values* (New York, 1929).

HOLCOMBE, ARTHUR N., *Human Rights in the Modern World* (New York, 1948).

DE JOUVENEL, BERTRAND, *Sovereignty: An Inquiry into the Political Good* (Chicago, 1957).

KELSEN, HANS, *What Is Justice?* (Berkeley, 1957).

LASKI, HAROLD J., *A Grammar of Politics* (London, 1925).

LERNER, DANIEL, and HAROLD D. LASSWELL, *The Policy Sciences* (Stanford, 1951).

LIPPMANN, WALTER, *An Inquiry into the Principles of the Good Society* (Boston, 1937). *Essays in the Public Philosophy* (Boston, 1955).

MARITAIN, JACQUES, *Man and the State* (Chicago, 1951).

VON MERING, OTTO, *A Grammar of Human Values* (Pittsburgh, 1961).

PARSONS, TALCOTT, *Structure of Social Action* (Glencoe, 1961).

PENNOCK, J. ROLAND, "Reason, Value Theory, and the Theory of Democracy," *American Political Science Review*, vol. 38 (1944), pp. 855–875. "Political Science and Political Philosophy," *American Political Science Review*, vol. 45 (1951), pp. 1081–1085.

PERELMAN, CHAIM, *Justice et Raison* (Brussels, 1963). *Justice* (New York, 1967).

RAHL, ROBERT A., and CHARLES E. LINDBLOM, *Politics, Economics and Welfare* (New York, 1953).

RAPHAEL, DAVID DAICHES, "Equality and Equity." *Philosophy*, vol. 21 (1946), pp. 118–132.

RAWLS, JOHN, "Justice as Fairness." *The Philosophical Review*, vol. 67 (1958), pp. 164–194.

RESCHER, NICHOLAS, *Distributive Justice* (New York, 1966).

RYAN, JOHN A., *Distributive Justice* (New York, 1916; 3rd ed., 1942).

RYAN, JOHN A., and F. B. BOLAND, *Catholic Principles of Politics* (New York, 1940).

SABINE, GEORGE H., *History of Political Theory* (New York, 1937).

SIDGWICK, HENRY, *Elements of Politics* (London, 1890; 2nd ed., 1897).

TAWNEY, R. H., *Equality* (London, 1931; 4th ed., 1952).

THOMSON, DAVID, *Equality* (Cambridge, 1949).

DEL VECCHIO, GIORGIO, *Justice* (Edinburgh, 1952).

WARD, L. R., *Philosophy of Value* (New York, 1930). [Has a short section on social value in the bibliography.]

WOLLHEIM, RICHARD, and ISAIAH BERLIN, Symposium: "Equality." *Proceedings of the Aristotelian Society*, vol. 56 (1955–1956), pp. 281–326.

4. Religion

ALLPORT, GORDON, *The Individual and His Religion* (New York, 1950).

BAUM, GREGORY, "Scriptural Faith and Cultural Values," in T. E. H. Reid (ed.), *Values in Conflict* (Toronto, 1963).

BONHOEFFER, DIETRICH, *Ethics*, English tr. by E. Bethge (New York, 1955).

BOURKE, VERNON J., *Ethics* (New York, 1951).

BRUNNER, EMIL, *The Divine Imperative* (Philadelphia, 1957).

BYERS, ROBERT PAYTON, *Transcendental Values* (Boston, 1925).

CLARK, W. H., "The Psychology of Religious Values." *Personality*, vol. 1 (1950), pp. 45–62.

DURKHEIM, ÉMILE, *The Elementary Forms of the Religious Life*, tr. by J. W. Swain (London, 1903).

FICHTER, JOSEPH H., "Religious Values and the Social Personality." *American Catholic Sociological Review*, vol. 17 (1956), pp. 100–116.

FLETCHER, JOSEPH FRANCIS, *Situation Ethics* (Philadelphia, 1966). *Moral Responsibility* (Philadelphia, 1967).

MÜNSTERBERG, HUGO, *The Eternal Values* (Boston, 1909).

NIEBUHR, H. RICHARD, "The Center of Value," in R. Anshen (ed.), *Moral Principles of Action* (New York, 1952). *Faith and Ethics* (New York, 1965).

NIEBUHR, REINHOLD, *An Interpretation of Christian Ethics* (New York, 1935). *Moral Man and Immoral Society* (New York, 1934).

PERRY, RALPH BARTON, "Religious Values." *The American Journal of Theology*, vol. 19 (1915), pp. 1–16.

RAMSEY, PAUL, *Basic Christian Ethics* (New York, 1952).

RASHDALL, HASTINGS, *Conscience and Christ* (London, 1933).

SORLEY, W. R., *Moral Values and the Idea of God* (Cambridge, 1918).

TAWNEY, R. H., *Religion and the Rise of Capitalism* (New York, 1926).

THOMAS, GEORGE F., *Christian Ethics and Moral Philosophy* (New York, 1955).

TILLICH, PAUL, *The Courage to Be* (New Haven, 1952). "Is a Science of Human Values Possible?" in A. H. Maslow (ed.), *New Knowledge in Human Values* (New York, 1958). *Morality and Beyond* (New York, 1963).

TROELTSCH, ERNST, *The Social Teachings of the Christian Churches*, tr. by O. Wyon (London, 1931).

WARD, LEO RICHARD, *Philosophy of Value* (New York, 1930).

WEBER, MAX, *The Protestant Ethic and the Rise of Capitalism*, tr. by Talcott Parsons (New York, 1930).

WILLIAMS, ROBIN M., "Religion, Value-Orientations, and Intergroup Conflict." *The Journal of Social Issues*, vol. 12 (1956), pp. 12–20.

C. The theory of practical reasoning

1. Aristotle

ARISTOTLE, *Ethica Nicomachea* Bk. III. Chaps. 1–5; Bk. VI, Chaps. 2, 5, 7–12.

MICHELAKIS, E. M., *Aristotle's Theory of Practical Principles* (Athens, 1961).

ROSS, W. D., *Aristotle* (5th ed., London, 1949), Chap. 7.

SCHILLER, F. S. C., "Aristotle and the Practical Syllogism." *The Journal of Philosophy*, vol. 14 (1917), pp. 645–653.

2. Kant

KANT, IMMANUEL, *Critique of Practical Reason* (New York, 1956).

PATON, H. J., *In Defence of Reason* (London, 1951). [Especially the chapter "Can Reason Be Practical?" See also the author's Henrietta Hertz Lecture of the same title in *Proceedings of the British Academy*, vol. 29 (1943), as well as the review thereof by R. Jackson in *Philosophy*, vol. 20 (1945), pp. 263–265.]

3. Recent discussions

ANSCOMBE, G. E. M., *Intention* (Oxford, 1958). [See especially the account of practical knowledge on pp. 57–61.]

BAIER, KURT, *The Moral Point of View* (Ithaca, 1958).

CHISHOLM, RODERICK, "The Descriptive Element in the Concept of Action." *The Journal of Philosophy*, vol. 61 (1964), pp. 613–625.

EDGLEY, ROY, "Practical Reason." *Mind*, vol. 294 (1965), pp. 174–191.

GAUTHIER, DAVID P., *Practical Reasoning* (Oxford, 1964). [Reviewed by J. Bennett in *Mind*, vol. 74 (1965), pp. 116–125.]

HALL, EVERETT W., "Practical Reasons and the Deadlock in Ethics." *Mind*, vol. 44 (1955), pp. 319–332.

HARE, R. M., *The Language of Morals* (Oxford, 1952).

JACKSON, REGINALD, "Practical Reason." *Philosophy*, vol. 17 (1942), pp. 351–367. [Primarily an analysis of the concept of "validity of choice."]

KENNY, A. J. P., "Practical Inference." *Analysis*, vol. 26 (1965–1966), pp. 65 ff.

MANFRED, MORITZ, "Der praktische Syllogismus und das juristische Denken." *Theoria*, vol. 20 (1954), pp. 78–127.

MOTHERSILL, MARY, "Anscombe's Account of the Practical Syllogism." *The Philosophical Review*, vol. 71 (1962), pp. 448–461.

MURPHY, ARTHUR E., *The Theory of Practical Reason* (LaSalle, 1964).

SELLARS, WILFRID, "Imperatives, Intentions, and the Logic of 'Ought,'" in H. Castaneda and G. Nakhnikian (eds.), *Morality and the Language of Conduct* (Detroit, 1963), pp. 159–218.

TOULMIN, STEPHEN, *The Place of Reason in Ethics* (Cambridge, 1950).

VON WRIGHT, G. H., *The Varieties of Goodness* (London, 1962). "Practical Inference." *The Philosophical Review*, vol. 72 (1963), pp. 159–179.

D. Deontic logic and the theory of norms

For a general introduction to this problem area, including a comprehensive bibliography of its literature see:

ANDERSON, A. R., "The Formal Analysis of Normative Systems," in N. Rescher (ed.), *The Logic of Decision and Action* (Pittsburgh, 1967), pp. 147–213.

A few contributions too recent for inclusion here are:

HANSON, W. H., "Semantics for Deontic Logic." *Logique et Analyse*, vol. 8 (1965), pp. 177–190.

HUND, WILLIAM B., "The Distinction Between Ought-to-Be and Ought-to-Do." *The New Scholasticism*, vol. 41 (1967), pp. 343–355.

RESCHER, NICHOLAS, "Semantic Foundations for Conditional Permission." *Philosophical Studies*, vol. 18 (1967), pp. 56–61.

ROBISON, JOHN, "Further Difficulties for Conditional Permission in Deontic Logic." *Philosophical Studies*, vol. 18 (1967), pp. 27–30.

VON WRIGHT, GEORG HENRIK, "Deontic Logics." *American Philosophical Quarterly*, vol. 4 (1967), pp. 136–143.

IV. Scientific approaches to value

A. The Psycho-biology of valuation

For a comprehensive bibliography of this domain see:

DUKES, WILLIAM, "Psychological Studies of Values." *The Psychological Bulletin*, vol. 52 (1955), pp. 24–50.

For the Allport-Vernon Test, which has dominated work in this area, see in particular:

ALLPORT, GORDON W., PHILIP E. VERNON, and GARDNER LINDZEY, *Study of Values* (New York, 1931; revised ed., Boston, 1951). *Study of Values: Manual of Directions for the Study of Values* (Cambridge, Mass., 1951).

BROGDEN, HUBERT E., "The Primary Personal Values Measured by the Allport-Vernon Test, 'A Study of Values'." *Psychological Monographs*, vol. 66 (1952), no. 16.

CANTRIL, HADLEY, and GORDON ALLPORT, "Recent Applications of the Study of Values." *Journal of Abnormal and Social Psychology*, vol. 28 (1933), pp. 259–273.

DUFFY, ELIZABETH, "A Critical Review of Investigations Employing the Allport-Vernon Study of Values and Other Tests of Evaluative Attitude." *The Psychological Bulletin*, vol. 37 (1940), pp. 597–612.

GAGE, N. L., "Review of Allport-Vernon Literature." *Fifth Mental Measurements Yearbook* (New Jersey, 1959), pp. 199–202.

HARRIS, DANIEL, "Group Differences in Values Within a University." *Journal of Abnormal and Social Psychology*, vol. 29 (1934), pp. 95–102.

HARTMANN, GEORGE W., "Six Differences in Valuational Attitudes," *Journal of Social Psychology*, vol. 5 (1934), pp. 106–112. "Value as the Unifying Concept of the Social Sciences," *Journal of Social Psychology*, vol. 10 (1939), pp. 563–575.

McGINNIES, ELLIOTT M., "Personal Values as Determinants of Word Association." *Journal of Abnormal and Social Psychology*, vol. 45 (1950), pp. 28–36.

MEEHL, PAUL, "Review of AVL Literature." *Third Mental Measurements Yearbook*, (New Brunswick, 1949).

SCHAFER, BENJAMIN R., "The Validity and Utility of the Allport-Vernon Study of Values Test." *Journal of Abnormal and Social Psychology*, vol. 30 (1936), pp. 419–422.

SHORR, J. E., "The Development of a Test to Measure the Intensity of Values." *Journal of Educational Psychology*, vol. 44 (1953), pp. 266–274.

SPOERL, DOROTHY TILDEN, "The Values of the Post-War College Student." *Journal of Social Psychology*, vol. 35 (1952), pp. 217–225.

VERNON, PHILIP E., and GORDON W. ALLPORT, "A Test for Personal Values." *Journal of Abnormal and Social Psychology*, vol. 26 (1931), pp. 231–248.

WHITELY, PAUL L., "A Study of the Allport-Vernon Test for Personal Values," *Journal of Abnormal and Social Psychology*, vol. 28 (1933), pp. 6–13. "The Constancy of Personal Values," *Journal of Abnormal and Social Psychology*, vol. 33 (1938), pp. 405–408.

Some other works in this area are:

AUERBACH, J. G., "Value Changes in Therapy." *Personality*, vol. 1 (1950), pp. 63–67.

BEEBE-CENTER, J. G., *The Psychology of Pleasantness and Unpleasantness* (New York, 1932).

BRICKNER, RICHARD M., "Man and His Values Considered Neurologically." *The Journal of Philosophy*, vol. 41 (1944), pp. 225–243.

CREEGAN, ROBERT F., "Recent Trends in the Psychology of Values," in A. A. Roback (ed.), *Present-Day Psychology* (New York, 1955), pp. 949–960.

DEMBO, TAMARA, *Investigation of Concrete Psychological Value Systems* (Washington, 1953; Report of the U. S. Public Health Service, Institute for Mental Health).

EHRLE, GERTRUD, *Aus dem Werterleben des Kleinkindes* (Münster in Westfalen, 1930).

GRAHAM, JAMES L., "Some Attitudes Towards Values." *Journal of Social Psychology*, vol. 12 (1940), pp. 405–414.

HAERING, THEODOR, "Untersuchungen zur Psychologie der Wertung." *Archiv für die gesammte Psychologie*, vol. 26/27 (1913), pp. 285–366.

HARDING, D. W., *Social Psychology and Individual Values* (London, 1953).

HARDING, LOWRY W., "A Value-Type Generalizations Test; A Value-Type Problemmaire," *Journal of Social Psychology*, vol. 19 (1944), pp. 53–79, 115–144. "Experimental Comparisons Between Generalizations and Problems as Indices of Value," *Journal of General Psychology*, vol. 38 (1948), pp. 31–50.

KELLY, E. LOWELL, "Interest-Values Inventory," in O. K. Buros (ed.), *The Third Mental Measurements Yearbook* (New Brunswick, 1949), pp. 53–54.

LALANDE, ANDRÉ, *La Psychologie des jugements de valeur* (Cairo, 1929).

LURIE, WALTER A., "A Study of Spranger's Value-Types by the Method of Factor Analysis." *Journal of Social Psychology*, vol. 8 (1937), pp. 17–37.

MILLER, DANIEL R., and MAX C. HUTT, "Value Interiorizations and Personality Development." *The Journal of Social Issues*, vol. 5 (1949), pp. 2–30.

MULLAHY, PATRICK, "Values, Scientific Method, and Psychoanalysis." *Psychiatry*, vol. 6 (1943), pp. 139–146.

MULLER, H. J., "Human Values in Relation to Evolution." *Science*, vol. 127 (1958), pp. 625–629.

PIAGET, JEAN, *Le jugement morale chez l'enfant* (Paris, 1932). Tr. as *The Moral Judgment of the Child* (New York, 1929).

RENDA, ANTONIO, *Theoria psicologica dei valori* (Rome, 1920).

ROSENTHAL, DAVID, "The Selection of Stimulus Words for Value." *Journal of Abnormal and Social Psychology*, vol. 50 (1955), pp. 403–404.

SNYGG, DONALD, "The Psychological Basis of Human Values," in A. D. Ward (ed.), *Goals of Economic Life* (New York, 1953), pp. 335–364.

STÖRRING, GUSTAV E., "Experimentelle Untersuchungen über das Werterlebnis." *Archiv für die gesamte Psychologie*, vol. 73 (1929), pp. 129–216.

THORNDIKE, EDWARD L., "The Value of Reported Likes and Dislikes for Various Experiences and Attitudes or Indications of Personal Traits," *Journal of Applied Psychology*, vol. 20 (1936), pp. 285–313. "Individual Differences in Valuation," *Journal of Abnormal and Social Psychology*, vol. 33 (1938), pp. 71–85.

THURSTONE, L. L., "The Measurement of Values." *Psychological Review*, vol. 61 (1954), pp. 47–58.

TROW, WILLIAM C., "The Value Concept in Educational Psychology." *Journal of Educational Psychology*, vol. 44 (1953), pp. 449–462.

URBAN, WILBUR MARSHALL, "Recent Tendencies in the Psychological Theory of Values." *Psychological Bulletin*, vol. 4 (1905), pp. 65–72.

VAN DUSEN, ALBERT C., STAN WIMBERLY, and CHARLES L. MOSIER, "Standardization of a Values Inventory." *Journal of Educational Psychology*, vol. 30 (1939), pp. 52–62.

WHITE, RALPH K., "Value Analysis: A Quantitative Method for Describing Qualitative Data," *Journal of Social Psychology*, vol. 19 (1944), pp. 351–358. *Value Analysis: The Nature and Use of its Methods* (Glen Gardner, N. J., 1951).

WOLFF, WERNER, *Values and Personality: An Existential Psychology of Crisis* (New York, 1950).

WOODRUFF, ASAHEL D., "Personal Values and the Direction of Behavior." *The School Review*, vol. 50 (1942), pp. 32–42.

B. **Anthropological and sociological studies**

1. **Comparative and general studies**
   Note: For a considerably more extensive bibliography of this area see:

ALBERT, ETHEL M., and CLYDE KLUCKHOHN, *A Selected Bibliography on Values, Ethics and Esthetics* (Glencoe, 1959).

ADLER, FRANZ, "The Value Concept in Sociology." *American Journal of Sociology*, vol. 62 (1956), pp. 272–279.

ANDERSON, ALAN ROSS, and OMAR K. MOORE, "The Formal Analysis of Normative Concepts." *American Sociological Review*, vol. 22 (1957), pp. 9–17.

BARTON, ALLEN, "Measuring the Values of Individuals." *Review of Recent Research Bearing on Religious and Character Formation* (Research Supplement to *Religious Education*, July–August, 1962).

BECKER, HOWARD, "Supreme Values and the Sociologist," *American Sociological Review*, vol. 6 (1941), pp. 155–172. *Through Values to Social Interpretation* (Durham, 1950).

BELSHAW, CYRIL S., "The Identification of Values in Anthropology." *American Journal of Sociology*, vol. 64 (1959), pp. 555–562.

BENEDICT, RUTH, "Configurations of Culture in North America," *American Anthropologist*, vol. 34 (1932), pp. 1–27. *Patterns of Culture* (New York, 1934).

BIDNEY, DAVID, "The Concept of Value in Modern Anthropology," in *idem* (ed.), *Anthropology Today* (Chicago, 1953), pp. 682–699.

BOUGLÉ, C., *L'Évolution des valeurs* (Paris, 1922). Tr. by H. S. Sellars as *The Evolution of Values* (New York, 1926).

BURGESS, ERNEST W., "Values and Sociological Research." *Social Problems*, vol. 2 (1954), pp. 16–20.

CARTER, ROY E., "An Experiment in Value Measurement." *American Sociological Review*, vol. 21 (1956), pp. 156–163.

CASE, CLARENCE MARSH, "The Value Concept in Sociology and Related Fields." *Sociology and Social Research*, vol. 23 (1939), pp. 403–430. *Essays in Social Values* (Los Angeles, 1944).

CATTON, WILLIAM R., JR., "Exploring Techniques for Measuring Human Values," *American Sociological Review*, vol. 19 (1954), pp. 49–55. "A Retest of the Measurability of Certain Human Values," *American Sociological Review*, vol. 21 (1956), pp. 357–359. "A Theory of Value," *American Sociological Review*, vol. 24 (1959), pp. 310–317.

COLLIER, JOHN, "Values and the Introduction of Change." *Merrill-Palmer Quarterly*, vol. 1 (1955), pp. 148–157.

DAHLKE, OTTO, *Values in Culture and Classroom: A Study of the Sociology of the School* (New York, 1958).

EASTON, DAVID, "Shifting Images of Social Science and Values." *Antioch Review*, vol. 15 (1955), pp. 3–18.

FALLDING, HAROLD, "A Proposal for the Empirical Study of Values." *American Sociological Review*, vol. 30 (1965), pp. 223–233.

FIRTH, RAYMOND, "The Study of Values by Social Anthropologists." *Man*, vol. 53 (1953), pp. 146–153.

GEIGER, GEORGE R., "Values and the Social Sciences." *The Journal of Social Issues*, vol. 6 (1950), pp. 8–16.

GEIGER, THEODORE, "Evaluational Nihilism." *Acta Sociologica*, vol. 1 (1955), pp. 18–25.

GOLDSCHMIDT, WALTER, "Values and the Field of Comparative Sociology." *American Sociological Review*, vol. 18 (1953), pp. 287–293.

GUTH, WILLIAM D., and RENATO TAGIURI, "Personal Values and Corporate Strategy." *Harvard Business Review*, vol. 43 (1965), pp. 123–132.

HARDING, D. W., *Social Psychology and Individual Values* (London, 1953).

HART, HARWELL, "A Reliable Scale of Value Judgments." *American Sociological Review*, vol. 10 (1945), pp. 473–481.

HERSKOVITS, MELVILLE J., "On the Values in Culture," *Scientific Monthly*, vol. 54 (1942), pp. 557–560. "Tender and Tough Minded Anthropology and the Study of Values in Culture," *South-Western Journal of Anthropology*, vol. 7 (1951), pp. 22–31.

HIMES, JOSEPH S., "Value Analysis in the Theory of Social Problems." *Social Forces*, vol. 33 (1955), pp. 259–262.

HYMAN, HERBERT H., "The Value Systems of Different Classes," in R. Bendix and S. M. Lipset (eds.), *Class, Status, and Power* (Glencoe, 1953).

INKELES, ALEX, "Industrial Man: The Relation of Status to Experience, Perception, and Value." *The American Journal of Sociology*, vol. 66 (1960), pp. 1–31.

KLUCKHOHN, CLYDE M., "Values and Value Orientations in the Theory of Action," in T. Parsons and E. A. Shils (eds.), *Toward a General Theory of Action* (Cambridge, Mass., 1951). "A Comparative Study of Values in Five Cultures," in E. Z. Vogt (ed.), *Navaho Veterans: A Study of Changing Values* (Cambridge, Mass., 1951; Publications of the Peabody Museum of Harvard University, vol. 41, no. 1). "Universal Values and Anthropological Relativism," in *idem, Modern Education and Human Values* (Pittsburgh, 1952), pp. 87–112. "Ethical Relativity," *The Journal of Philosophy*, vol. 52 (1955), pp. 663–677. "Toward a Comparison of Value-Emphases in Different Cultures," in L. D. White (ed.), *The State of the Social Sciences* (Chicago, 1956), pp. 116–132. "The Scientific Study of Values and Contemporary Civilization," *Proceedings of the American Philosophical Society*, vol. 102 (1958), pp. 469–476.

KLUCKHOHN, FLORENCE R., "Dominant and Variant Value-Orientations," in C. Kluckhohn, H. Murray, and D. Schneider (eds.), *Personality in Nature, Culture, and Society* (New York, 1953), pp. 342–357. "Value Orientations," in R. R. Grinker (ed.), *Toward a Unified Theory of Human Behavior* (New York, 1956). *Variations in Value Orientations* (Evanston, 1961).

KOLB, WILSON L., "The Changing Prominence of Values in Modern Sociological Theory," in H. Becker and A. Boskoff (eds.), *Modern Sociological Theory*, (New York, 1957).

KROEBER, ALFRED L., "Values as a Subject of Natural Science Inquiry." *Proceedings of the National Academy of Sciences*, vol. 35 (1949), pp. 261–264.

LEWIN, KURT, and PAUL GRABLE, "Conduct, Knowledge, and Acceptance of New Values." *The Journal of Social Issues*, vol. 1 (1945), pp. 53–64.

LINTON, RALPH, "The Problem of Universal Values," in R. F. Spencer (ed.), *Method and Perspective in Anthropology* (Minneapolis, 1954).

LIPSET, SEYMOUR, "The Value Patterns of Democracy: A Case Study in Comparative Analysis." *American Sociological Review*, vol. 28 (1963), pp. 515–531.

MASLOW, ABRAHAM, *New Knowledge in Human Values*, ed. by A. Maslow (New York, 1959).

von Mering, Otto, *A Grammar of Human Values* (Pittsburgh, 1961).

Miller, David L., "Norms, Values, and the Social Sciences." *Southwestern Social Science Quarterly*, vol. 32 (1951), pp. 132–149.

Mitchell, E. T., "Values, Valuing, and Evaluation," in R. Lepley (ed.), *Value: A Comparative Inquiry* (New York, 1949), pp. 190–210.

Mogar, Robert E., "Value Orientations of College Students: Preliminary Data and Review of the Literature." *Psychological Reports*, vol. 15 (1964), pp. 739–770.

Mukerjee, Radhakamal, *The Social Structure of Values* (London, 1953). "The Sociology of Values," *Sociology and Social Research*, vol. 31 (1946), pp. 101–109.

Myrdal, Gunnar, *Value in Social Theory* (New York, 1958).

Parsons, Talcott, "The Place of Ultimate Values in Sociological Theory," *Ethics*, vol. 45 (1935), p. 285. "Evolutionary Universals in Society," *American Sociological Review*, vol. 29 (1964), pp. 339–357.

Parsons, Talcott, and Edward A. Shils, "Values, Motives, and Systems of Action," in T. Parsons and E. A. Shils, (eds.), *Toward a General Theory of Action* (Cambridge, Mass., 1951).

Partridge, P. H., "Value Judgments and the Social Sciences." *Australian Journal of Politics and History*, vol. 1 (1956), pp. 210–222.

Rettig, Salomon, "Changes in Moral Values as a Function of Adult Socialization," *Social Problems*, vol. 7 (1959), pp. 117–125. "Moral Value Structure and Social Class," *Sociometry*, vol. 24 (1961).

Riesman, David, "Values in Context." *American Scholar*, vol. 22 (1952), pp. 29–39.

Rose, Arnold M., "Values in Social Research," in *idem*, *Theory and Method in the Social Sciences* (Minneapolis, 1954). "Sociology and the Study of Values," *British Journal of Sociology*, vol. 7 (1956), pp. 1–17.

Roshwald, M., "Value-Judgments in the Social Sciences." *British Journal for the Philosophy of Science*, vol. 6 (1955), pp. 186–208.

Schellenberg, James, "Social Choice and Similarity of Personal Values." *Sociology and Social Research*, vol. 41 (1957), pp. 270–273.

Schwarzweller, Harry, "Value Orientations in Educational and Occupational Choices," *Rural Sociology*, vol. 24 (1959), pp. 246–256. "Values and Occupational Choice," *Social Forces*, vol. 39 (1960), pp. 126–235.

Scott, William A., "Factors Affecting the Learning of Personal Values Through Social Reinforcement," *American Psychologist*, vol. 11 (1956), pp. 407–408. "Empirical Assessment of Values and Ideologies," *American Sociological Review*, vol. 24 (1957), pp. 299–310.

Seeley, John, Alexander Sim, and Elizabeth Loosley, "Differentiation of Values in a Modern Community." *The Family*, (New York, 1960).

Siegel, Bernard J., "Currents of Anthropological Theory and Value Concepts." *South-Western Journal of Anthropology*, vol. 4 (1948), pp. 199–210.

Spranger, Edward, *Types of Men* (Halle, 1928).

Tagiuri, Renato, "Value Orientations and the Relationships of Managers and Scientists." *Administrative Science Quarterly*, vol. 9 (1965), pp. 39–51.

Tiryakian, Edward A., *Sociological Theory, Values and Sociological Change*, ed. by E. Tiryakian (New York, 1963).

Tolmain, Edward C., "Value Standards, Pattern Variables, Social Roles, Personality," in T. Parsons and E. A. Shils (eds.), *Toward A General Theory of Action* (Cambridge, Mass.; 1951), pp. 343–354.

TURNER, RALPH H., "The Quest for Universals in Sociological Research," *American Sociological Review*, vol. 18 (1953), pp. 604–611. "Value Conflict in Social Disorganization," *Sociology and Social Research*, vol. 38 (1954), pp. 301–308.

VEROFF, JOSEPH, and M. R. B. KLINGER, "Cross-Cultural Dimensions." *Personnel and Guidance Journal*, vol. 42 (1964), pp. 899–903.

VOGT, EVON Z., and JOHN M. ROBERTS, "A Study of Values." *The Scientific American*, vol. 195 (1956), pp. 25–31.

VOGT, EVON Z., and THOMAS F. O'DEA, "A Comparative Study of the Role of Values in Social Action in Two Southwestern Communities." *American Sociological Review*, vol. 18 (1953), pp. 645–654.

WARREN, ROLAND L., "Philosophy and Social Science in the Field of Values." *The Journal of Philosophy*, vol. 38 (1941), pp. 404–409.

WEBER, MAX, *The Methodology of the Social Sciences*, E. A. Shils and Henry A. Finch (eds.) (Glencoe, 1949).

WEIGEL, WENZEL, *Vom Wertreich des Jugendlichen*, 2 vols. (Leipzig, 1926).

WESTERMARCK, EDWARD A., *Origin and Development of the Moral Ideas*, 2 vols. (New York, 1906).

WHITE, RALPH K., *Value Analysis* (Glen Gardner, N. J., 1951).

WIEMAN, HENRY N., "Science in Service of Values." *The Journal of Social Issues*, vol. 6 (1950), pp. 33–38.

WILKENING, EUGENE A., "Techniques of Assessing Farm Family Values." *Rural Sociology*, vol. 19 (1955), pp. 39–49.

2. Special studies of American values

Note: For a considerably more extensive bibliography of this area see:

ALBERT, ETHEL M., and CLYDE KLUCKHOHN, *A Selected Bibliography on Values, Ethics and Esthetics* (Glencoe, 1959).

ALBERT, ETHEL M., "Conflict and Change in American Values: A Culture-Historical Approach." *Ethics*, vol. 74 (1963), pp. 272–279.

ALBRECHT, MILTON C., "Does Literature Reflect Common Values?" *American Sociological Review*, vol. 21 (1956), pp. 722–729.

BAIER, KURT, and NICHOLAS RESCHER, *Values and the Future: The Impact of Technological Change in American Values*, ed. by K. Baier and N. Rescher (New York, 1968).

BARRETT, DONALD N., *Values in America*, ed. by D. N. Barrett (Notre Dame, 1961).

CUBER, JOHN F., and ROBERT A. HARPER, *Problems of American Society: Values in Conflict* (New York, 1948; new ed. with William F. Kendal, 1956).

DuBOIS, CORA, "The Dominant Value Profile of American Culture." *American Anthropologist*, vol. 57 (1955), pp. 1232–1239.

GILLIN, JOHN P., "National and Regional Cultural Values in the U.S." *Social Forces*, vol. 34 (1955), pp. 107–113.

GREENSTEIN, FRED I., "New Light on Changing American Values." *Social Forces*, vol. 42 (1964), pp. 441–450.

HERMAN, ABBOT P., "Values of Individualism." *Sociology and Social Research*, vol. 33 (1949), pp. 196–203.

HYMAN, HERBERT H., "The Value Systems of Different Classes: A Social Psychological Contribution to the Analysis of Stratification," in Reinhard Bendix and S. M. Lipset (eds.), *Class, Status, and Power* (New York, 1953).

JACOB, P. E., *Changing Values in College* (New York, 1957).

JOHNS-HEINE, PATRICK, and HANS H. GERTH, "Values in Mass Periodical Fiction: 1921–1940." *Public Opinion Quarterly*, vol. 13 (1949), pp. 103–113.

KLUCKHOHN, CLYDE M., "The Evolution of Contemporary American Values," *Daedalus*, vol. 87 (1958), pp. 78–109. "Shifts in American Values," in E. Morison (ed.), *The American Style* (New York, 1958). "Have There Been Discernible Shifts in American Values During the Past Generation?", in E. Morison (ed.), *The American Style* (New York, 1958), pp. 145–217. "Shifts in American Values," *World Politics*, vol. 11 (1959), p. 261.

KLUCKHOHN, FLORENCE R., "American Women and American Values," in L. Bryson (ed.), *Facing the Future's Risks* (New York, 1953), pp. 175–199.

LIPSET, SEYMOUR MARTIN, "The Value Patterns of Democracy." *American Sociological Review*, vol. 28 (1963) pp. 515–531.

MEAD, MARGARET, *And Keep your Powder Dry* (New York, 1942).

PARSONS, TALCOTT, "American Values," in *idem, On American Society* (Glencoe, 1956).

PARSONS, TALCOTT, and WINSTON WHITE, "Continuity and Change in American Values," in S. M. Lipset and L. Lowenthal (eds.), *Culture and Social Character; The Work of David Riesman Reviewed* (Glencoe, 1961).

RESCHER, NICHOLAS, "The Dynamics of Value Change," in K. Baier and N. Rescher (eds.), *Values and the Future* (New York, 1968).

RETTIG, SALOMAN, and BENJAMIN PASANMONICH, "Changes in Moral Values Among College Students: A Factorial Study." *American Sociological Review*, vol. 24 (1959), pp. 856–863.

ROSENBERG, MORRIS, EDWARD A. SUCHMAN, and ROSE K. GOLDSEN, *Occupations and Values* (Glencoe, 1952).

ROTHS, LOUIS, "Appraising Changes in Values of College Students." *Journal of Educational Research*, vol. 35 (1942), pp. 557–564.

WILLIAMS, ROBIN, *American Society; A Sociological Interpretation* (New York, 1951; 2nd ed., 1960).

C. Economic valuation and related topics

1. Theory of economic value

ARROW, KENNETH J., *Social Choice and Individual Values* (New York, 1951; 2nd ed., New Haven, 1963).

BALZ, ALBERT G., *The Value Doctrine of Marx* (New York, 1943).

BAUMOL, WILLIAM M., *Welfare Economics and the Theory of the State* (Cambridge, 1952).

BOULDING, KENNETH, *Principles of Economic Policy* (Englewood, 1958).

BOWER, HOWARD B., *Toward Social Economy* (New York, 1948).

CARVER, THOMAS N., *Essays in Social Justice* (Cambridge, Mass., 1925).

COWLES COMMISSION FOR RESEARCH IN ECONOMICS, *Rational Decision-Making and Economic Behavior.* 19th Annual Report, 1950–1951 (Chicago, 1951).

DANHOF, CLARENCE H., "Economic Values in Cultural Perspective," in A. O. Ward (ed.), *Goals of Economic Life* (New York, 1953), pp. 84–117.

EDGEWORTH, F. Y., *Mathematical Psychics* (London, 1881; New York, 1961).

FETTER, FRANK A., "Value and the Larger Economics." *Journal of Political Economy*, vol. 31 (1925), pp. 790–803.

FLUBACHER, JOSEPH FRANCIS, *The Concept of Ethics in the History of Economics* (New York, 1950).

GRAFF, JOHANNES DE VILLIERS, *Theoretical Welfare Economics* (Cambridge, 1957).

HANEY, LEWIS H., *Value and Distribution* (New York, 1939).

HEIMANN, EDUARD, *History of Economic Doctrines* (New York, 1945).

HICKS, J. R., "The Foundations of Welfare Economics," *Economic Journal*, vol. 69 (1939), pp. 696–712. *The Social Framework: An Introduction to Economics* (London, 1942). *Value and Capital* (Oxford, 1946), 2nd ed. *The Theory of Wages* (London, 1951).

HOBSON, JOHN A., *Economics and Ethics: A Study in Social Values* (Boston, 1929).

HUTCHINSON, T. W. A., *A Review of Economic Doctrines* (Oxford, 1953).

JEVONS, W. STANLEY, *The Theory of Political Economy* (London, 1885; 4th ed., 1911).

KALDOR, NICHOLAS, "Welfare Propositions in Economics," *Economic Journal*, vol. 69 (1939), pp. 549–552. "Alternative Theories of Distribution," *Review of Economic Studies*, vol. 23 (1955–1956), pp. 83–100. *Essays on Value and Distribution* (London, 1960).

KEYNES, JOHN MAYNARD, *The General Theory of Employment, Interest and Money* (London, 1936). *Essays in Biography* (New York, 1933).

KEYNES, JOHN NEVILLE, *The Scope and Method of Political Economy* (London and New York, 1891).

LANGE, OSKAR, "The Foundations of Welfare Economics." *Econometrica*, vol. 10 (1942), pp. 215–228.

LEVIN, HARVEY J., "Standards of Welfare in Economic Thought." *Quarterly Journal of Economics*, vol. 70 (1956), pp. 117–138.

LITTLE, IAN M. D., *A Critique of Welfare Economics* (Oxford, 1950; 2nd ed. 1957).

LOWE, ADOLPH, *On Economic Knowledge* (New York, 1957).

MARSHALL, ALFRED, *Principles of Economics* (London, 1890; 8th ed., 1920). See especially Chap. 6 on "Value and Utility."

MYINT, HLA, *Theories of Welfare Economics* (London, 1948).

MYRDAL, GUNNAR, *An International Economy: Problems and Prospects* (New York, 1956). *Beyond the Welfare State* (London, 1960).

OLIVER, HENRY M., JR., *A Critique of Sociao-Economic Goals* (Bloomington, 1954). "Economic Value Theory as a Policy Guide," *Ethics*, vol. 68 (1958), pp. 186–193.

PARETO, VILFREDO, *Manuel d'économie politique*. Tr. from Italian by Alfred Bonnet (Paris, 1909).

PIGOU, A. C., *Wealth and Welfare* (London, 1912). *The Economics of Welfare* (London, 1920; 4th ed., 1932). "Some Aspects of Welfare Economics," *American Economic Review*, vol. 41 (1951), pp. 287–302.

RESCHER, NICHOLAS, *Distributive Justice* (New York, 1966).

ROBBINS, LIONEL, *An Essay on the Nature and Significance of Economic Science* (London, 1932).

ROTHENBERG, JEROME, *The Measurement of Social Welfare* (Englewood Cliffs, 1961). "Values and Value Theory in Economics," in *The Structure of Economic Science* (Englewood Cliffs, 1966).

SAMUELSON, PAUL ANTHONY, *Foundations of Economic Analysis* (Cambridge, 1947).

SCHUMPETER, JOSEPH A., *Capitalism, Socialiam and Democracy* (London, 1943). "On the Concept of Social Value," in R. V. Clemence (ed.), *Essays* (Cambridge, 1951), pp. 1–20.

SCITOVSKY, TIBOR, *Welfare and Competition* (London, 1952). *Papers on Welfare and Growth* (London, 1964).

SENIOR, NASSAU, *Four Introductory Lectures on Political Economy* (London, 1852).

SMART, WILLIAM, *An Introduction to the Theory of Value on the Lines of Menger, Wieser, and Böhm-Bawerk* (London, 1931).

SMELSEN, NIEL J., *The Sociology of Economic Life* (Englewood Cliffs, 1963).

SPRANGER, E., *Über die Stellung der Werturtheile in der Nationalökonomie* (Munich, 1914).

STIGLER, GEORGE J., "The New Welfare Economics," *American Economic Review*, vol. 33 (1943), pp. 355–359. "The Economists and Equality," in *idem*, *Five Lectures on Economic Problems* (London, 1949). *The Goals of Economic Policy* (Chicago, 1958).

SWEEZY, ALAN R., "The Interpretation of Subjective Value Theory in the Writings of the Austrian Economists." *Review of Economic Studies*, vol. 1 (1934), pp. 176–185.

THOMPSON, WILLIAM, *Inquiry into the Principles of the Distribution of Wealth* (London, 1824; 2nd ed., 1850).

WALRAS, LÉON, *Eléments d'économie politique pure.* 2 vols. (Lausanne, 1874–1877).

WEISSKOPF, WALTER A., "Hidden Value Conflicts in Economic Thought." *Ethics*, vol. 61 (1951), pp. 195–204.

WICKSTEED, PHILIP HENRY, *An Essay on the Co-ordination of the Laws of Distribution* (London, 1894). *Common Sense of Political Economy* (London, 1910; revised edition, London, 1933).

WIESER, FRIEDRICH VON, *Natural Value*, tr. by C. A. Mallock (New York, 1930).

2. Utility theory

Note: This listing is highly selective, and addresses itself more to the content of the utility concept than to the formal machinery of its implementation. The following three works may be consulted for fuller bibliographic data:

EDWARDS, WARD, "The Theory of Decision Making." *Psychological Bulletin*, vol. 5 (1954), pp. 380–417.

LUCE, R. DUNCAN, and HOWARD RAIFFA, *Games and Decisions* (New York, 1957).

SAVAGE, LEONARD J., *The Foundations of Statistics* (New York, 1954).

ADAMS, E. W., "A Survey of Bernouillian Utilities and Applications." *Technical Report No. 9 of the Behavioral Models Project* (Columbia University, 1954).

ARMSTRONG, W. E., "Uncertainty and the Utility Function," *Economic Journal*, vol. 58 (1948), pp. 1–10. "The Determinateness of the Utility Function," *Economic Journal*, vol. 49 (1939), pp. 453–467. "Utility and the Theory of Welfare," *Oxford Economic Papers*, N. S. No. 3 (Oxford, 1951), pp. 259–271.

BAUMOL, W. J., "The Neumann-Morgenstern Utility Index: An Ordinalist View." *Journal of Political Economy*, vol. 59 (1951), pp. 61–66.

BOHNERT, HERBERT G., "The Logical Structure of the Utility Concept" in Robert M. Thrall et al. (eds.), *Decision Processes* (New York, 1954).

BOULDING, KENNETH E., "Some Contributions of Economics to the General Theory of Value." *Philosophy of Science*, vol. 23 (1956), pp. 1–14.

COOMBS, CLYDE H., "Psychological Scaling Without a Unit of Measurement," *Psychological Review*, vol. 57 (1950), pp. 145–158. "Social Choice and Strength of Preference," in R. M. Thrall et al. (eds.), *Decision Processes* (New York, 1954).

DAVIDSON, DONALD, J. C. C. MCKINSEY, and PATRICK SUPPES, "Outlines of a Formal Theory of Value." *Philosophy of Science*, vol. 22 (1955), pp. 140–160.

EDGEWORTH, F. Y., *Mathematical Psychics* (London, 1881; reprinted New York, 1961).

EDWARDS, WARD, "Utility, Subjective Probability, Their Interaction and Variance Preferences." *Journal of Conflict Resolution*, vol. 6 (1962), pp. 42–51.

FRIEDMAN, MILTON J., and L. J. SAVAGE, "The Utility Analysis of Choices Involving Risk," *Journal of Political Economy*, vol. 56 (1948), pp. 279–304. Reprinted with a correction in G. S. Stigler and K. E. Boulding (eds.), *Readings in Price Theory* (Chicago, 1952). "The Expected-Utility Hypothesis and the Measurability of Utility," *Journal of Political Economy*, vol. 60 (1952), pp. 463–474.

GEORGESCU-ROEGEN, NICHOLAS, "Choice, Expectations and Measurability." *Quarterly Journal of Economics*, vol. 68 (1954), pp. 503–534.

HARSANYI, JOHN C., "Cardinal Welfare, Individualistic Ethics, and Interpersonal Comparisons of Utility." *Journal of Political Economy*, vol. 63 (1955), pp. 309–321.

HERSTEIN, I. N., and JOHN W. MILNOR, "An Axiomatic Approach to Measurable Utility." *Econometrica*, vol. 21 (1953), pp. 291–297.

HOUSNER, MELVIN, "Multidimensional Utilities," in R. M. Thrall, C. H. Coombs and R. L. Davis (eds.), *Decision Processes* (New York, 1954).

HOUTHAKKER, H. S., "Revealed Preference and the Utility Function," *Economica*, vol. 17 (1950), pp. 159–174. "Additive Preferences," *Econometrica*, vol. 28 (1960), pp. 244–257.

LANGE, OSCAR, "The Determinateness of the Utility Function." *Review of Economic Studies*, vol. 1 (1934), pp. 218–225.

LITTLE, I. M. D., *A Critique of Welfare Economics* (Oxford, 1950).

LYONS, DAVID, *Forms and Limits of Utilitarianism* (Oxford, 1965).

MCNAUGHTON, ROBERT, "A Metrical Conception of Happiness." *Philosophy and Phenomenological Research*, vol. 14 (1954), pp. 172–183.

MARKOWITZ, HARRY, "The Utility of Wealth." *Journal of Political Economy*, vol. 60 (1952), pp. 151–158.

MARSHAK, JACOB, "Rational Behavior, Uncertain Prospects, and Measurable Utility." *Econometrica*, vol. 18 (1950), pp. 111–141.

MARSHALL, ALFRED, *Principles of Economics* (London, 1890).

MOSTELLER, FRIEDERICH, and PHILIP NOGEE, "An Experimental Measurement of Utility." *Journal of Political Economy*, vol. 59 (1951), pp. 371–404.

VON NEUMANN, JOHN, and OSKAR MORGENSTERN, *Theory of Games and Economic Behavior* (Princeton, 1953).

PARETO, VILFREDO, *Manuel d'économie politique*. Tr. from Italian by Alfred Bonnet (Paris, 1909).

PIGOU, A. C., and N. GEORGESCU-ROEGEN, "Marginal Utility of Money and Elasticities of Demand." *Quarterly Journal of Economics*, vol. 50 (1936), pp. 532–539.

RADER, TROUT, "The Existence of a Utility Function to Represent Preferences". *Review of Economic Studies*, vol. 30 (1963), pp. 229–232.

RESCHER, NICHOLAS, *Distributive Justice* (New York, 1966).

ROBBINS, LIONEL, "Interpersonal Comparisons of Utility: A Comment," *Economic Journal*, vol. 68 (1938), pp. 635–641. *An Essay on the Nature and Significance Economic Science* (London, 1930; 2nd ed., 1935).

ROBERTSON, D. H., *Utility and All That* (London, 1952).

RUBIN, HERMAN, *The Existence of Measurable Utility and Psychological Probability* (Chicago, 1949; Cowles Commission Discussion Paper, *Statistics*, N. 331.)

SAMUELSON, PAUL ANTHONY, *Foundations of Economic Analysis* (Cambridge, Mass., 1947).

SONNENSCHEIN, HUGO, "The Relationship Between Transitive Preference and the Structure of the Choice Space." *Econometrica*, vol. 33 (1965), pp. 624–634.

STIGLER, GEORGE J., "The Development of Utility Theory." *Journal of Political Economy*, vol. 58 (1950), pp. 307–327.

SUPPES, PATRICK, and MURIEL WIMENT, "An Axiomatization of Utility Based on the Notion of Utility Differences." *Management Science*, vol. 1 (1955), pp. 259–270.

SUPPES, PATRICK, "Behavioristic Foundations of Utility." *Econometrica*, vol. 29 (1961), pp. 186–202.

THRALL, ROBERT M., "Multidimensional Utility Theory," in R. M. Thrall et al., (eds.), *Decision Processes* (New York, 1954).

UZAWA, HIROFUMI, "Preference and Rational Choice in the Theory of Consumption." *Proceedings on a Symposium on Mathematical Methods in the Social Sciences* (Stanford, 1960).

WOLD, HERMAN O. A., "Ordinal Preferences or Cardinal Utility?" *Econometrica*, vol. 20 (1952), pp. 661–664.

3. The theory of games
The classic of this field is:

VON NEUMANN, JOHN, and OSKAR MORGENSTERN, *Theory of Games and Economic Behavior* (Princeton, 1946; 2nd ed., 1953).

A very comprehensive bibliography of game theory is given in the following three works, the second of which provides an excellent introduction to the field:

HANDY, ROLLO, and PAUL KURTZ, *A Current Appraisal of the Behavioral Sciences*, Sec. 7, Supplement to *American Behavioral Scientist*, vol. 7, no. 7 (Great Barrington, 1964). Chap. 13, "Game Theory," pp. 121–125.

LUCE, R. DUNCAN, and HOWARD RAIFFA, *Games and Decisions: Introduction and Critical Survey* (New York, 1957).

SHUBIK, MARTIN, *Readings in Game Theory and Political Behavior* (New York, 1954).

A few important items too recent to be listed in the above works are:

RAPOPORT, ANATOL, *Fights, Games, and Debates* (Ann Arbor, 1960).

SCHELLING, T. C., *The Strategy of Conflict* (Cambridge, Mass., 1960).

SHUBIK, MARTIN, *Game Theory and Related Approaches to Social Behavior* (New York, 1964).

4. Decision theory and cost-benefit analysis

A useful bibliography of decision theory is given in the work by R. D. Luce and H. Raiffa cited in Sec. 3 above. As regards cost-benefit analysis, see:

DONVITO, P. A., *Annotated Bibliography of Systems Cost Analysis* (Santa Monica, 1967; RAND Corporation Research Memorandum RM-4848-1-PR).

a. Formal models (general theory, statistical approaches, operations research)

ACKOFF, RUSSELL L., "The Development of Operations Research as a Science," *Operations Research*, vol. 4 (1956), pp. 265–295. *Progress in Operations Research* (New York, 1961).

ARROW, KENNETH J., "Alternative Approaches to the Theory of Choice in Risk-Taking Situations," *Econometrica*, vol. 19 (1951), pp. 404–437. *Social Choice and Individual Values* (New York, 1951).

BATES, JAMES, "A Model for the Science of Decision." *Philosophy of Science*, vol. 21 (1954), pp. 326–339.

BLACKWELL, DAVID and M. A. GIRSHIK, *Theory of Games and Statistical Decisions* (New York, 1954).

BROSS, IRWIN, *Design for Decision* (New York, 1953).

CHURCHMAN, C. WEST, *Prediction and Optimal Decision* (Englewood Cliffs, 1961).

CHURCHMAN, C. WEST, RUSSELL L. ACKOFF, and ELEONARD ARNOFF, *Introduction to Operations Research* (New York, 1957).

CLARK, JOHN J., "The Economics of Systems Analysis." *Military Review*, vol. 44 (1964), pp. 25–31.

COWLES COMMISSION FOR RESEARCH IN ECONOMICS, *Rational Decision-Making and Economic Behavior*. 19th Annual Report, 1950–1951 (Chicago, 1951).

DAVIDSON, DONALD, PATRICK SUPPES, and SIDNEY SIEGEL, *Decision-Making: An Experimental Approach* (Stanford, 1957).

ENKE, STEPHEN, *Defense Management* (Englewood Cliffs, 1967).

GIRSHIK, MEYER A., "An Elementary Survey of Statistical Decision Theory." *Review of Educational Research*, vol. 24 (1954), pp. 448–466.

HANDY, ROLLO, and PAUL KURTZ, *A Current Appraisal of the Behavioral Sciences*, Sec. 7. Supplement to *American Behavioral Scientist*, vol. 7, no. 7 (1964). Chap. 14, "Decision-Making Theory," pp. 126–130.

HITCH, CHARLES J., "An Appreciation of Systems Analysis." *Journal of the Operations Research Society of America*, vol. 3 (1955), pp. 466–481.

JACOBS, PHILIP, "Functions of Values in Policy Decisions." *American Behavioral Scientist*, Supplementary vol. 5, no. 9 (1962).

JEFFREY, R. C., *The Logic of Decision* (New York, 1965).

MCKEAN, R. N., *Efficiency in Government through Systems Analysis* (New York, 1958).

NOVICK, DAVID, ET AL., *Program Budgeting, Program Analysis, and the Federal Budget* (Cambridge, Mass., 1965).

OPPENHEIM, FELIX E., "Rational Choice." *The Journal of Philosophy*, vol. 50 (1953), pp. 341–350.

SASIENI, MAURICE, ARTHUR JASPUR, and LAWRENCE FRIEDMAN, *Operations Research: Methods and Problems* (New York, 1959).

SIMON, HERBERT A., *Models of Man, Social and Rational* (New York, 1957). See especially Chaps. 14–16.

SMITH, NICHOLAS M., JR., STANLEY S. WALTERS, FRANKLIN C. BROOKS, and DAVID H. BLACKWELL, "The Theory of Value and the Science of Decision: A Summary." *Journal of the Operations Research Society of America*, vol. 1 (1953), pp. 103–113.

SNYDER, RICHARD C., H. W. BRUCK, and BURTON SAPIN, *Decision-Making as an Approach to the Study of International Politics* (Princeton, 1954). "A Decision-Making Approach to the Study of Political Phenomena," in *Approaches to the Study of Politics* (Evanston, 1958), pp. 3–38.

SUPPES, PATRICK, "The Philosophical Relevance of Decision Theory." *The Journal of Philosophy*, vol. 58 (1961), pp. 605–614.

THRALL, ROBERT M., CLYDE H. COOMBS, and ROBERT L. DAVIS, *Decision Processes* (New York, 1954).

WASSERMAN, PAUL, *Bibliography on Decision-Making* (Ithaca, N. Y., 1957). Dittoed.

WILLNER, DOROTHY, AND NORMAN F. WASHBURN (eds.), *Decision, Values and Groups*. Reports of an Interdisciplinary Research Conference, University of New Mexico, vol. I (Albuquerque, 1960), vol. II (Albuquerque, 1962).

b. Empirical studies

COOMBS, CLYDE H., "Social Choice and Strength of Preference," in R. M. Thrall et al. (eds.), *Decision Processes* (New York, 1954).

COOMBS, CLYDE H., and DAVID C. BEARDSLEY, "On Decision-Making Under Uncertainty," in R. M. Thrall et al. (eds.), *Decision Processes* (New York, 1954).

DAHL, ROBERT A., "Hierarchy, Democracy, and Bargaining in Politics and Economics," in *Research Frontiers in Politics and Government, Brookings Lectures* (Washington, D. C., 1955), pp. 45–69.

EDWARDS, WARD, "The Theory of Decision Making." *Psychological Bulletin*, vol. 51 (1954), pp. 380–417.

RAUP, R. BRUCE, "Choice and Decision in Social Intelligence." *The Journal of Social Issues*, vol. 6 (1950), pp. 45–49.

SIEGEL, SIDNEY, "Level of Aspiration and Decision-Making." *Psychological Review*, vol. 64 (1957), pp. 253–262.

SIMON, HERBERT A., *Administrative Behavior: A Study of Decision-Making Processes in Administrative Organization*, 2nd ed. (New York, 1957).

5. Preference aggregation and social welfare functions

ARROW, KENNETH J., *Social Choice and Individual Values* (New York, 1951); Cowles Commission Monograph No. 12; 2nd ed. (New Haven, 1961). "The Meaning of Social Welfare: A Comment on Some Recent Proposals," *Technical Report No. 2 of the Department of Economics and Statistics, Stanford University* (Stanford, 1951).

BLACK, DUNCAN, "On the Rationale of Group Decision Making," *Journal of Political Economy*, vol. 56 (1948), pp. 23–24. *The Theory of Committees and Elections* (Cambridge, 1958).

BLAU, J. H., "The Existence of Social Welfare Functions." *Econometrica*, vol. 25 (1957), pp. 302–313.

BUCHANAN, JAMES M., "Individual Choice in Voting and the Market," *Journal of Political Economy*, vol. 62 (1954), pp. 334–343. "Social Choice, Democracy, and Free Markets," *Journal of Political Economy*, vol. 62 (1954), pp. 114–123.

COOMBS, C. H., "Social Choice and Strength of Preference," in R. M. Thrall, C. H. Coombs, and R. L. Davis (eds.), *Decision Processes* (New York, 1954), pp. 69–86.

GOODMAN, L. A., "On Methods of Amalgamation," in R. M. Thrall, C. H. Coombs, and R. L. Davis (eds.), *Decision Processes* (New York, 1954), pp. 39–48.

GOODMAN, L. A., and HARRY MARKOVITZ, *Social Welfare Functions Based on Rankings*, Cowles Commission Discussion Paper, Economics, N. 2017 (New York, 1951). "Social Welfare Functions Based on Individual Rankings," *American Journal of Sociology*, vol. 58 (1952), pp. 257–262.

HILDRETH, CLIFFORD, "Alternative Conditions for Social Orderings." *Econometrica*, vol. 21 (1953), pp. 81–94.

KEMENY, JOHN G., and J. LAURIE SNELL, "Preference Rankings: An Axiomatic Approach," in J. G. Kemeny and J. L. Snell (eds.), *Mathematical Models in the Social Sciences* (New York, 1962), pp. 9–23.

MAY, K. O., "Intransitivity, Utility, and the Aggregation of Preference Patterns." *Econometrica*, vol. 22 (1954), pp. 1–13.

RESCHER, NICHOLAS, *Distributive Justice* (New York, 1966).

ROTHENBERG, JEROME, *Measurement of Social Welfare* (Englewood Cliffs, 1961).

WELDON, J. C., "On the Problem of Social Welfare Functions." *Canadian Journal of Economics and Political Science*, vol. 18 (1952), pp. 452–463.

D. The logic of preference

ÅQVIST, LENNART, "Deontic Logic Based on a Logic of 'Better'." *Acta Philosophica Fennica*, vol. 16 (Helsinki, 1963), pp. 285–290.

ARISTOTLE, *Topics*, book 3. [For historical stagesetting.]

ARROW, K. J., *Social Choice and Individual Values* (New York, 1951; 2nd ed., New Haven, 1961). [The classical treatment of the economists' approach to preference.]

BAYLIS, CHARLES, "Tranquility is Not Enough." *Pacific Philosophy Forum*, vol. 3 (1965), pp. 84–95.

BROGAN, A. P., "The Fundamental Value Universal." *The Journal of Philosophy, Psychology and Scientific Methods*, vol. 16 (1919), pp. 96–104.

CHISHOLM, RODERICK M., "The Descriptive Element in the Concept of Action." *The Journal of Philosophy*, vol. 61 (1964), pp. 613–625.

CHISHOLM, RODERICK M., and ERNEST SOSA, "On the Logic of Intrinsically Better," *American Philosophical Quarterly*, vol. 3 (1966), pp. 244–249. "Intrinsic Preferability and the Problem of Supererogation," *Synthese* vol. 16 (1966), pp. 321–331.

DAVIDSON, DONALD, J. C. C. MCKINSEY, and PATRICK SUPPES, "Outlines of a Formal Theory of Value, I." *Philosophy of Science*, vol. 22 (1955), pp. 140–160.

FRANKENA, WILLIAM K., "G. H. von Wright on the Theory of Morals, Legislation, and Value." *Ethics*, vol. 76 (1966), pp. 131–136.

HALLDÉN, SÖREN, *On the Logic of 'Better.'* (Uppsala, 1957).

HANSSON, BENGT, *Topics in the Theory of Preference Relations* (Lund, 1964).

HOUTHAKKER, H. S., "Revealed Preference and the Utility Function," *Economica*, vol. 17 (1950), pp. 159–174. "The Logic of Preference and Choice," in A. T. Tymieniecka (ed.), *Contributions to Logic and Methodology in Honor of J. M. Bochenski* (Amsterdam, 1965), pp. 193–207. [An attempt to draw together the interests of logicians and economists.]

JEFFREY, R. C , *The Logic of Decision* (New York, 1965).

KATKOV, GEORG, *Untersuchungen zur Werttheorie und Theodizee* (Brünn, 1937).

KEMENY, J. G., and J. L. SNELL, *Mathematical Models in the Social Sciences* (Boston, 1962).

KRAUS, OSKAR, *Die Werttheorien* (Brünn, 1937).

LUCE, R. D., and H. RAIFFA, *Games and Decisions* (New York, 1957). [Presents the mathematicians' approach to utility and preference theory.]

MARTIN, RICHARD M., *Intention and Decision* (Englewood Cliffs, 1963).

MOORE, G. E., "A Reply to My Critics," in P. A. Schilpp (ed.), *The Philosophy of G. E. Moore* (Evanston, 1942).

RESCHER, NICHOLAS, "Semantic Foundations of the Logic of Preference," in N. Rescher (ed.), *The Logic of Decision and Action* (Pittsburgh, 1967).

SCHELER, MAX, *Der Formalismus in der Ethik und die materiale Wertethik* (Halle, 1921; 4th ed., Bern, 1954).

SCHWARZ, HERMAN, *Psychologie des Willens zur Grundlegung der Ethik* (Leipzig, 1900).

TIMUR, M., "*Better* as the Value Fundamental." *Mind.* vol. 64 (1955), pp. 52–60.

VON WRIGHT, G. H., *The Logic of Preference* (Edinburgh, 1963). [The principal treatise on the subject.]

V. Bibliographies

ALBERT, ETHEL M., and CLYDE KLUCKHOHN, *A Selected Bibliography on Values, Ethics, and Esthetics in the Behavioral Sciences and Philosophy: 1920–1958* (Bloomington, 1959).

DASHIELL, J. FREDERICK, "An Introductory Bibliography on Value." *The Journal of Philosophy*, vol. 10 (1913), pp. 472–476.

EATON, HOWARD O., *The Austrian Philosophy of Values* (Norway, 1930). [Pp. 373–375 give a bibliography of writings on value theory by Brentano, Ehrenfels, and Meinong.]

FERRATER MORA, JOSÉ, "Valor" in *idem*, *Diccionario de Filosofia*, vol. II (5th ed., Buenos Aires, 1965), pp. 867–872.

HARTMAN, ROBERT S., "General Theory of Value," in R. Klibansky (ed.), *Philosophy in Mid-Century*, vol. 3 (Firenze, 1956), pp. 3–41.

HEYDE, J. E., "Gesammtbibliographie des Wertbegriffes." *Literarische Berichte aus dem Gebiet der Philosophie*, publ. by A. Hoffmann, fasc's 15–20 (1928–1929); A *Nachtragsheft* was issued in 1930.

VON MERING, OTTO, *A Grammar of Human Values* (Pittsburgh, 1961). [See the bibliography on pp. 265–282.]

REID, T. E. H., *Values in Conflict*, ed. by T. E. H. Reid (Toronto, 1963). [See the selected bibliography on pp. 125–130.]

VARET, GILBERT, *Manuel de bibliographie philosophique*, vol. II (Paris, 1956). [See pp. 864–910, devoted to "Philosophies de l'Être et de la Valeur."]

WARD, LEO RICHARD, *Philosophy of Value: An Essay in Constructive Criticism* (New York, 1930). [See the bibliography on pp. 233–259.]

Index of Symbols

Index of Names

Subject Index